Organisation Management in the Digital Economy

Organisation Management in the Digital Economy

Globalization Challenges

Anna Brzozowska

Dagmara Bubel

Larysa Nekrasenko

CRC Press
Taylor & Francis Group
Boca Raton London New York

CRC Press is an imprint of the
Taylor & Francis Group, an **informa** business

First edition published 2022
by CRC Press
6000 Broken Sound Parkway NW, Suite 300, Boca Raton, FL 33487-2742

and by CRC Press
4 Park Square, Milton Park, Abingdon, Oxon, OX14 4RN

CRC Press is an imprint of Taylor & Francis Group, LLC

ISBN: 978-1-032-22156-4 (hbk)
ISBN: 978-1-032-22158-8 (pbk)
ISBN: 978-1-003-27134-5 (ebk)

DOI: 10.1201/9781003271345

Typeset in Times
by SPi Technologies India Pvt Ltd (Straive)

Contents

List of Figures ix

List of Tables xiii

Authors xv

Introduction xvii

Chapter 1 The Nature of Informatics Technology in the Era
of Globalisation 1

    1.1 Versatility of Information Technology 1

    1.2 Information System vs. Informatics System 10

    1.3 Data–Information–Knowledge Relations 17

Chapter 2 Information as a Database in an Organisation 35

    2.1 Information as an Element Which Determines
the Success of an Organisation 35

    2.2 Model of Utilisation of Information Technique in an
Organisation 48

    2.3 Applications of Information Technology
in Organisations and Public Institutions 55

    2.4 Smart Organisation in the Modern World 63

    Notes 68

Chapter 3 Determinants Related to Threats in Information and
Informatics Systems 69

    3.1 Threats Related to Information Technique 69

    3.2 Information Security Management 75

    3.3 IT Risk Management 89

    3.4 Advanced Informatics Solutions Supporting
Risk Management in an Organisation. 99

    3.5 Problems of Personal and Social Threats Arising from
Utilisation of Information Technologies
in the Modern World 107

    Notes 122

Chapter 4 How Information Technology Is Changing E-Business
on the Way to the Digital Economy 123

    4.1 E-Commerce Business Models and Global Trends
in Their Development 123

        4.1.1 E-commerce Basic Definitions and Features 123

4.1.2   E-commerce Sectors and Their Features 126
4.1.3   Business-to-Business 127
4.1.4   Business-to-Consumer/Consumer-to-Business........ 128
4.1.5   Consumer-to-Consumer... 129
4.1.6   Business-to-Government... 129
4.1.7   Government-to-Citizen 130
4.1.8   Direct-to-Consumer (D2C) 130
4.1.9   Global Trends in the E-commerce Development..... 131
4.1.10   Mobile Shopping and Mobile Payments................. 132
4.1.11   PWA for E-commerce 133
4.1.12   A New Level of Logistics 133
4.1.13   Headless and API-driven E-commerce 133
4.1.14   Voice Commerce 134
4.1.15   AI and Machine Learning 134
4.1.16   The Rise of Virtual Reality 135
4.1.17   Augmented Reality Enhances the Reality
         of Online Shopping 136
4.1.18   B2B Is Growing 136
4.1.19   A focus on Direct-to-Consumer (D2C)................... 136
4.1.20   New Ways to Pay 137
4.2 Features of E-Commerce in Small- and Medium-Sized
     Businesses.. 139
4.2.1   Electronic Exchange to Improve B2B Activity........ 142
4.2.2   Mechanical Trading System as Example
         of B2C activity 143
4.2.3   Analyse Trading Signals 145
4.2.4   MetaStock Explorer 146
4.2.5   Enhanced System Tester 146
4.2.6   Charting.. 147
4.2.7   The Expert Advisor 148
4.2.8   Indicator Builder 148
4.3 The Types of Settlements: Advantages and Security Rules..... 150
4.3.1   E-commerce Payment Systems: Advantages and
         Security Rules 153
4.3.2   Mobile Digital Wallets 157
4.3.3   Smart Cards and Their Use 160
4.3.4   E-money Advantages 162
4.3.5   Safety Rules, When Using the Card......................... 164
4.3.6   Internet Banking Services and Rules 164
4.3.7   Internet Banking Vulnerabilities and Security 167
4.3.8   Digital and Virtual Money System Is an
         Alternative to C2C and D2C Models....................... 170
4.3.9   Decentralised Electronic Money Systems................ 170
4.3.10   Difference between Digital, Virtual and
         Cryptocurrencies... 171
4.3.11   Virtual Currency... 172

4.3.12   Cryptocurrency 172
4.3.13   Types of Cryptocurrencies and Their
          Classification.. 173
4.3.14   The Advantages of Cryptocurrency 176
4.3.15   Vulnerabilities 176
4.3.16   Risks of the Cryptocurrency Market......................... 177
4.3.17   Race Attack 178
4.3.18   History Modification.. 178
4.3.19   Deanonymisation of Clients...................................... 178
4.3.20   Data in the Blockchain... 179
4.3.21   Security 180
4.4   Payment Systems Worldwide: Risks, Threats and
       Data Protection 180
4.4.1   Fedwire Is the US Federal Reserve Banking
          Network.. 180
4.4.2   CHIPS (Clearing House Interbank Payment
          System) 181
4.4.3   BACS 182
4.4.4   Clearing House Automated Payment System
          (CHAPS)... 182
4.4.5   International Payment System TARGET 183
4.4.6   The SWIFT in the Global B2B 185
4.4.7   Challenges for SWIFT 188
4.4.8   Vulnerabilities and Fundamental Principles
          of the Functioning of Payment Systems 190
4.4.9   Payment Systems and Payment-Processing
          Services 192
4.4.10   Data Protection in E-commerce 202

Summary 209

References 213
Index 223

Figures

1.1 Three definitions of information technology provided in UNESCO documents 4
1.2 Key skills according to Kuszewski's interpretation 8
1.3 Key skills for information technologies 9
1.4 Basic concepts of the theory of information by B. Langefors 10
1.5 Place and role of information technique in organisation management 13
1.6 The DIKW hierarchy 18
1.7 Interpretation of the concept of knowledge according to Panasiewicz 23
1.8 Picture of wisdom 24
1.9 Quality of information arising from its attributes 27
1.10 Data, messages, information 28
1.11 Factors that affect information needs arising from the information gap 29
1.12 Information gap 29
1.13 Shaping of knowledge 31
1.14 Relations between data, information and knowledge 32
2.1 Definitions of information 36
2.2 Description of data 37
2.3 Criteria of evaluation of information quality 37
2.4 Types of information from the infological point of view in terms of management needs 38
2.5 Classification of information by impact on operations and nature of its effect 39
2.6 Classification of information by time criterion 39
2.7 Defined system components 40
2.8 System components 40
2.9 Models of informatics systems 42
2.10 Functional division of information systems in an organisation 42
2.11 Division of informatics systems by functions realised by them 43
2.12 New generation informatics systems 44
2.13 Division of expert systems 45
2.14 Development of expert systems 45
2.15 Levels of integration of utilisation of informatics systems 46
2.16 Features of integrated informatics systems 47
2.17 Management support 49
2.18 Active participation in work on modernisation of the organisation 50
2.19 7S organisation framework 51
2.20 Necessary technical changes to eliminate threats 53
2.21 Purposes and advantages of using information technique in an enterprise 56
2.22 Objectives and advantages of using information technique in an enterprise 57
2.23 Areas of IT applications in an enterprise 58

2.24 Factors which determine choice of IT..61
2.25 Forms of IT use...62
2.26 Key attributes of smart organisations...64
2.27 Informatics technology support for the fundamental structures
of an organisation and the online implementation of the concept of
"now economy"..65
2.28 Four pillars of SMAC systems...66
2.29 Attributes of SMAC systems 67
3.1 The primary function of an informatics system – provision
of information 70
3.2 Types of states of unavailability or reduced availability of system
resources 70
3.3 Enterprises after loss of information resources..............................70
3.4 Main causes of loss of data 71
3.5 Levels of informatics system security against data loss in relation
to the price...71
3.6 Critical redundancy areas..72
3.7 Disaster and system recovery...73
3.8 Recovery Point Objective mechanisms offered by two basic
technologies RPO and RTO 74
3.9 Hierarchy of an organisation's operating policies..........................75
3.10 A set of the best practices in the area of informatics security 76
3.11 Security management system measures..78
3.12 Information security management structure according to BS EN
ISO/IEC 27002:2017 78
3.13 Standard ISO ISO/IEC 27005:2018..79
3.14 Four domains of ICT process management according to the COBIT
methodology 80
3.15 Main advantages of the information security standardisation 80
3.16 A model dedicated to small organisations (minimum financial
expenditures)...81
3.17 A model dedicated to organisations of any size (optimised financial
expenditures)...81
3.18 A model dedicated to organisations of any size (a certificate of
conformity with PN-I-07799-2:2005)..82
3.19 Conduct of a risk analysis (BS7799) 82
3.20 Actions of an organisation focusing on developing an effective
information processing system 83
3.21 Elements of an informatics system 84
3.22 Layers of protection 85
3.23 Key risks related to security of informatics systems.....................86
3.24 Database storage guidelines..87
3.25 Contents of a Security Book 90
3.26 Stages in the process of IT risk management.................................90
3.27 Four strategies for selecting risk management methods 92
3.28 Risk analysis criteria...94

3.29 Relation between the security level and the cost of a safeguard 95
3.30 Relation between the risk value expressed in a currency unit
and the cost of a safeguard 95
3.31 Safeguard cost, risk value expressed in a currency unit, sum of risk
value expressed in a currency unit and safeguard cost 96
3.32 Risk treatment on the basis of a risk map 98
3.33 Definitions of risk management 99
3.34 Integrated approach to GRC 101
3.35 Stages of implementation of the risk management process according
to the FERMA standard 101
3.36 Integrated risk management according to the COSO standard 102
3.37 Maturity models 103
3.38 Levels of an organisation's maturity in terms of risk management 104
3.39 GRC concept in the SAP system 105
3.40 Proposal for comprehensive risk management support 106
3.41 Threats 109
3.42 Internet Addition Syndrome (IAS) 111
3.43 Internet-induced mental addictions 111
3.44 The most addictive Internet content 112
3.45 Dimensions of the digital divide 115
4.1   E-commerce models 126
4.2   B2B sector 127
4.3   B2C sector 128
4.4   C2C sector 129
4.5   B2G sector 129
4.6   D2C sector 131
4.7   The retail E-commerce sales 2014–2023 (in billion US dollars) 132
4.8   MTS work model 145
4.9   The Enhanced System Tester 146
4.10   Charting 147
4.11   The Expert Advisor 148
4.12   Indicator builder 149
4.13   Cashless transactions by country in 2019 151
4.14   Make payments with electronic money 153
4.15   Credit card payments scheme 155
4.16   Money circulation scheme in electronic money system 158
4.17   Scheme of interaction between participants in the card project 160
4.18   Scheme of settlements using Smart Card (SC) "electronic wallet" 161
4.19   SWIFT architecture 187

Tables

1.1 Characteristics of Information and Informatics System 15

1.2 Summary of Selected Definitions of Information and
the Related Functions 28

2.1 A Systemic Structure of Areas of Technological Support
of Enterprises 58

3.1 Definitions of Security Attributes 77

3.2 Comparison between the Traditional and Integrated Approaches
to Risk Management 100

4.1 Features of the Demand and Supply of Goods in the Internet
Environment 125

4.2 Advantages and Disadvantages that the Online Store Provides
to Customers and Sellers 141

4.3 The Types of Settlements for Different Sectors of E-commerce 150

4.4 Centralised and Decentralised Electronic Money Systems 171

4.5 Payment Systems and Payment-Processing Services 194

Authors

Anna Brzozowska obtained a PhD in economics, in the discipline of management science. Currently, she works at the Department of Logistics at the Faculty of Management of the Czestochowa University of Technology as an assistant professor. Since 2000, Anna's research and teaching activity has been associated with the Czestochowa University of Technology, where she worked as a teaching and research assistant, and since February 2005 as an assistant professor. Anna is the author or co-author of about 180 scientific publications. Until 2018, she was the editor of the EUREKA Social and Humanistic magazine. Between the years 2018-2021, Anna was the editor-in-chief of Scientific Journals of the Czestochowa University of Technology Management. Her scientific and research activity focuses on organization of management and logistic processes, marketing, information, and IT aspects. Anna's research is primarily concerned with how the institutional environment influences management in light of integration activities. The main directions of Anna's research include four key issues: the broadly understood concept of marketing and logistics management, IT in business, EU project management, management and marketing in agribusiness and the processes of integration with the EU. She systematically investigates these issues by conducting national and international research, participating in thematic groups, research and development teams, as well as through cooperation with business and local and regional authorities. As part of her scientific and educational work, Anna cooperated with the Mechanical Engineering Faculty, University of Miskolc, Hochschule Wismar University of Applied Sciences Technology, Technical University of Ostrava, Poltava State Agrarian Academy Ukraina, King Abdulaziz University Saudi Arabia.

Dagmara Bubel, PhD in Humanities, Professor of Sciences in Economics, Director of the Main Library of Czestochowa University of Technology. Academic teacher teaching courses in science studies.

My interests, both theoretical, empirical and in the application area, concentrated around the issues of intellectual capital management in organizations. As the concept of intellectual capital management regards people as the most valuable potential of an enterprise, directly related to its strategy, in this respect, I conducted analysis of selected aspects of the functioning of small and medium-sized enterprises.

Initially, my scientific studies addressed the problems of the following issues: management in organizations, management including management of knowledge, information and communication. Additionally, the subject of my scientific studies oscillated around logistics management and management in agribusiness. It should be stressed that active activity of an organization is one of the most important characteristics of the democratic society, an element that ties and activates local community.

My research interests were connected with broadly understood restructuring of enterprises, which undergo changes not only in the aspect of material resources, but also intangible ones, i.e. organisational culture. When designing an organisation, it is necessary to take into account elements of the structure and ties that connect them. Decision-making powers and responsibility are assigned, and then executory processes are formalised. I presented exploitive concepts, i.e. diagnostic approach to designing an organisation.

Larysa Nekrasenko was born on 28 April 1965 in Kremenchuk, Ukraine. She graduated from Kharkiv University, receiving a master's in Biology in 1989. In 1998, she graduated from Kremenchuk State Polytechnic University in business economics. In addition, in 2009 she graduated from Poltava Agrarian Academy, in Finance and Accounting.

From 1990 to 1994 she worked in the Botanical Garden of Kharkov State University as Associate Research employee.

From 1994 to 2000 she worked in Kremenchuk affiliate of Joint Stock Company Prominvestbank of Ukraine on position economist. Then from 2000 to 2001, she worked at JSC Kremenchuk Wheel Plant as an economist in the Economics Department. She has been teaching at Poltava State Agrarian Academy since 2001 on a bachelor and master's levels. She received a PhD in 2004 and she got an Associate Professor of Finance and Credit in 2010. As an Associate Professor of the Department of Finance and Credit, she created the following courses: Information Systems and Technologies in Finance; Payment Systems; Budgeting of Business Entities.

Since 2013, she headed the educational research laboratory of the Department of Finance and Credit. She was responsible for the assigned duties of conducting laboratory and practical work using specialized software to study business processes. Her main scientific interest is Information Systems and Technologies in Finance; Payment Systems; E-commerce.

She has 67 publications, including 39 research and 22 teaching character. She is the co-author of two monographs, 2 handbooks for higher education students that have a stamp of the Ministry of Education and Science of Ukraine. She got a "Special Prize" from VoxUkraine and publication on the blog the article "The environmental tax policy in Ukraine and Sweden".

Introduction

At the turn of the 21st century, the field of information systems is nearly as important for civilisational development as information technique. It is certainly more significant to those who, while utilising information technique, influence economic development, thus creating opportunities for utilising the full acquired knowledge of also other, auxiliary disciplines. Comprehensive study as well as development and utilisation of information systems allows utilisation of the information technique potential. Computerisation-like actions, i.e. "implementation of informatics" (creation of informatics systems), represent avoidance of making necessary changes in the management system and therefore bear all hallmarks of ostensible activity.

Perceiving an information system as the key component of the management system is the condition for making any changes. Development of an informatics system on the basis of an existing organisation oriented to achieve other objectives must lead to degeneration of the system. The hindrance lies not in the limited nature of information technique, but in the inability to use it to solve organisational problems and difficulties. Unambiguous and accurate definition of problems and objectives at the very start of a project makes it possible to properly direct further work and achieve the desired effects. Conversely, imprecise or inaccurate definition of actions will make the complete success of any project unachievable.

Problems and objectives can be identified fully, precisely and accurately only on the basis of a thorough analysis of the situation which underpins the decision to undertake a project. All short-cuts (preconceptions) which may direct further work in an unwarranted manner should be eliminated. Such preconceptions can be represented by building an informatics system (the use of a computer, specific software) when one considers *a priori* (although no specific objective is known) that a specific tool will be employed without taking the necessary steps. Thus, one leaves the management system unchanged while building something that will fit the "existing conditions" – hence resigning from the change. The resulting system is incoherent with the objectives of the organisation as a whole. Since what is produced is a perfect tool of an undefined and still inefficient system, the entire system will continue to operate with limited efficiency due to the resignation from creating an information system.

This approach leads to designing an informatics system which is a super-modern solution of non-defined functions, for it is not possible to define any functions of a system which is not subjected to studies – a decision-making system (a decision-making information system).

1 The Nature of Informatics Technology in the Era of Globalisation

1.1 VERSATILITY OF INFORMATION TECHNOLOGY

Scientific maturity of any discipline is demonstrated by its methodological maturity, which is built of unambiguity and awareness of the nomenclature used.

The issue of key information technology skills, which is pertinent not only to the informatics methodology, requires a detailed consideration, mainly due to its methodological convention. The following terms require clarification: technology, information technology, skills, key skills and information technology skills.

When developing its own conceptual framework, every scientific discipline draws from the colloquial language and terminologies used in interoperable and similar disciplines. In addition to the subject and range of studies, own language is always a measure of development of a scientific discipline and even of its right to exist on its own.

A correctly codified terminological convention of a discipline provides for meeting the requirements of the principle of intersubjective communicability of its terms (Chan et al. 2019, pp. 1–8). The reality described in scientific statements must be independent from the language of those statements – and therefore from any discretion of their interpretation. Uncritical transfer of one discipline's terminology into another must not be accepted.

Further conditions of terminological correctness are related to the principle of intersubjective verifiability of statements. Their obviousness does not require any interpretation.

The quality of a terminological convention determines its communicability and instructive value of its statements. Only unambiguous terminological conventions can provide for translatability of findings into the language of related theories. Trans-communicability allows verification of the findings and also responds to practical needs through formulating praxeological rules. No such rules can be formulated when a given discipline lacks the necessary and precise conceptual apparatus. In this light, concepts of a given discipline must be accurately explained, clear, explicit and operational. This is why it is necessary to indicate their designata, define the scope of their contents (denotation) and clarify polysemous and synonymous terms.

The matter of key information technology skills requires detailed methodological consideration and definition of the content range. It is therefore necessary to discuss the meaning of concepts such as technology, information technology, skills, key skills and information technology skills. It should also be highlighted that each of the aforementioned concepts is polysemous and represents a node of a conceptual framework.

The issue of key information technology skills requires refining due to the terminological convention of each separate concept and the double-category concepts, i.e. key skills and information technology. Not only do the growing information civilisation and efforts to build information society imply the need to deal with these issues, but they also demonstrate the vast extent of the subject.

However, the following terms must be explained first (Arana-Solares et al. 2019, pp. 81–95):

- technology
- information technology
- skills
- key skills
- information technology skills

The concept "technology" can be used within a narrow meaning with respect to a specific phenomenon, e.g. the information acquisition technology. "Technology" can be understood broadly and referred to the definition of a scientific discipline. If various technologies are considered in line with the state of the art of contemporary technical sciences, as scientific disciplines, then they should meet the necessary methodological requirements. They should also realise the tasks arising from the methodological functions of scientific studies (Gräfrath, Huber, Uhlemann 2020).

In the Polish terminological convention, the concept of technology is too often regarded as synonymous to the praxeological understanding of the concept of technique (in its functional meaning). In classical terms, the concept of technology meant an applied science that concerned the processes of production of products from raw materials. Indeed, every human production activity is accompanied by the following three basic questions: What? What from? How?

The first question is answered by defining the subject of production, or the primary objective of the technology concerned, and by naming the creation (product) or any other deliverable. Therefore, in most general terms, there are technologies which lead to tangible products, transformed energy, or transformed (processed) information (Aasheim, Lixin, Williams 2019, p. 10).

The answer to the second question (what from?) categorises technologies by the raw material subjected to technological processing. Effects of these technologies are effects of production, extraction, storage, processing, transfer, carriage, transmission. The raw material from which these effects will be produced can be matter (either animate or inanimate), energy (which cannot be only produced), information. Notably, each of these raw materials can have a different appearance, or input form, which in turn will affect the structure of the related "treatment" processes.

The third question (how?) is regarding ways (methods), forms of their organisation and technical means which serve the purpose of technological processing. The answer to that question includes the answer to the question of how something is processed (and sometimes produced), stored, transmitted and used. It should be added, however, that it is not about a one-off phenomenon but a method which is conscious, systematically repeated, unambiguous and sufficiently precise. This is how such a technology is characterised in qualitative and praxeological terms (Ullah, Sepasgozar 2019, pp. 469–484).

The developing, widely understood informatics, implies the need to perceive various phenomena differently. The systemic, total and global nature of informatics phenomena puts researchers in a situation that is new to them; hence, the concepts must be reinterpreted.

Taking the above references to informatics phenomena, the concept of technology must include two groups of phenomena (Berdowska, Mikuláš 2020, pp. 126–147):

- all technical actions related to methods of designing, constructing and producing technical means of informatics. For the purpose of standardisation of the terminological convention, all these technologies will be referred to as informatics technologies;
- all methods and means of "treatment" (processing) of information, including *inter alia* searching for, gathering, recording, storing, processing, transmitting and erasing information. These technologies will be referred to as information technologies. Notably, they form whole families of technologies – there are different information processing needs and processes (including methods and technical means) employed by them. Indeed, in every sphere of activity, e.g. storage of information, various technologies can be identified and used for data compression (depending on the type of data) and recording on different media – therefore involving different technologies and technical means of their application.

In reference to the above questions (what, what from, how), it can be said that information technologies take usable processing, storage, transmission, or erasure of any type of information (data) as their primary objective.

Today, the concept of information (what from?) is also significantly broader. Forms in which it appears are not neutral to the processes of information processing, i.e. specific technologies. Each of them represents a separate information technology and therefore requires application of a specific technological process (organisation and means of informatics technique). It also requires persons involved to have appropriate skills.

It can also be recognised that the concept of information technologies is significantly expanding at present as the methods and technical means expand and the information processing needs change. The view that there is one universal information technology is therefore not legitimate. The interpretation provided here implies that information technologies include entire sets of detailed technologies.

Information technologies serve versatile search, gathering, utilisation, processing, storage and transmission of various types of information. This versatility applies to sources, range, purposes and ways of utilisation of information through various technical means and their systems.

The term "information technology" (IT) refers to a bundle of industries related with informatics technologies. Therefore, IT covers production of hardware, production of software, hardware and software consultancy, data processing and database creation, software and hardware sales and maintenance as well as education in informatics technologies. They are high-technology industries which currently determine the efficiency of nearly all traditional branches of economy. They support both small and medium organisations of various fields as well as the financial sector, public administration, transport, power engineering, telecommunications, pharmacy, scientific institutions, food industry, retail chains and petrol stations and many other institutional and private customers.

Information technology is defined as a combination of informatics proper with well-established communications techniques – teleinformatics and telematics (Osterhage 2018, pp. 139–151). This definition, albeit very general, shows characteristic relations which are constantly developed and refined within this area of science.

Even before informatics tools and means are introduced on a mass scale, Marz Oliver writes that the term refers to a structured set of methods, means and latest targeted actions oriented to realisation of all information processes in the society (Marz et al. 2019, pp. 7–1).

Mammes Ingelore defines information technology as all methods and tools for information processing, including methods of searching, selecting, gathering, recording, storing, processing, transmitting and erasing information. The author also writes that information technology represents all technical actions related to methods of designing architecture and producing technical means of informatics (Mammes et al. 2019, pp. 93–109).

UNESCO documents include three definitions of information technology (Biehl 2020, pp. 3–23) – they are shown in Figure 1.1.

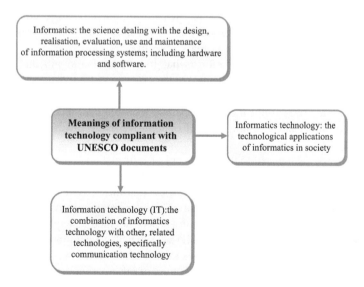

FIGURE 1.1   Three definitions of information technology provided in UNESCO documents.

Source: Own work based on: Biehl 2020, pp. 3–23.

Information technology can be defined also as a set of modern devices used in the process of communication. It is generally agreed that the capabilities of information technology can be characterised by the skills of effective use of means, tools and sources of information for analysing, processing and presenting information as well as modelling, measuring and controlling devices and events.

In organisations, information technologies have two main functions: services and innovation. The service function allows organisations to pursue their strategies in a more effective manner. The innovation function provides organisations with new growth opportunities which would not be available without IT. Both these functions have a profound impact on the level of the rate of return on capital invested in an organisation and on its ability to grow. This, in turn, translates into future financial flows, which determine the value of the organisation.

Information technologies (IT) play an important role in organisations with state-of-the-art management, penetrating into virtually every aspect of their operations. They have a tremendous impact on the manner in which modern organisations are managed. Thanks to deployment of state-of-the-art information technologies, organisations are modernised and improve on earlier management methods, thus contributing to the development of their innovation and competitive edge on the global market.

Information technologies cover not only various forms of information itself but also informatics equipment and knowledge as well as telecommunication. At present, the concept also covers those technologies that have emerged from the combination of informatics with communication techniques (information and communication technologies). In order to differentiate between them, it is proposed to use the concept of telematics to mark the process of inclusion of telecommunication technologies into the needs of information technologies and *vice versa*. This field of science and technology is believed to combine the achievements of informatics and telecommunications, which opened the way to the rapid development of informatics applications. D. Zumkeller uses the concept of teleinformatics interchangeably for the concept of telematics. He defines teleinformatics as a combination of informatics with other fields and technologies that cooperate with it and affect its application in society (Zumkeller 2002, pp. 00–4).

Information technologies are now the foundation for all actions of the modern-day science and economy, as well as a chance for economisation and rationalisation of efforts on the global scale.

Information technologies have radically changed the nature of labour and organisation of production. Labour relationships and employment conditions are changing. Organisations are becoming more flexible and less centralised in their operations. Effects of information technologies include search for new flexible form of action, intensified cooperation in utilisation of the global information network, increased use of subcontracting and enhanced teamwork.

The analysis clearly indicates that skills of the human operator are the concepts that constitute all types of technologies. When speaking of skills related to information technologies, one should see a broad spectrum of issues in which they are located.

In informal speech, the meaning of the concept of skills seems obvious. However, some difficulties arise when one makes it a scientific term. The main cause lies in the fact that the term "skills" concerns different planes of deliberations and therefore different conceptual circles. One can say that the term "skills" is multi-dimensional and its sense depends on which plane of deliberation is assumed.

According to T. Nowacki, a skill is the ability to perform appropriate actions under specific conditions. On the one hand, that ability concerns subjective factors, and then it is referred to in praxeology as the internal ability. On the other hand, it concerns factors rooted in the environment that determine the possibility to act, and then it is called the external ability. In the structure of the internal ability, one can distinguish, in particular, the subject's intellectual readiness, motivational readiness and skill readiness to undertake and execute actions. Based on this definition, one can understand the term "skills" as the readiness to undertake a specific type of action while providing for adjusting it to the changing conditions in which it will be executed (Furmanek 2002, p. 250).

M. Kęsy defines "skill" as the ability to act sensibly (consciously), effectively and efficiently, manifested when solving and performing tasks which require adapting the method of action to the changing conditions. It is possible only when one has operative knowledge of objects and phenomena which are involved in action. The level of command of skills is expressed by achieving successful results despite the volatility of operating conditions (Kęsy 2019, pp. 120–134).

A skill is demonstrated by a person who has strong situation-specific motivation. A skill is the proficiency in using information in action for the purpose of accomplishing specific tasks. This means that every skill is based on its intellectual foundation. That foundation is built in different ways and can have a different content. Research shows that excess of intellectual superstructure is the condition for flexible and effective action in variable conditions (Blickle 2019, pp. 235–249).

Proficiency can be regarded as a parameter which determines the level of command of a specific skill. The emotional and motivational component manifested in that readiness to act determines a person's propensity to act. Such a syndrome of features of skills gives them a special educational meaning.

One should note the relation between knowledge and skills. The knowledge element is a passive and static structure which is manifested and whose manifestation makes sense only when an activity is being performed. A skill, in turn, is an active and dynamic structure – it is simply the structure of any activity.

Information skills are related to efficiency in using knowledge to solve information tasks (Ferstl, Sinz 2019). They require specific knowledge which is their intellectual foundation. It is used in the form of normative knowledge as laws, principles, rules, methods or patterns of action.

When defined as above, knowledge of informatics is the necessary component of every information technology. Information skills represent the readiness to tackle information issues (tasks) with the ability to adapt to the changing conditions in which a specific task is to be executed. In this sense, they have subjective nature; they always belong to someone and are based on the subjective knowledge of the person undertaking an action. However, they are always clearly related to a specific operation which constitutes an element in the process of a given information technology. It should be noted that such understanding of information skills means that they are a category which expresses a specific form of human behaviour in a situation which requires use of information or which involves the necessity to process information.

B. Siemieniecki defines information skills as ones that concern acquisition of knowledge from various sources as well as the ability to evaluate and use the acquired information. He also notes that there are many attitudes to defining information actions (Jacob 2019).

The concept of information skills cannot be linked solely with knowledge acquisition skills, for they have much broader sense and content which arise from the interpretation of the concept of information technologies. Information skills have intellectual and practical character. For instance, the interpolation or extrapolation skills concern activity of a person within a certain sequence of data. They have purely intellectual character. Deployment of suitably designed software (algorithmisation of actions) to handle extrapolation or interpolation processes provides for machine execution of these actions. The skills of utilising informatics hardware for this purpose are informatics skills of practical or practical-intellectual character.

P. Hügelmeyer and A. Glöggler define key skills as skills which are necessary to effectively perform tasks related to learning, working and social obligations. They include intellectual and social skills required to understand and master knowledge which is not contained in the current curriculum, as well as practical proficiency (Hügelmeyer, Glöggler 2020, pp. 171–194).

As rightly noted by D. Kalisz and A. Szyran-Resiak, key skills are an inherent element of all qualifications rather than separate type of qualifications within a system of various types of qualifications arising from horizontal and lateral division of work. Key skills are to be a part, an element of all qualifications, and in this sense the term does not mean a new type of qualifications but rather characteristics of a part of qualifications, i.e. skills arising from the needs of the volatile present (Kalisz, Szyran-Resiak 2019).

A review of a number of different definitions of key skills shows that their authors highlight that they are those types of skills that help a person to cope with the new and changing social and economic reality. Key skills belong to the family of skills which are characterised by wide transfer, which is manifested through multiple possibilities to apply them to many various situations (Rozkrut et al. 2018, pp. 347–360). They have transferable character, hence they are relatively universal.

It is proposed to include the skills enumerated in Figure 1.2 to key skills (Klinkel, Rahn, Bernhard 2017, pp. 267–280).

The first two groups of skills require specific use of information. The model of the communication process includes the following skills: encoding (translation of intentions, thoughts and feelings into information); transmission of a signal through a communication channel; decoding a signal (translation of received signals into meaningful content and assigning meaning to received messages); interpretation (decoding the intentions which the recipient attributes to the sender). This model clearly illustrates that even such communication skills – which are components of this relatively simple process of conveying information – are complex skills. The process of their development requires a shift to the level of functional and elementary skills (Klinkel, Rahn, Bernhard 2017, pp. 267–280).

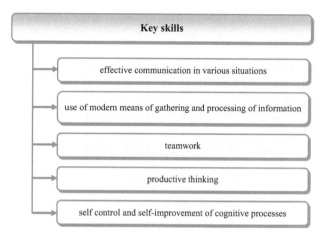

FIGURE 1.2 Key skills according to Kuszewski's interpretation.

Source: Own work based on: Klinkel, Rahn, Bernhard 2017, pp. 267–280.

Communication which takes place through the media is more complex and thus can have a different nature. According to A. Kühn and F.H. Kühn, one can distinguish: intermediate interpersonal communication, simulated interpersonal communication, communication between a person and a computer and unicommunication (Kühn, Kühn 2017, pp. 481–540). It is evident that each type of communication requires different complex information skills. The question is: how that complexity of information skills should be understood? How should this concept be connected with the concept of information technologies. Can each of them, when manifested in a situation of use of information technologies, be regarded as an information technology skill? It seems that it should be so. There can be no question of a single information technology. One cannot regard the said catalogue of skills (searching for, structuring and using information) as a single skill.

In a person's private and professional situations, even the simplest ones, one can distinguish two types of systems. One includes relatively constant, stereotypical and repetitive systems which quickly become automated, and the other includes volatile, non-stereotypical systems that trigger and require active thinking. They appear most clearly in the processes of planning, ongoing control of work and removal of obstacles and rectification of defects. In this light, one can distinguish the use of information in typical situations and the ability to use knowledge in non-stereotypical situations. Key skills always concern operating in non-stereotypical situations.

In today's dynamically changing reality – so, in fact, in non-stereotypical situations – it is important to have skills which can be widely applied in various fields. Providing a full list of key information technology skills requires adopting a relatively simple model that would be common to these technologies. Therefore, one can say that in order to function in an information situation, a person requires to acquire information, process information and emit the results of such processing.

In this context, it is necessary to have skills which are shown in Figure 1.3.

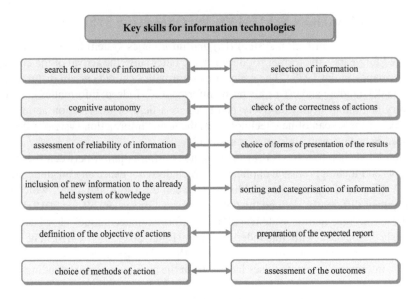

FIGURE 1.3   Key skills for information technologies.

Source: Own work based on: Kühn, Kühn 2017, pp. 481–540.

Since information technologies involve integration of information processing requirements with processes of operation of various technical means adjusted to one's needs, key information technology skills include a wide variety of skill sets. Classifications of those sets, although covering diverse skills, do not include all situations that must be taken into consideration. To illustrate, one may recall the concept of development of information skills (Çoklar, Yaman, Yurdakul 2017, pp. 1–9) which includes definition of the subject, location of information, selection of information, organisation of information, evaluation of information, work with outcomes obtained as well as formulation and analysis of needs, definition and evaluation of possible sources, access to information resources, examination, evaluation and selection of information, examination of sources, gathering of information, interpretation, analysis, synthesis, evaluation and division of individual sources of information, choice of information, reproduction and recording of information.

The issue of categorisation of key information technology skills should be referenced to the general praxeological model of human actions (Gasparski 2019, pp. 5–28). It includes seven types of skills which enable a person to act efficiently, effectively and economically in changing conditions. They concern recognition of situation and formulation of the objective of actions; analysis of information in the starting situation; designing the final situation; planning of actions; preparation of the necessary resources; execution; evaluation of the outcomes and return (rationalisation of the actions).

Adoption of any solution suggested herein can by no means be fully satisfactory and requires further analyses and studies. The question of which information technologies should be regarded as primary remains particularly important.

1.2 INFORMATION SYSTEM VS. INFORMATICS SYSTEM

The concepts of information system (IS) and informatics system have been known and used for years – the former for decades, the latter since the arrival of the concept of informatics in the 1970s. The concept of informatics caused certain disturbances in the understanding and use of the term "information". Indeed, informatics has from the very beginning been intuitively perceived as a field of information actions. In the wake of the spread of new technologies, the term "information system" (IS) was replaced by a new term "informatics system".

The global literature has led to unambiguous differentiation between these two concepts and their appropriate application which does not cause any misunderstandings. A number of studies were published between the 1960s and 1990s which precisely, albeit differently, defined the field of information systems (Lutz 2019).

The terms "information system" (IS) and "information technique" have been continuously associated with misunderstandings (Baun 2019, pp. 3–13). The same applies to the concepts of information system (IS) and informatics system. The cause of those interpretation errors arises largely from the ambiguous understanding of the concept of information which is frequently considered as synonymous to the concept of data. Information is an abstract concept which means something that changes the entropy. In the interpretation of management systems, it reduces ignorance and unawareness. Figure 1.4 shows basic concepts of the information theory. Data is a physical representation of the elementary portion of information. It is used for recording and transmitting information. In the everyday language practice, the terms information and data are used interchangeably in order to simplify communication, which may result in the aforementioned misunderstandings.

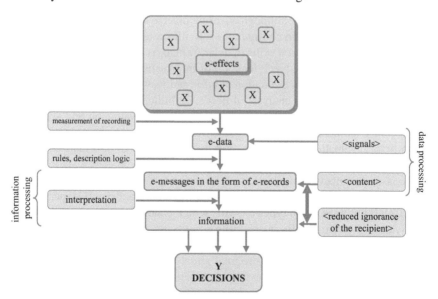

FIGURE 1.4   Basic concepts of the theory of information by B. Langefors.

Source: Own work based on: Langefors 1980, pp. 17–32.

If one agrees and accepts the above definition of information, then, on its basis, another definition can be assumed – the organisational information system (OIS), a complex creation which is meant to ensure access to information for every member of an organisation in accordance with his or her authorisations arising from his or her role in that organisation. Such findings are insufficient and it is necessary to systematise the related concepts and establish relations between them, thus complementing the accepted and used terminology in the area of information systems.

Another concept whose meaning is not used clearly is "data", i.e. a physical representation of the elementary portion of information in the form of which the latter is recorded and (or) transmitted. Data plays an important role in an IS, for information must first be recorded to be stored and made available on multiple occasions. To this end, it is necessary to use a physical form of representation to ensure transfer in time and space – hence the significant role of data and all data processing functions (measurement, recording, transmission, gathering, storage, search, presentation, emission, distribution). Processing of data was a type of operation "on information" which had been noticed earlier and for the purpose of which computer technique had been employed (Langefors 1980, pp. 17–32). The theory of information systems formulated by B. Langefors at that time became the basis for employing computers to process data. Thus, from the very first attempts, an error was made involving incomplete understanding and not fully correct use of the concept of information and its unfounded identification with data. That practical approach, arising from the overlapping meanings and efforts to simplify communication, resulted in imprecise use of the concepts and, in consequence, distortion of that communication.

Misunderstandings started when the concept "information processing" was introduced as a synonym of "data processing". It is incorrect in that only signals, i.e. representation of information, are processed, whereas information processing concerns processes that take place in human brain. The point of our interests in the context of information processes in the area of management is the processing of data meant to adapt it to the needs and perception abilities of the recipients (persons authorised to make organisational decisions). Information can be processed only by humans through mental processes – which have yet to be adequately explored and, as such, are difficult, or even impossible, to quantify and formalise.

Therefore, an IS as a system of human actions covers two spheres: the sphere of data processing and the sphere of information processing in individual or group thinking processes. The former appears relatively easy to structure and consequently to formalise and use a computer technique. The latter – the sphere of mental processes, more complex and poorly explored – is still too difficult to formalise and use computer technique support. However, one must be aware of the complexity and limitations regarding deployment of computer support of information processes. Its scope is currently limited to support of data processing, while all efforts should focus on creating the best information systems possible. When designing information systems, one needs to remember that information technique solutions, even the finest ones, will never replace an organisation. At best, one can expect adaptation of computerised system solution to the most effective organisation of processes while ensuring the desired human behaviour. Only a fully coordinated entirety of information systems can ensure desired effects – i.e. the accomplishment of objectives set by the organisation.

An information system means "processing systems and information channels" (Elm 2018). According to this definition, an information system is therefore any complex system whose elements include processing and transmitting components (But do they include information?). However, if it were to process information, then the definition is incorrect, for only a human being could be such a processing system, but humans are not covered by the definition. Such a definition seems to be overly laconic for the purpose of examining a complex object like a management information system.

The definition proposed by Calvo-Amodio and Rousseau (2019, pp. 91–99) is equally simple, but it indicates more details that are essential for researchers. They defined the information system as a human activity system which is comprises elements of five classes: data, methods, technique (technology employed – technical equipment), organisation, people. Adopting such an approach shows clearly that the nature of the information system does not allow categorising it in the class of artificial systems (artefacts). Based on this definition, one can conclude that the informatics system is not a synonym of the information system, for it is an artefact (a technical solution) used for performing (in an automated process) a certain subset of functions of all functions expected of the information system.

An informatics system is a set of technical and logical/logistical means which serve the purpose of gathering, storing and processing information. This definition appears useless, and in fact incorrect, particularly where it indicates information as the subject of processing – for according to the current deliberations, information is the exclusive preserve of the human being and cannot be stored by technical equipment, etc. At the same time, it is inconsistent with other definitions (the informatics system is an automated information system or a part thereof). Neither does the definition show any relations with management, so it is useless from the perspective of our interests. A question which should be asked is a question about the informatics system itself, which is a solely technical solution.

Functions performed by informatics systems normally represent only the elementary scope of IS functions related to proper data processing. In basic terms and taking into account the priority needs of an organisation and the limited abilities to satisfy them, these functions relate solely to data processing. An ideal informatics system can therefore include such basic information functions as interpretation of data and, for more advanced informatics systems, process modelling, indication of action variants, suggesting "a decision" (selection of a variant) as well as assessment and indication of the most favourable solutions. Such functions of an informatics system (or rather an information system for decision making) should be individualised (adjusted to the needs of a specific decision-maker). The requirements set for information systems, albeit completely rational, are unreachable given the current scientific and technological progress and economic development. Building new organisations which compete for position on the global market, one should deliberately prepare to understand and accept new information needs and new possibilities to satisfy them. Information awareness should be built for users who fully and correctly understand the concept of information and realise the objectives and tasks of the information system as a human activity system whose relations with organisation (and object and structuring) play a decisive role. It is by no means aided by consolidating the habit of using the term "informatics system", which is not adapted to organisational conditions and therefore fails to reflect the substance of the matter in question. A computerised data processing system as an integral element of the information system is a technical solution that includes selected components (data, methods and technical means). Such a system offers limited possibilities for full implementation of the software (Lutz 2019).

Only when this order is maintained can one ensure that a coherent framework of information systems for decision making can be created while maintaining the desired relations between the component subsystems. It is evident that such an intention may occur unattainable through linear action.

Due to the complexity of tasks and financial limitations and the necessity to apply complicated management methods, this approach is being defeated by relatively simple methods employed by computer specialists. The research simplism (Kilian et al. 2018, pp. 37–58), while justified from the point of view of a computer specialist who does not understand management, is truly lethal for the management system modernisation discussed here. It is necessary to fully understand the concepts, ensure their full consistency and maintain the relations between them. Therefore, there are no "typically informatic methods" which can be used as proxy to build a new organisation in which the computer will fully take over the information role. Given the accuracy of such a claim, the only way to attain the intention is through application of new methods that ensure successful cooperation within an interdisciplinary team of representatives of various management specialisations and computer specialists (Figure 1.5).

In fact, problems of similar complexity are solved by using methodologies other than hard system methodologies – e.g. soft system methodology (SSM) (Irawan et al. 2019). The said methodology was created to solve complex problems and tackle messy situations. Its application in the conditions of implementing "an informatics system", destabilising the organisation, offers an opportunity to redefine the objectives, identify particularly problematic areas, define systems needed to prevent disturbances and thus bring the organisation back to health. Originating from organisational design, the SSM is a methodology for designing IS which offers other

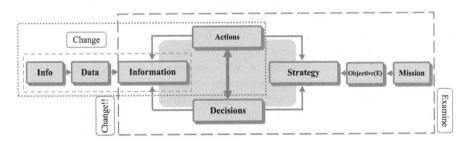

FIGURE 1.5   Place and role of information technique in organisation management.

Source: Own work based on: Lutz 2019.

solutions regarding the use of hard methods by computer specialists, which is the main source of errors. Such weak areas include ignorance of the rights that govern organisations, inability to accurately formulate objectives (uncritical acceptance of objectives) and the belief in algorithmic nature of actions taken by people active in the area of IS. The soft approach makes it possible to know, understand and modify the behaviour of people who co-create information systems, notice and understand user problems, identify major systems, properly define (redefine) system objectives and accurately choose design methods and techniques. A system created through the application of such an approach includes a design of the working system – it assumes effecting an organisational change – which, when omitted by the designers who can see only the computer role in their system, often becomes the cause of the ultimate failure.

In practice, the existence of the information system was not noticed, and its field was defined as economy, not management. In the wake of the growing interest in the use of computers to support data processing and access to the world's literature on information system, the concept of informatics system emerged. It became to reflect the subject of interest of creators of informatics systems, i.e. technicians who were proficient in computers and used them to support data processing. Informatics systems have not been defined by researchers, for they have adopted a simplifying assumption that an informatics system is synonymous to an information system. Since it is clear that the concept of informatics system remains undefined, a simplified definition has been assumed – for the sake of "order" – according to which it is a computerised part of the IS. However, no definition of IS is universally known or used to define the nature, field, objectives or structure of the subject. Furthermore, such a simplified definition of an informatics system fails to indicate what part of the IS is separated and under what criteria, and what it means to be "computerised". It is often assumed that an unconscious, perceived, defined, purposefully designed and functioning OIS performs IS's tasks and that this role has been taken over by the informatics system.

The characteristics of both systems presented in Table 1.1 confirm that the informatics system is a system only in "technological" terms (programming). At the same time, it may lead to an ascertainment that it "suffices" to focus on developing computerised solutions for they are bound to replace humans anyway.

Experiences of organisations advanced in using information techniques demonstrate clearly that a new technique does not change an organisation in which people remain the most important element. Understanding that only a human being can have (create, process and use) specific information is an important change that one needs to make to adapt to new conditions. Organisations are reengineered to cope with new requirements of hyper-competition in the conditions of "new economy". In the "information economy" conditions, information technique is no longer a factor that ensures competitive advantage (Hoffmann 2019). Although information technique as a standard good must be used, it is the ability to innovate that is the main factor behind competitive advantage (Korombel, Nowicka-Skowron 2017, pp. 9–19). A company which does not use any information technique is bound to lose to its competitors. Only organisations that are able to effectively and efficiently utilise information technique stand a chance to survive on the market.

TABLE 1.1

Characteristics of Information and Informatics System

Characteristic	IS – Information System	Informatics System
Field	information as an important factor; systems that process and transmit information	data – recorded, transmitted, stored, searched for, processed, presented, delivered to recipients
Objective of actions, outputs produced	information for every member of the organisation; operational objectives based on manager needs	structures of output data, reports accepted to date
System class	human activity system – social system	artificial system (artefact)
Components	people, artificial components (data, technical means) and abstract components (methods, organisation)	artificial systems (artefacts) – data, methods and abstract components,
Class of problems tackled	typical management problems, organisational problems	well-structured problems of computer specialists formulated according to the needs of data recipients
Characteristic	IS – information system	Informatics system
Methods of system examination, analysis and development	variety of methods, prevalence of hard methods (to date), increasing awareness of the need to employ the soft approach	hard methods
System owner	top management	head of the informatics system and line managers
Worldview	need to provide information	need to accomplish the tasks assigned
Data	all data useful to the recipient	data identified according to the old organisation template
Techniques and "technology"	all techniques suitable to adjust data for consumption by recipients	information technique, i.e. computer technique
Methods	all methods suitable to provide information	quantitative methods supported by computer technique
Technique, technology	all organisational, social and communication techniques adapted to OIS needs	computer techniques and available organisational techniques (as a supplement)
Organisation	new organisation subordinated to the objectives arising from the objectives of the organisation as a whole	inherited organisation to which the informatics system is adapted
People	people who adapt to new objectives/needs/requirements of the adapting organisation	people who are learning new technical solutions
Human role	human being as an IS component is a conscious and responsible factor thereof	human being is treated as a technical element

Source: Own work.

Data is still representation of information. Data processing functions are strictly technical matters which can be efficiently solved today, thanks to information technique. This does not mean, however, that performing all operations on the representation of information has dominated the sphere of creating, adapting and using information. Therefore, the field of information should be perceived, in particular, in the area of management in which it exists, and shaped by that area according to the needs.

IS should become an area of studies that adapt decades-long solutions to new opportunities created by the scientific and technical progress. Information systems are developed to streamline and improve organisations rather than to make them more modern. Development of IS requires application of methods that allow utilising the great ability of information technique to improve operations of people and their teams. Operating in "full information" conditions within their organisations, they are able to achieve incomparably better results. Such aspiration is by all means justified. If organisations want to achieve great economic objectives, they must change radically to cope with competitors and take the lead as soon as possible. One must have information and should be able to use it, even to just evaluate the situation accurately.

Organisational changes which are bound to take place in the near future represent another challenge which must be met by information systems. An organisational change is indeed perceived as another frontier in the development of information systems, not informatics systems (Neuhaus 2019, pp. 73–126). Information systems, the awareness of their importance and the ability to create and use them offer opportunities to adapt to new conditions arising from competition.

An informatics system "is designed on the basis of an inventory" (Kura et al. 2019, pp. 1821–1839) of a data processing system. Designed informatics systems demonstrate contradiction between the manner of perceiving informatics (as a usable field of operations) and business management – not as an applied art, but as means of political influence (ruling over people). Information systems belong to the field of management and as such have a decisive impact on its effectiveness and efficiency. Adopting the technical point of view on IS means dominance of the tool over the user and, in consequence, loss of opportunities related to the ability to draw quick gains thanks to changes. They will materialise, but only when computer specialists begin to notice management and make changes that give competitive advantage. Indeed, such are objectives of management, and information systems are supported by IT so that they could give an organisation a competitive advantage. Information technique does not offer such an advantage any longer.

Information technique employed in the area of management comes together with improvement (modernisation) of management rather than computerisation of management (because it is impracticable and inadvisable). Thus, information systems, as an area of management, should be the most important area both in the sphere of studies and didactics. Their replacement with informatics systems means that, for management, the tool is more important than identification of objectives and ensuring methods to attain them. At present, management's reliance on information is becoming increasingly evident, and the emergence of new approaches and methods shows that competitors are active in their attempts to win advantage. Such an approach should serve the purpose of maintaining and gaining competitive advantage both in the field of studies and education.

While entailing the necessity of thorough organisational restructuring to use all opportunities offered by the new medium (information technique) to its users, studies in applications of information technique to support organisations require submission to a different paradigm. Changing the paradigm is related to a different approach to information technique, which implies the necessity to perceive it in its new role of new energy that has never been used before (Anderl 2018, pp. 1997–2011). Therefore, while studying the needs of IS in the new era, one must realise that data alone does not satisfy the need of information, although it can help to do so.

Knowledge which provides for adapting data to ensure generation of information which is necessary to take actions is an important component of every information and decision- making system. Development of information technique applications clearly reflects the intentions to make integrated use of knowledge to support data processing in methods which ensure more effective acquisition of information by data recipients, which is taking place at present.

Actions taken should focus on management issues. Management has a decisive influence on needs, which is why changes must be sought for in this particular area, while application of information technique is a derivative of the needs and issues which are to be tackled by new information system solutions.

This direction of studies was and continues to be more promising for the future. Although the notion of informatics sounds more attractive, focusing on information systems better reflects the essence of the matter while at the same time not eliminating information technique. Since application of information technique is indispensable in studies and in the practice of IS development, this remains an important tool in the sphere of scientific interest.

The above analysis of concepts of information, information systems and informatics systems leads to presenting the following conclusions and methods of utilising them.

IS is and will remain the fundamental management concept, and its meaning is becoming ever more significant in the changing management conditions. Dissemination of information technique (computer technique) as support for management processes not only checks the human being from playing the key role but it also requires humans to meet greater requirements. At the same time, it means that the information system and human being as an element of that system face tasks that are more complex and advanced than simple computing activities. These new tasks increasingly often include management and analytical tasks. Exclusion of humans from execution of information tasks (replacement of IS with informatics systems) is an illusion.

1.3   DATA–INFORMATION–KNOWLEDGE RELATIONS

Rapid growth of globalisation tendencies in economy as well as political transformations and dynamic development of the Internet – phenomena which have been particularly noticeable since the beginning of the 1990s – have made everyone clearly aware of the role played by information in the life of modern-day societies. The electronic revolution, bringing the birth of information society, has become a fact. However, it must be highlighted that although the concept of information society is relatively new and somewhat surprising to an average citizen, it was anticipated already in the 1960s. Visions of futurologists and sociological studies emerged from a clearly noticeable new paradigm which was closely related to the concept of information society.

The available literature lack an unequivocal definition of information society, for the concept is of an interdisciplinary nature belonging to the fields of sociology, economy and technical sciences. Unfortunately, the matter of information society is quite frequently brought down to the purely technological dimension. Although no one challenges contemporary information techniques as a factor which makes it possible to transform industrial society into information society, it is wrong to put too much emphasis on ensuring adequate infrastructure while underestimating the sphere of sociology, law and economy (Krebs 2019). One definition of information society indicates the attribute of a specific form of social organisation in which information generation, processing and transmission become the fundamental sources of productivity and power because of new technological conditions emerging in this historical period (Capurro 2017, pp. 127–148).

The most important concepts regarding information society include, undoubtedly, the terms "data", "information" and "knowledge". Unfortunately, they are used interchangeably and often inaccurately. The lack of accuracy frequently causes wrong understanding of the essence of information society and information economy. Understanding these terms is particularly important now, when the volume of information collected and made available is virtually limitless. The excessive volume of data and large amounts of useless information were already signalled by Christian Möller. He claimed that in view of large amounts of data handled by organisations, selection and meaning compression of excessive amounts of information would be a particularly valued functionality of information systems (Möller 2019, pp. 155–193).

The terms "data", "information" and "knowledge" are considered to be difficult to define due to their primary nature. They are used interchangeably in the informal speech. As they represent a special subject of interest of two disciplines – knowledge management and theory of information – the name of the hierarchy of cognitive concepts differs from discipline to discipline and is either the pyramid or hierarchy of knowledge or pyramid or hierarchy of information. There is also the term DIKW (Figure 1.6) – which is an acronym for the terms data, information, knowledge and wisdom.

FIGURE 1.6   The DIKW hierarchy.

Source: Own work.

The theory of information constantly struggles with the problem of lacks in definitions of its primary concepts. The hierarchy of cognitive concepts consists of four levels: data, information, knowledge and wisdom. Unfortunately, although no one challenges the hierarchy itself or the direction of generalisation, no clear, satisfactory and generally acceptable definitions of the concepts have been developed yet. Since the last of the DIKW concepts – wisdom – belongs to the realm of philosophy, it is not discussed here.

The literature quite often provides the concept of the cognitive chain data – information – knowledge – wisdom. One may raise doubts regarding the addition of the term wisdom to that chain or the term value – which is sometimes also added, because of the differing bases adopted to define them.

A question also arises whether the chain exhausts all concepts which exist in informatics and, potentially, management, and which also form its part, and how they can be defined consistently and in harmony with other concepts.

Isabel Steinhardt and Christian Schneijderberg describe data as objects, facts on which one can rely in their deliberations. As regards information, they assume that it can be defined as structured data (…) Structuring of data according to a certain key means that it can form the basis for formulating conclusions or predictions. As regards knowledge, they write that, in practical terms, knowledge can be defined as usable information. As for wisdom, they assume that it is the ability to take prudent and appropriate actions in a specific situation, based on ethical problem solving in accordance with one's system of beliefs (Steinhardt, Schneijderberg 2019, pp. 183–204).

It is not difficult to notice that the authors have not avoided certain inconsistencies and inaccuracies. Namely, given the aforementioned interpretation of the concept of information, it is impossible to determine *a priori* whether a set of figures – e.g. data obtained from a statistical yearbook – is already information or whether it requires further structuring. Furthermore, in this perspective, information is always a subjective concept, as it is obtained through the said structuring according to a subjective criterion assumed arbitrarily by the user.

This position significantly reduces the scope of the meaning of the term information – it excludes, e.g. the existence of objective (potential) information independent from the subjective interpretation of a specific recipient.

Knowledge, as usable information, has also been greatly reduced. Such an approach raises at least two reservations (North, Brandner, Steininger 2016, pp. 5–8):

- It is impossible to establish in advance whether a granule of information is usable or not. It becomes substantiated to assume that there will always be a recipient for whom a granule received is usable to a certain degree, while other recipients will find it as information noise.
- The scope of knowledge interpreted in this manner fails to include rich resources of data which is unstructured and therefore represents non-information and, in consequence, non-knowledge. This becomes particularly aggravated in the absence of any criteria of such restructuring.

Doubts are raised also by the reduction of wisdom to merely the ability to take prudent and appropriate actions in a specific situation – even if it is based on a specific system of beliefs. Indeed, it is difficult to reduce all actions only to decision-making. It is therefore important to notice the need for searching for the bases for developing clearer and more precise statements and definitions in this respect. Lacks in the often-quoted idea of Shannon's mathematical theory of communication are particularly noticeable. Competitive to Shannon's work (Sienkiewicz 2019, pp. 593–599) and more appropriate in the area of information systems is the so-called Langefors infological theory (Gryncewicz 2007, pp. 158–168). This idea can be described in short by the so-called infological equation formulated by Langefors which assumes that information is a certain function of the process of interpretation of data taking into account the recipient's knowledge and time they need to make that interpretation (Stefanowicz 2017, pp. 11–22).

This encourages one to analyse these concepts taking into account the common plane of analysis offered by the infological approach and the concept of infological relation. The Langefors's infological equation reflects the idea of searching for a way to record large data sets on media so that its content can be analysed according to individual needs of the user, assuming that the complex and ambiguous concept of information should be treated as a derivative concept based on auxiliary concepts – data. Sundgren introduced an auxiliary concept of message M as a structured set (Zakrzewski, Kamińska 2010, pp. 11–37):

$$M : \langle O, X, x, t \rangle \tag{1.1}$$

where:

O object is the main element (subject) of the message; O may mean any tangible or intangible (virtual) object, process, event, abstract concept, ownership of another object, relation taking place between objects studied, etc. – so everything which in the natural language can be named with the use of a noun,

X attribute due to which object O is described in the message concerned,

x value of attribute X,

t time in which object O takes value x of attribute X.

Sundgren termed elements of message M as data. According to this concept, no data carries any content, as the latter arises only from the combination of the elements provided in (1.1), i.e. data. Message M defined in the form of formula (1.1) can be read as follows: "object O has value x of attribute X in time i". When combined in one whole in accordance with formula (1.1), the component pieces of data are given certain sense (meaning) by the message through binding them with a certain relation. This relation is called infological relation which provides content referred to as information. In other words, information is a relation defined on elements of message M in accordance with formula (1.1). Sundgren calls it information at the datalogical, or objective, level. At this level, information carried by M can be written as I(M). Symbol I in I(M) means information contained in M regardless of the recipient (Maciąg 2008, pp. 271–286). It should be added that both I(M) and other symbols are provided only for the purpose of shortening the text and do not represent an attempt at formalising the narration.

In practice, information takes on meaning in the context of its use by specific recipients. It is therefore appropriate to complement information I(M) with another component – user U. This can be shown in the form of formula (1.2):

$$I(M,U):\langle M,U\rangle \tag{1.2}$$

where:

M means a message defined in accordance with relation (1.1),
U means the specific recipient of the content (information) of the massage.

Formula (1.2) defines information in the infological sense – i.e. information in the subjective sense. Information I(M) at the objective level does not require the existence of a specific addressee, the recipient, as the necessary condition.

In its original form, the Sundgren formula is based on the sign notation. At the same time, in a broader perspective, the concept of information goes beyond the framework of sign representation of data that includes all other multimedia forms. The infological formula can be used to express information through sound (music) and graphics (image).

The infological formula (1.1) refers directly only to the concept of information. However, it can be generalised and expanded to include other complex concepts (non-primary, derivative) which are conceptually built of certain components – auxiliary concepts.

This approach is based on the assumption that synergy – as the source of the effect (added value) achieved as a result of combining individual components that cannot be achieved by either of them individually – is a universal property of reality. In particular, it justifies development of all kinds of systems, including informatics systems, when it becomes needed to acquire a new property or function which is not provided by any component on its own – be it devices, technologies, organisation, etc.

In the context of these deliberations, synergy – manifested as a result of conceptual (semantic) combination of a set of component concepts within the defining formula (*definiens*) – brings to existence a new concept (*definiendum*) which could not emerge if the component concepts concerned were separated. For instance, in the infological perspective, none of the elements of the message (1.1) on its own provides information in separation from the others. Combining the component elements contained therein, the formula creates a new relation – the infological relation.

It can generally be assumed that a combination of any several concepts, even selected at random, provides a certain "added value" (information) – it either explains something or brings to light a new complex concept, although we may not comprehend it.

The infological approach assumes that the *definiendum* is given as an unknown complex concept and an infological relation must be built to explain its meaning. This implies the necessity to construct the *definiens* as a set of known auxiliary concepts which give specific content to the unknown concept concerned. This requires searching for "allies" that will contribute to explaining the *definiendum* and calls for noticing and discovering specific logical relations between them (i.e. the infological relation), which normally is the most difficult part. Naturally, in the general case, these may be very different structures. The infological relation does not assume any limitations regarding the content or quantity of the concepts referenced. However, a case should be brought to attention where the quantity of such concepts is reduced to just a single concept – then one can say that the new concept (*definiendum*) is defined as a synonym of the concept which is provided in the *definiens*. It should be also emphasised that an excessively long list of defining concepts is, for obvious reasons, inconvenient and difficult to understand – instead of explaining, it often leads to chaos and ambiguity.

Based on these assumptions, in the following paragraphs the author discusses the concepts of knowledge and wisdom as concepts whose meaning is described through the infological relation.

As regards knowledge, there are numerous definitions and interpretations in the literature. However, it is difficult to regard any of these definitions and interpretations as unequivocally convincing in every respect. The term continues to be ambiguous. Not embarking on a broad analysis, let this discussion be limited to the formula proposed by Thomas H. Davenport and Laurence Prusak:

> Knowledge is a fluid mix of framed experience, values, contextual information, and expert insight that provides a framework for evaluating and incorporating new experiences and information. It originates and is applied in the minds of knowers. In organisation, it often becomes embedded not only in documents or repositories but also in organisational routines, processes, practices, and norms
>
> (Glinkowska 2012, pp. 339–350)

Leszek Panasiewicz interprets this as the assumption that knowledge is *płynna mieszanka wyrażonego doświadczenia, wartości, informacji wypływających z kontekstu i eksperckiej wnikliwości, które dostarczają podstaw do oceny i przyswajania nowych doświadczeń i informacji* (Panasiewicz 2019, pp. 12–17).

This thought can be captured more briefly in the infological form:

$$\text{knowledge} : \langle \text{information} + \text{experiences} + \text{context} \rangle \qquad (1.3)$$

where "+" is the symbol of a logical link between the auxiliary concept in this formula.

The formula (1.3) shows an infological relation built on the auxiliary concepts of information, experiences and context. According to it, knowledge manifests itself only as a result of joining information with experiences, having regard to the context in which the information and experiences are taken into account. Knowledge is value added to information through experiences and ability to comprehend its true potential.

There is also an opinion that knowledge means structured information. Each of these cases is covered by formula (1.3) – one just needs to add new elements (concepts) or remove the existing ones. Thus, it is easy to reduce the formula to the

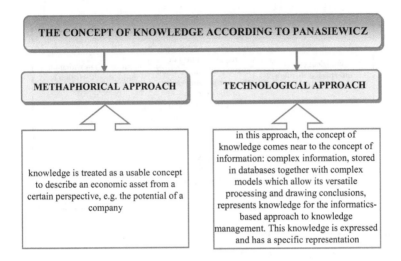

FIGURE 1.7   Interpretation of the concept of knowledge according to Panasiewicz.

Source: Own work based on: Panasiewicz 2004, pp. 42–49.

sentence saying that knowledge is information which is applied to solve a problem. Panasiewicz presents several approaches to interpreting the concept of knowledge, in particular the ones shown in Figure 1.7.

Based on these opinions, it is not difficult to deduce that formula (1.3) does not exhaust all variants and that its structure and the content of the *definiens* can be changed and other elements can be added and existing ones removed. Therefore, if experiences and context are removed from formula (1.3), the only information is left. Nevertheless, formula (1.3) will remain an infological relation, albeit a single-element one, which leads to a thesis that knowledge can be interpreted as a synonym of information.

It is easy to notice that infological formula (1.3) provides for a multi-faceted analysis of knowledge as defined above taking into account all the listed components. Based on (1.3), it can be deduced that experiences allow noticing both individual knowledge (when they relate to a specific person) and collective knowledge (when they are experiences of a team of cooperative persons).

Opinions on knowledge held by a number of authors lead to an assumption that there are no grounds to challenge or prefer either of them. In fact, when put together, they contribute a greater cognitive input to knowledge than either of them separately. In the context of these deliberations, particular attention should be brought to the opinion by Andreas Suchanek that the "sum" of personal knowledge and experience, enriched with knowledge and experiences of others, is a characteristic property of wisdom (Suchanek 2020, pp. 109–123).

Based on this, one can build a picture of wisdom (marked as Ω) as synergy created by combining the three components shown in Figure 1.8.

Context C is similar to context C taken into consideration in the case of knowledge. In this case, however, it is enriched with values taken by the individual such as moral, religious and ethical values based on which a person builds his or her vision of the

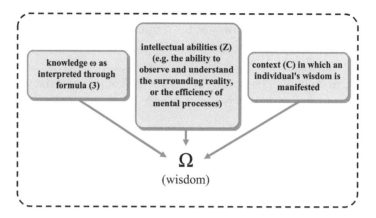

FIGURE 1.8 Picture of wisdom.

Source: Own work based on: Thielscher 2020, pp. 15–49.

world and rules of conduct. In this regard, context C consists of two areas: permanent principles (ethical, moral, religious) and principles arising from life and ongoing activity. The former can be called the fixed context and the latter – the variable context. The variable context determines the manifestation of wisdom in specific situations which are, however, consistent with the individual's wisdom arising from the fixed context.

With these assumptions, wisdom Ω can be symbolically represented as follows:

$$\Omega : \langle \omega, Z, C \rangle \qquad (1.4)$$

Within the framework of the above-defined relation, knowledge is interpreted as the effect of a joint consideration of information (I), experiences (E) and context (C) according to formula (1.3), whereas information (I) is the content describing an object (O) due to a specific property (X) which takes value X in time t – in accordance with formula (1.1). Wisdom can also be interpreted as the content of a slightly more complex structure in the form of formula (1.4). Therefore, all three concepts – information, knowledge and wisdom – are interpreted in a similar manner: as the content of a certain sentence-relation. In the case of information, such a sentence is relatively simple (namely, it is formula (1.1)); in the case of knowledge (formula (1.3)), the sentence becomes more complex, as it includes formula (1.1); and in the case of wisdom (formula (1.4)), it is even more complex.

Methodology based on the infological relation understood as a structure that joins purposefully selected known auxiliary concepts shows the way to explaining and defining a complex derivative concept, as demonstrated by the example of information, knowledge and wisdom. The infological relation appears in every structure in which combination of the concepts included is accented, regardless of its form. The infological relation allows flexible treatment of the structure of the *definiens* by offering the freedom to add new concepts. Thus, one can expand formula (1.1) by adding additional components to provide a more precise description of an object, particularly units of measurement attributed to measurable properties.

The infological relation operationalises the concepts defined – through providing *explicite* a set of known components of the *definiens*, it allows one to design processes for utilising these components according to one's needs and even to deploy modern information and communication technologies in these processes, such as developing information systems together with their components in the form of databases and knowledge repositories. Explanation of differences and convergences between various terms and concepts is important both in theoretical and practical terms. In the first case, it allows building consistent theories and theoretical ideas. In the latter, it reduces ambiguities and, frequently, confusion among decision-makers regarding organisation of information systems and pooling of resources tailored to the actual needs, in particular, actual gathering of information under the heading of knowledge, which to a certain degree may ennoble the efforts undertaken. It allows logical structuring of concepts concerned in a common sequence, such as the cognitive sequence covering the title concepts. Unfortunately, the infological relation does not ensure unambiguity of the *definiendum* – anyone can draft the *definiens* according to their own idea and select appropriate components. However, it still offers the ability to consistently analyse any idea and search for convergent elements as well as elements that differentiate one definition from another.

Further deliberations will focus around the matters of signal transmission through an information channel, taking into account the information noise, stochastic nature of the process and properties of the recipient of a message. Inspired by the concept of entropy taken from thermodynamics, C.E. Shannon claimed that a reduction of the user's entropy (uncertainty, ignorance) is a characteristic property of information. Although Shannon's theory did not define information itself – only its quantity – it contributes much to these deliberations, for it highlights the fact that information always reduces entropy. Shannon's theory identifies information with data and is specific to technical sciences, in particular the theory of codes and teletransmission (Kärtner 2019, pp. 116–135).

The so-called infological theory of Langefors is competitive for C.E. Shannon's work and more appropriate to the field of information systems (Lombardi, Holik, Vanni 2016, pp. 1983–2012). Contrary to the datalogical approach, the infological approach clearly differentiates between information and data and puts strong emphasis on taking user requirements into account. B. Langefors claims that information can come into being in a human mind through a process of data interpretation. B. Langefors is the author of the so-called infological equation which is expressed in the following formula:

$$I = i(D,S,t) \tag{1.5}$$

where:

I   information,
i   process of interpretation,
D   data,
S   pre-knowledge,
t   time.

Interpreting the Equation 1.5 shown above, one can say that information is a process of interpretation of data on the basis of knowledge *a priori* in time. One should note the subjective nature of information, i.e. the fact that specific data may lead different people to draw different information.

In addition to the theories specified above, there are also a great number of definitions of information. An analysis of those definitions shows that some of them are closer to the concept of data, while others to the concept of knowledge. A great many of these definitions draw attention to the close relation between information and decision-making. Information is life-giving blood in the organism of management – it is the basis for the right management decisions. If no appropriate information can be acquired, decisions must be based on presumptions, feelings or guessing (Lyre 2017, pp. 477–493).

Information is the fundamental factor affecting decision-making in all spheres of life, not only in management. As the foundation for information, data must first of all be comprehensible and should contain news for the recipient. Defining information in the context of the information system (IS), Y. Kautt notices that information is what changes and supports understanding, whereas data represents the entrance to the communication channel. Data is tangible and consists of numbers, words, telephone calls or computer printouts, either sent or received. Data will only provide information when humans use it to better understand a specific matter (Kautt 2019, pp. 31–42). Information systems in an organisation should provide information rather than data.

In an organisation, information is the foundation for building knowledge for all people involved in the process of its acquisition and use, shaping the awareness of the phenomena which take place within the organisation and its surrounding. It allows the organisation to adapt to the changing reality and transform that reality in order to ensure efficient operations. Thanks to information, the organisation can realise the existing problems and search for solutions.

When examining the role and significance of information to the recipient, one also needs to point out that quality, resulting from certain properties of information, is its important attribute (Figure 1.9).

A detailed business and process-oriented model of information technique management in organisations first defines the following, partially overlapping, criteria which any information provided must meet (Tiemeyer 2020):

- effectiveness – concerns ensuring relevant, pertinent and usable information delivered in a timely, correct and consistent form,
- efficiency – concerns the provision of information through the optimal (economical) use of resources,
- confidentiality – concerns the protection of sensitive information from unauthorized disclosure and use,
- integrity – relates to the accuracy and completeness of information as well as to its validity in accordance with business expectations,
- availability – makes information available when required by a specific business process at a specific time; it also concerns the safeguarding of necessary resources and associated capabilities,

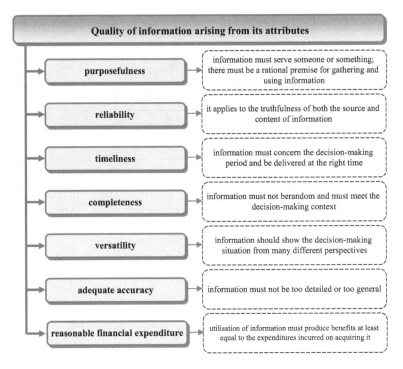

FIGURE 1.9 Quality of information arising from its attributes.

Source: Own work based on: Jecker, Huck-Sandhu 2020, pp. 351–371.

- compliance – deals with externally imposed requirements, laws, regulations, agreements as well as specific internal requirements and policies,
- reliability – relates to the provision of appropriate information in order to meet governance responsibilities.

Information is one of the key elements of decision-making. Lack of relevant information entails uncertainty. Changes in the surrounding and non-routine or interdependent technologies may cause uncertainty and increase situational ambiguity among managers. Uncertainty means absence of information – the higher the uncertainty, the more the need to acquire and process information. Quantity of information means the plurality of data on the organisation's operations gathered and interpreted by members of that organisation. In a high uncertainty situation, data can be gathered to reduce that uncertainty. (…) Ambiguity of information means that a situation cannot be analysed and understood objectively; no additional information can be gathered to solve the problem (Klinger et al. 2020, pp. 185–199) (Figure 1.10 and Table 1.2).

Information needs arise from the information gap (Figure 1.11) and depend on a number of factors.

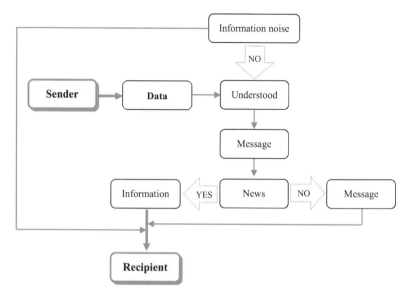

FIGURE 1.10   Data, messages, information.

Source: Own work.

TABLE 1.2
Summary of Selected Definitions of Information and the Related Functions

Authors	Definition of Information	Main Functions of Information
N. Wiener (1961)	A content taken from the outside world in the process of our adaptation to it and making our senses adjusted to it.	Representation of the past, present and future. Creation and alteration of the reality.
H. Greniewski (1982)	A message obtained by a person through observation or mental activity, subject to transmission in the sender-recipient system.	
Z. Gackowski (1977, p. 37)	Properties of a signal or message reduce ambiguity of the situation or its further developments.	
T. Wierzbicki (1981, p. 9)	A content taken from the outside world which increases knowledge or decreases the decision-maker's ignorance, uncertainty and ambiguity of the decision-making situation.	
J. Lyons (1984, p. 60)	A content with specific meaning about something, for someone and due to something, expressed through linguistic and/or non-linguistic signs.	Presentation of events, states, things, objects, etc., from the perspective of the past, present or future.
T. Kasprzak (definition from 1971)	Reflection of what exists in the material sense (the so-called reflection relation) and a factor defining, to a certain degree, the form of future things and phenomena (the so-called realisation relation)	Identification and anticipation. Reduction of the degree of uncertainty. Definition of the degree of system organisation.
Z. Mesner (1971)	Data on economic processes and phenomena used in the decision-making process.	Identification and solution of problems.

Source: Own work based on: Klinger et al. 2020, pp. 185–199.

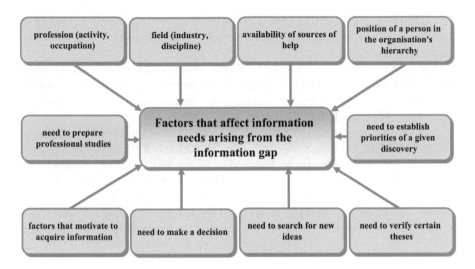

FIGURE 1.11   Factors that affect information needs arising from the information gap.

Source: Own work based on: Eickhoff et al. 2019, pp. 45–108.

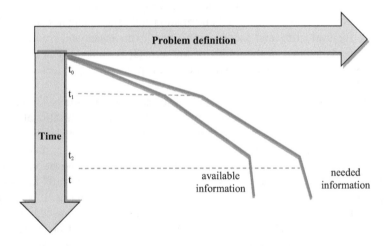

FIGURE 1.12   Information gap.

Source: Own work.

The information gap is primarily related to the uncertainty factor and availability of information at the time for making a decision (Figure 1.12). Decision-makers never have full information regarding a specific subject. Decision-making is therefore always related to risk, but information of adequate quality can reduce that risk.

Perceiving information as processed data leads to ignoring the important role of interpretation of information. A unit of data is one or more symbols used for representing something. Information is interpreted data. Information is data put in a meaningful context. Information has a subjective nature and must always be considered in the context of its recipient. The same data can be interpreted differently depending on knowledge, and knowledge is obtained from information through its integration with the existing knowledge.

Although there are many definitions of knowledge, most sources point out ambiguity of this term which is understood as all information acquired through learning, a resource of information from a certain field, awareness of something (Skowron-Grabowska, Szczepanik, Besta 2019, pp. 1012–1019).

It seems that a complete definition of data, information and knowledge has been presented by T.H. Davenport and L. Prusak. They clearly differentiate between the three concepts while focusing on knowledge, which they define as information in action. According to Davenport and Prusak, data is a set of discrete, objective facts about events. In technological terms, data is most often stored in the form of a set of records which represent specific transactions made by an organisation. Data alone has no purpose or meaning. In turn, information is "data which makes the difference". Data can be transformed into information through adding value to it. This can be done through contextualisation, categorisation, calculation, correction and condensation of data (Gibbons, Prusak 2020, pp. 187–92). As already mentioned, knowledge can be obtained from information through comparing situations, conversing with the recipients and defining consequences or connections with other information. The definition of knowledge by Davenport and Prusak appears as a fluid mix of framed experience, values, contextual information and expert insight that provides a framework for evaluating and incorporating new experiences and information. It originates and is applied in the minds of knowers. It is embedded in documents, repositories as well as organisational procedures, processes, practices and norms (Brătianu 2017, pp. 477–479).

The definition of knowledge proposed by Davenport and Prusak is similar to the concept of "hard knowledge" presented by I. Nonaka. In the organisational context, Nonaka distinguishes two types of knowledge – tacit or hidden knowledge and "hard" or concrete knowledge. He claims that it is tacit knowledge, hidden in the minds of people, which is extremely important in the process of innovation. Through its expression and application, tacit knowledge can evolve into "hard" knowledge, i.e. explicit, articulated knowledge captured in procedures and norms. It is common to underestimate tacit knowledge while overestimating "hard" knowledge which is identified with data and information. As people "plough through" data, they continuously interpret it either as "noise" (ignored and insignificant) or information (important in a certain sense). When data reaches their minds, they attribute a certain meaning to it. This shows how important human role is in transformation of data into information. Information is data which refers to the recipient's situation (Nonaka, Nishihara 2018, pp. 1–15).

Knowledge is also the potential to act effectively and cannot be transformed into an object or given by one person to another. Knowledge is transformed only in the process of learning, when a person creates new potential to act effectively. Information technique, which is crucial for dissemination of information, cannot gather or store knowledge. Only people can do that (Nonaka, Nishihara, Kawada 2018, pp. 1–21).

Based on such assumptions, one can conclude that the main task of knowledge management should be to provide people with appropriate – in terms of time, form and relevance – data. It must be adapted to the recipients' existing potential, i.e. their current knowledge, as well as to their ability to learn. Only then can data be transformed into information and subsequently remembered and gathered as the recipient's knowledge. "Hard" knowledge, although objective, does not necessarily expand the recipients' knowledge and sometimes may cause chaos when it is misunderstood and misinterpreted.

The multitude and ambiguity of definitions – particularly ones regarding information and knowledge – require clarification of the respective concepts. Taking the above deliberations into account, one can formulate the following functional definitions of data, information and knowledge.

Data represents facts. In computer-aided management systems, data is coded with appropriate symbols. It can be recorded, processed and transmitted. Since data is transmitted to the recipient's consciousness in the form of a message, every message contains data. Although data alone has no meaning or purpose, selection of appropriate symbols can imply or suggest specific interpretation.

Information is data contained in a message which is interpreted by and is meaningful for the recipient and therefore reduces the recipient's ignorance. For data to become information, there must be a recipient who will decide, firstly, whether he or she wants to interpret it and, secondly, whether he or she comprehends it and to what extent. Then data becomes message for that recipient. Next, the recipient determines whether the message is a repetition of something he or she already knows or whether it is a new element, in which case the message becomes information. Since information depends on the recipient's interpretation ability, it has a subjective nature.

Knowledge arises from information which is relevant to the recipient and has been verified in practice (Figure 1.13).

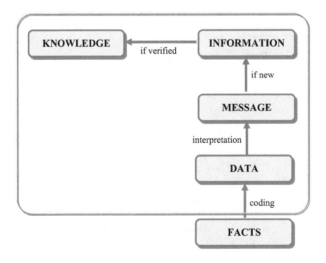

FIGURE 1.13 Shaping of knowledge.

Source: Own work.

Verification involves establishing whether conclusions drawn in the process of interpretation conform to the reality; hence, knowledge is information that is relevant and empirically verifiable. Other information, i.e. irrelevant and short-lived (e.g. today's data), does not represent knowledge.

The recipient's existing knowledge is decisive for the interpretation and understanding of data and relevance of information. In this light, data is objective whereas information is subjective. This is so because its emergence is decided by either a human being or a specific organisational context. It is also difficult to describe knowledge as a subjective feeling of the recipient, although knowledge is indeed shaped in the recipient's mind and cannot be considered in separation from the subjective process of thinking. However, there are facts, methods and procedures which have already been verified in practice by many people and organisations. One can say that they are binding and therefore carry objective knowledge. For organisations, such carriers of relevant knowledge are the so-called "good practices", i.e. procedures and processes which have proven their worth in many organisations but will not necessarily work everywhere. However, the fact that a procedure has been tested in a number of situations becomes the objectifying factor. They can be described as "hard knowledge" which, when captured in the form of data, methods and procedures, can be stored in an organisation's information systems.

The so-called tacit knowledge of individual nature, which cannot be stored as such, is a separate matter. Acquisition of information and shaping of tacit knowledge has a dynamic character (Figure 1.14). From the perspective of a specific recipient, information which is relevant today will become unimportant and unneeded after some time. They carry a certain load of knowledge which will become the recipient's knowledge once absorbed. However, the same data can become the basis for shaping the knowledge of another recipient.

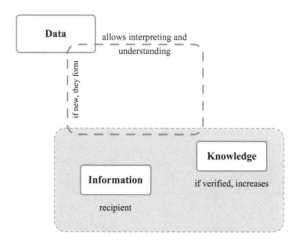

FIGURE 1.14   Relations between data, information and knowledge.

Source: Own work.

Transformation of a person's knowledge into data which can, and even should, increase knowledge of other people is a separate issue. It involves representation of knowledge in the form of data which is sufficiently universal for many recipients to be able to comprehend the data and then correctly interpret and absorb it as their own knowledge. The said interpretation is a significant barrier for it is specifically bound with the recipient's existing knowledge and ability to learn.

The concept of knowledge itself and its definition generates many problems and controversies, and consequently more problems are related to knowledge management, firstly as a term and secondly as a sphere of organisational activity. Information technique provides numerous tools which enable more effective dissemination of data and information, and therefore it has potential to increase knowledge of individual entities, in particular in times when excess of data and efficient selection of data are very problematic. At present, finding required information takes a long time, which reduces time left for fathoming information. However, the manner in which data is used depends solely on the recipients' abilities, intellect and knowledge.

2 Information as a Database in an Organisation

2.1 INFORMATION AS AN ELEMENT WHICH DETERMINES THE SUCCESS OF AN ORGANISATION

The changing environment and the pace of those changes make information an important element which determines the success of all ventures. Large, often excessive, quantities of various types of information require it to be appropriately gathered, processed and made available to the recipients in an appropriate form and extent, which currently is accomplished with the use of information systems, which have been largely determined by informatic solution. Effectiveness of utilisation of information resources is determined not only by the quality of an information system but also by the ability to properly use information, which to a significant extent is based on knowledge and experience.

Initiated by the civilisational development, the volatility of operating conditions, market competition and globalisation trends make any activity dependent on the necessity to hold adequate data and information resources, which the aforementioned conditions show as a typically economic dimension.

Every organisation operating in free market competition represents an open system whose activity is strongly dependent on the conditions and circumstances created by the so-called external environment. This dependence requires a continuous flow of information between the organisation and its external environment. It also shows the importance attributed to information gathering and processing systems, particularly where the external environment is characterised by instability and unpredictability. Nowadays, information becomes not only a factor that determines operations but it is also the primary source an organisation's competitive advantage, adding to its market value in the area of the so-called intangible assets. It is not just about any information, but about information that will enable an organisation to predict phenomena and processes which are important for its operations. This applies particularly to information which signals opportunities and risks that appear outside or inside an organisation.

Although there are many definitions of information, none of them is fully universal and generally acceptable. Information is normally presented in a descriptive form, for instance as in Figure 2.1.

DOI: 10.1201/9781003271345-2

a factor which increases our knowledge about the surrounding reality

combination of data in an abstract model of a real object

INFORMATION

a type of resources which allows us to increase our knowledge about us and the surrounding world

virtually everything which can be captured electronically, i.e. recorded in the form of a sequence of bits

FIGURE 2.1　Definitions of information.

Source: Own work based on: Bergemann, Morris 2019, pp. 44–95.

Information is considered according to two approaches – quantitative and qualitative. While the quantitative approach describes information processes in terms of uncertainty and probability, the qualitative approach describes information and studies its properties and meaning in terms of use. Deliberations regarding the qualitative approach evolve in several directions, mainly in datalogical and infological terms (Podolski et al. 2019, pp. 112–133).

In datalogical terms, information is depersonified and is carried only by data. In infological terms, information is considered through its practical usability in strict relation with the author – sender and/or the user – recipient of information. Information is defined as meaning – the content that can be attributed to data with appropriate interpretation. Here, interpretation means the process of giving sense and relevance to data which is driven by psychological, sociological, semantic and linguistic factors (Bombała 2017, p. 2).

Information is a result of data processing, a product of transformation of data taking place during the so-called information process. Information arises from data through arithmetical, logical, merger and division operations leading to a better understanding or presentation of a matter, problem or situation. Being a result of result of data processing, it normally has greater value than data alone, which is the basis for its creation.

In the information process, information is based on data resources which often have various forms and contents. Data alone is only an element of information and does not have any information value. Data is a set of parameters, symbols, records of events, processes or states. It normally is represented by figures, records of facts, descriptions of situations or events.

Data can describe facts and phenomena in various ways, as shown in Figure 2.2.

Data processing does not always lead to the emergence of information. This is the case when a result of data transformation cannot be utilised by the user, e.g. to make a decision, demonstrating its uselessness. Information which emerges through data processing can be further processed, becoming input data in another information process. There are also cases when processed data represent information in a specific context, while in other contexts it is useless or require further processing. Quality of information is considered in terms of its decision-making usability and operational suitability.

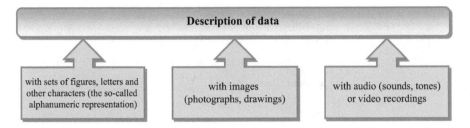

FIGURE 2.2   Description of data.

Source: Own work.

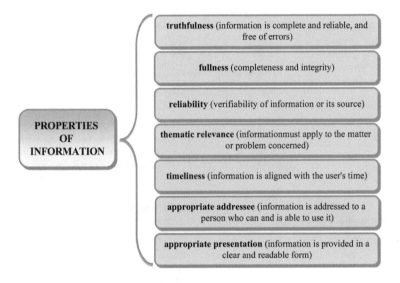

FIGURE 2.3   Criteria of evaluation of information quality.

Source: Own work based on: Kollmann 2019, pp. 139–258.

Due to multiple criteria applicable to the concept of quality, the manner of select-ing quality properties of information and understanding the content of each of them depend on the user. Indeed, the user's personality and experience affect both the selection of quality criteria and the scale of their value. Quality of information can be evaluated according to the properties shown in Figure 2.3.

The variety of approaches to and interpretations of information, as well as different criteria assumed, have led to the emergence of inconsistent classification profiles.

When considering the term "information" from the infological point of view and limiting its scope only to the purposes of the management process, one can distin-guish the types of information shown in Figure 2.4.

Taking into account the impact of information on how organisations operate and the nature of its effect, one can distinguish the following groups of information (Figure 2.5).

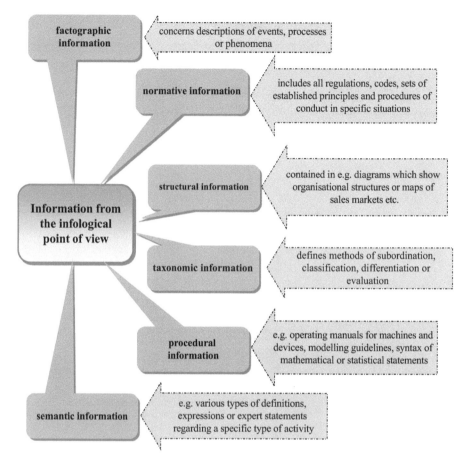

FIGURE 2.4 Types of information from the infological point of view in terms of management needs.

Source: Own work based on: Tiemeyer 2020.

The above classification profile of the concept of information, limited to operations of an organisation and presented in generic and functional terms, does not include a criterion that is crucial for information processes, namely the passing time. Taking the time criterion into account, information can be divided as shown in Figure 2.6.

In information processes, the greatest importance is attributed to current information, pointing out the significance of how fast it can be acquired and used. Generally, belated information has low value or is useless. Although this view appears appropriate for civilisational threats and opportunities, it ignores the importance of retrospective and prospective information resources. Decision-making processes often require retrospective, current and prospective information alike – provided that it meets the basic quality standards.

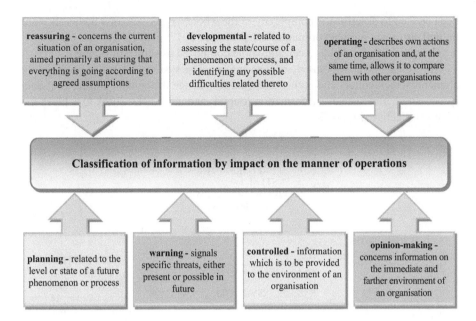

FIGURE 2.5 Classification of information by impact on operations and nature of its effect.

Source: Own work based on: Kels 2019, p. 34.

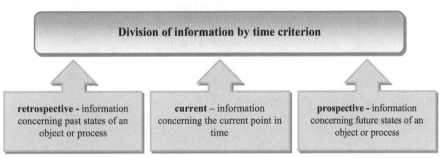

FIGURE 2.6 Classification of information by time criterion.

Source: Own work based on: Meggle 2019, pp. 29–53.

As regards functioning of an organisation, information can have four basic functions – namely, an informative function, a decision-making function, a steering function and a consumer function. Because of these functions, and due to the importance attributed to it, information is often treated as an economic resource which is at least as important as traditional production resources. In economic aspect, information is considered in terms of *inter alia* a productive factor, a product, a service, a commodity or a consumer good.

Defined on the basis of observations of similarities between technique, nature and organisation of human society, the concept of system is among the fundamental concepts of contemporary science. Based on these similarities, a common concept has been created to describe the complexity of the whole – regardless of whether they are natural, artificial, animate or inanimate (Dallinger 2017, p. 237).

The system is defined as a certain whole composed as shown in Figure 2.7.

According to the systems theory, an information system is a set of cooperating elements which collect and gather data (input), change the content and form of data (processing), emit data and information (output) and provide feedback to achieve the desired objective (Figure 2.8).

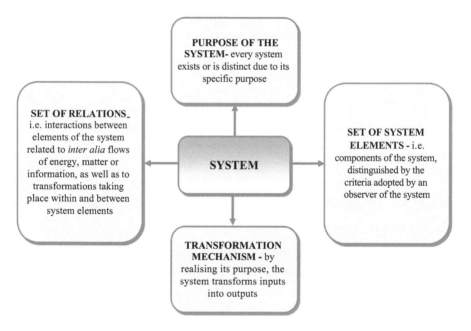

FIGURE 2.7   Defined system components.

Source: Own work.

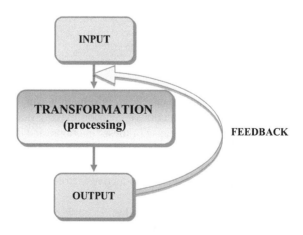

FIGURE 2.8   System components.

Source: Own work.

Of many definitions of the information system, one can distinguish two basic approaches which present it in static and dynamic terms.

In static terms, the information system can be defined as a multi-level structure which allows the user to transform specific input information into desired output information by means of appropriate procedures and models. In turn, the dynamic approach defines the information system as a set of information streams described on its organisational structure, i.e. the structure of the sphere of real processes and the sphere of management processes (Urbanowska-Sojkin 2017, pp. 240–256). Both approaches concern different aspects of information systems, representing a different perspective of the same matter.

The growing complexity of processes conducted within organisations and ever faster pace of changes induced by civilisational transformations and market competition entail the necessity to process more and more data and use various types of information in management (decision-making) processes and real action processes.

Data processing and analysis processes can take place spontaneously in the human mind, but they can also be aided by technical solutions. However, it happens ever more frequently that due to the quantity and variety of data (the effect of scale) and the necessity for fast decision-making or process responses (the time criterion), information processes make wide use of computer hardware and software, which in some cases minimises the human decision-making or operational subjectivity.

Application of informatics systems to decision-making or the so-called real action processes causes synergies arising from the combination of human intelligence and creativity with the capabilities of information technology. The computing power, speed and level of complexity of data processing demonstrate the potential of informatics solutions which indeed goes beyond human abilities. On the other hand, human activity is characterised by decision-making subjectivity, quick adaptability and learning skills.

A contemporary information system is automated and makes wide use of computer hardware and software. A separate computerised part of an information system is called an informatics system. It is a system which is comprised of computer hardware, software, database, devices and means of communication, people and procedures. In theory and practice, in addition to informatics systems there is also the concept of a computer system, which is defined as a set of computer hardware, data and data processing algorithms as well as people who operate in that environment.

Informatics systems could not function without informatics technologies. Purposes and functional scopes of informatics systems are determined by technologies available at a given stage of development of informatics together with information needs of organisations. In turn, subsequent models of informatics systems are the basis and catalyst, as shown in Figure 2.9.

Informatics systems represent a large group of systems that support operations of organisations. Taking into account the criterion of their functions, one can distinguish a group of systems which support management systems and a group of systems which automate real action processes. The former is represented by systems which support decision-making processes and transaction-recording systems which are substantively related with processes that form the basis for control and evaluation of organisations' operations. The latter includes systems which support, coordinate and optimise production processes, including manufacturing, supplies and distribution.

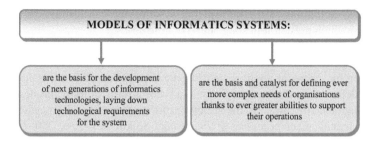

FIGURE 2.9   Models of informatics systems.

Source: Own work.

As regards manufacturing processes, one can distinguish a group of systems which support design and production planning and control processes.

Taking into account the information currency criterion, one can distinguish information systems which are based on retrospective, current and prospective information. Informatics systems are also adapted to the organisation management level.

The scope and form of required information depends on the management level (strategic, tactical, operational) and area of operations (management, production). This entails various directions of development of informatics systems in terms of their purpose, substantive scope and functional and technical complexity (Figure 2.10).

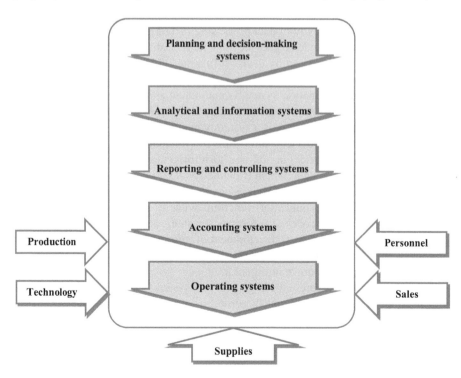

FIGURE 2.10   Functional division of information systems in an organisation.

Source: Own work.

Due to the area of their application, management informatics systems represent a special class of information systems. Such systems are often used within the scope of broadly understood management. They can be divided according to the basic criteria, i.e. the substantive scope of the informatics system, intended use, functional and technical complexity or the scope of functions realised.

Taking into account the substantive scope criterion, one can distinguish area-specific systems, sub-systems and comprehensive systems (Stroińska, Trippner-Hrabi 2017, pp. 261–270). In terms of their intended use, they include recording, information and regulation systems. An analysis of their functional and technical complexity shows simple, complex and particularly complex systems (Hernes et al. 2019, pp. 77–87).

In turn, an analysis of their functions leads to distinguishing the following types of informatics systems (Figure 2.11).

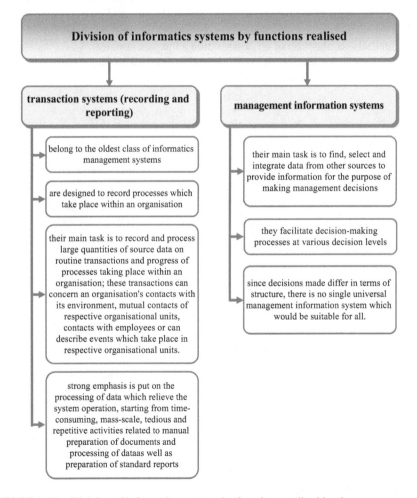

FIGURE 2.11   Division of informatics systems by functions realised by them.

Source: Own work based on: Urbanowska-Sojkin, Weinert 2019, pp. 58–67.

As information technology developed in informatics systems, efforts were made to implement various optimisation, statistical, simulation and artificial intelligence-based methods such as knowledge databases, genetic algorithms, semantic or neuron networks. This led to the development of new generations of informatics systems, as shown in Figure 2.12.

Expert systems can be divided into the following basic groups (Figure 2.13).

Development of expert systems involves mainly transformation of information provided by an expert into a set of rules, facts or semantic networks. The key element of expert systems, the database, allows facts and rules from a specific field to be processed by the reasoning module, and the results are sent to the user interface software in order to enable the final presentation of the results (Figure 2.14).

Integration is one of the basic features of contemporary information systems. It can be interpreted as connection of elements of an organisation's informatics with the use of informatics technologies. As regards utilisation of informatics systems in an organisation, integration takes place at two levels (Figure 2.15):

- internal – connection of an organisation's internal systems,
- external – connection of an organisation internal systems with systems which cooperate with the environment.

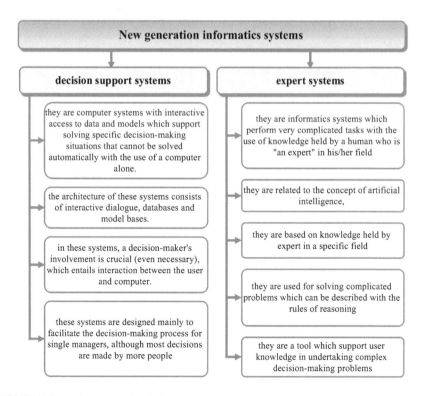

FIGURE 2.12 New generation informatics systems.

Source: Own work based on: Sala, Tańska 2019, pp. 198–208.

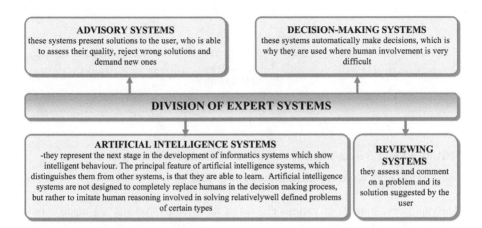

FIGURE 2.13 Division of expert systems.

Source: Own work based on: Gunia 2019.

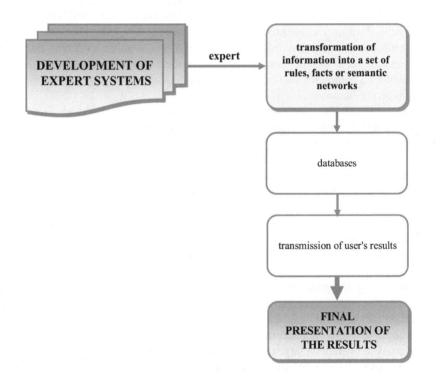

FIGURE 2.14 Development of expert systems.

Source: Own work.

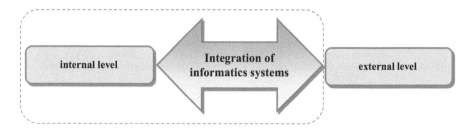

FIGURE 2.15   Levels of integration of utilisation of informatics systems.

Source: Own work based on: Glenc 2020, pp. 108–125.

The rapid development of various classes of information systems has made it possible to deploy them virtually anywhere within an organisation's area of functioning. However, comprehensive management would be very difficult with only one system. This has given rise to the need for a new generation of systems which integrate data processing within the entire organisation in order to optimise its functioning.

Integration of informatics systems can take place on two planes, namely the functional and physical planes. In the former case, various functions are realised as if they were realised within a single process. This allowed an authorised user to use all functions realised in integrated informatics systems via a single coherent interface enabling him/her to switch between different system tasks. In turn, physical integration involves a comprehensive combination of components of integrated informatics systems on the hardware/software plane.

However, full integration was only possible on the basis of the most advanced class of informatics systems – namely the module systems (Gadatsch 2020, pp. 87–151). The dynamic advances in the area of computer equipment, database systems, processing technologies, operating/system/tool software and management systems has allowed meeting the requirements regarding cooperation in which the ultimate usability of informatics solutions is fuller than the sum of components of informatics systems.

The main features of integrated informatics systems are shown in Figure 2.16.

Integration between organisations is becoming increasingly important due to the globalisation of operations and abilities offered by contemporary informatics technologies.

Functioning of organisations in the conditions of rapid technical development and free market competition shows that information resources are becoming a very important factor which determines economic effectiveness. The pace of technological changes and turbulent nature of the external environment of organisations make it necessary to operate on large quantities of various data and facts, indicating that the problem lies with excess of information rather than lack or deficit thereof. Excess of information often becomes the reason for attention poverty, hence the need for transforming it so that it is suitable for a specific application, which can be achieved by deployment of customised informatics systems.

The development of informatics technique and the associated continuous decrease in the prices for hardware and software, as well as mindset changes in the modern-day

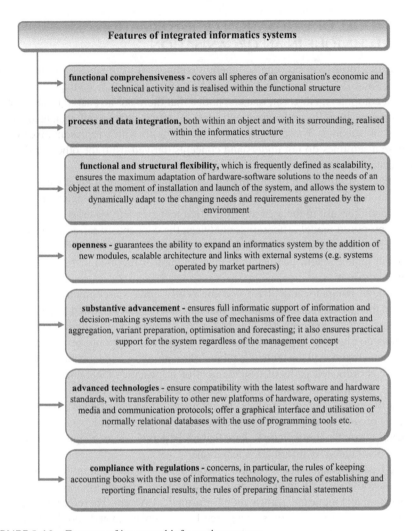

FIGURE 2.16   Features of integrated informatics systems.

Source: Own work based on: Gunia 2019.

society, cause that informatics solutions find broad applications in virtually every area of human life. As regards information processes, this manifests through the universal use of various informatics system solutions.

Every informatics system which supports information procedures in the area of management shows certain sociotechnical dualism. Isolation of the dualistic nature of the informatics system is relevant as the efficiency of the system will depend both on the users' competences and literacy, and the quality of applications. The dualistic method of assessment of the informatics system appears to be gaining in importance in view of the prevalence of integration and ever greater complexity and substantive interdisciplinarity of informatics systems.

2.2   MODEL OF UTILISATION OF INFORMATION
TECHNIQUE IN AN ORGANISATION

Informatics tools have become an inherent component of organisation management systems, and it is difficult today to imagine an organisation management system without computers. However, one can notice that there are no shared basic concepts which would be fully understood and used by representatives of management and applied informatics. There are opinions according to which representatives of one of these disciplines do not understand concepts derived from the other, or that they depreciate them.

A model of utilisation of information technique should be a good workshop providing tools to build a framework of basic concepts shared by management and informatics and their use in the area of information management systems.

The proposed model differentiates between the concepts of information and data. When creating a model that is to help in common understanding of the role of informatics in management, one needs to take account of the area of management and applied informatics.

Although computer tools have become nearly universal component of management, in the last 25 years, one can say that they are not fully adapted to organisations (Brenner, Broy, Leimeister 2017, pp. 602–606). In many cases, advanced informatics solutions go ahead of organisations, which is equivalent to unnecessary costs. One can assume that the advancement is taking place along two independent and unsatisfactorily coordinated paths of development of informatics tools and organisational changes. Examples of such shortcomings are numerous, and the fact that effective actions to ensure integration of these two elements of organisation is most disturbing. Leaving organisation and informatics as autonomous and independent disciplines does not allow their integration. This feature is perceived as a significant value of management aided by information technique.

The basic concepts which require thorough consideration, definition and precise use in accordance with their meanings include *inter alia* information, informatics, information technique and information (informatics) system. Therefore, it is required to perform a synthesis and present a general model covering and coordinating useful concepts from the area of management, organisation, data processing and creation and use of information.

Incomplete comprehension of capabilities offered by informatics is most often demonstrated by its perception as a tool that accelerates data processing and potentially replaces the human being in an organisation. This is so because computer specialists, belittling the complexity of processes in which humans take part, perceive mainly processes that are formalised and well structured where tasks performed by clumsy humans can be taken over by a computer which automatically (and faultlessly) performs complex actions. This error arises from misunderstanding of the essence of processes which must often be subordinated to the rhythm set by humans – the ultimate recipients of data, based on which they generate and use required information. Automation provides for beneficial changes in the human activity system (HAS) where they are advisable, fully coordinated and adapted to human needs. Therefore, the computer does not change the system (information system), but it can become an important factor which allows a change. Such a change can be identified, designed and implemented only by the human, not by the computer.

Information technique – a tool – cannot replace the human, for the human is the administrator of the process and the creator and user of information who intentionally uses an unmatched data processing tool. That tool should streamline and improve work in a coordinated and orchestrated manner. Functions of information technique are by all means desired, but, as shown by experience, their identification, development and implementation requires advanced actions as well as adequate expenditures and time. Experience shows that a holistic view of intentions from the organisation perspective is required. In order to support management, one needs to consider the processes shown in Figure 2.17.

The holistic view of the organisation and organisational management should ensure better understanding of the basic concepts and relations between them as well as the structure of the related component processes. The necessary demand should be active participation in work on modernisation of the organisation, in particular as shown in Figure 2.18.

Information technique can and should have impact on future organisational solutions, creating opportunities for winning competitive advantage. Indeed, this is the objective and task of management, and therefore it cannot be entrusted to computer specialists who have no insight into management and who have no liability in this respect.

The above recommendations are meant to ensure cohesion of the entire system which is, and should remain, an organisation together with its components. It should be noted that they include systems of all four classes (natural, artificial, abstract and human action systems). Such an ascertainment leads to the conclusion that an

FIGURE 2.17 Management support.

Source: Own work based on: Lenk 2017, pp. 87–100.

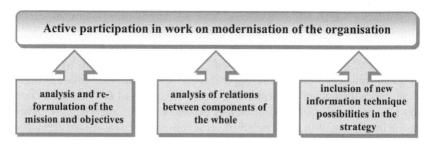

FIGURE 2.18   Active participation in work on modernisation of the organisation.

Source: Own work.

organisational change bringing competitive advantage through application of informatics (information technique) should be the main objective of the task.

Introducing information technique alone to an unchanged organisation does not produce any advantages other than extensive ones, which are moderately associated with achieving the organisation's objectives. Competitive advantage can be ensured only by an organisational change through application of information technique serving the purpose of achieving the organisation's mission and objectives. This is the only definition of the purpose of modernisation of the organisation's information system that justifies any expenditures on information technique.

Applications of informatics as tools must be subordinated to the entire management system and embedded in that system which is necessary to ensure its integrity and cohesion. It is important because, as many other functions in an organisation, informatics shows tendencies to become autonomous.[1] Given the status of this tool, it should not be allowed.

The technical development has entailed a tremendous increase in applications of computers for management purposes. Strong impulses associated with this field have stimulated the development of hardware and software as well as innovative management methods. This rapid progress has been somewhat restrained by the indolence of information system developers who think in accordance with classical models from one field (either informatics or management) and have a limited view of the general (common) model of the processes being subject to management. That field of interest – managing an organisation with the use of the potential offered by computer technique – requires cooperation among information system developers.

From the management perspective, information system, which includes all components important for an organisation, is the priority.[2] The presented conceptual model is the basis for considering management information systems and includes concepts of management in computer data processing. It is a general view of relations between the fundamental concepts of management and its tools.

There are still difficulties in linking the basic concepts presented and demonstrating the relation between management and informatics. The cause may be the superficiality and lack of analytical perception of management, on the one hand, and the façade nature of the vision of informatics as "a science of computers", on the other.

Creating an information system is primarily about creating a system of work (Elm 2018), which is a task of creators of organisation who use all available tools. This can by

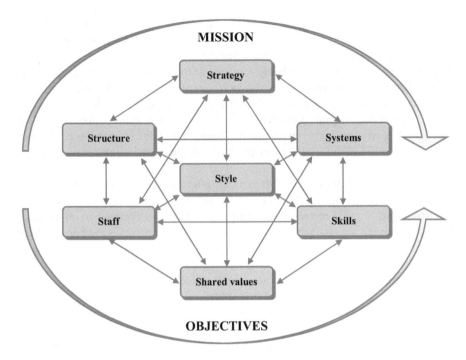

FIGURE 2.19 7S organisation framework.

Source: Own work.

no means be substituted by the use of a computer with all its equipment (software), for it will not ensure creativity – a crucial factor in modernisation. An organisational system is a network of elements which belong to 7 classes: strategy – structure – systems – staff – skills – style – shared values (Figure 2.19).

None of these components can represent the concept of organisation on its own. Only their combination, ensuring coordination, efficiency and effectiveness of the whole, can be accepted. An informatics system, so important nowadays, must be aligned with all other elements in order to approve as meeting the organisational requirements. Only harmonisation of the organisational whole including components at various levels of advancement can lead to achieving a satisfactory result. The development of a component (partial development) does not have to entail any improvement in efficiency of the entire organisation – it can even become a cause of dissonance.

Taking into account all important, albeit non-homogeneous, components is necessary to maintain the nature of the model (a human activity system, a soft system). Its structure is to ensure a holistic and teleological view of creation and utilisation of a simple deterministic informatics system in an extremely complex and non-deterministic system such as organisation (a human activity system).

The greatest significance in the model is held by the link, i.e. information, which plays an important role in managing an organisation. This is why information may not be replaced with data, which is a simplification. Being only a carrier of information, data can be misinterpreted by the recipient, and so it is not information. A technical solution does not guarantee the desired interpretation of data or acquisition of information or knowledge on its basis. Such interpretation is a product of intellect, an immanent property of a thinking being. Creation of information in the thought process (comprehension – interpretation – validation – verification – qualification – critical assessment of data and its internalisation) is a necessary factor to understand the role of information in an organisation. While data has a material nature, information is an abstract being whose natural environment is human mind. It can be recorded through data, but creation of information on the basis of data requires the use of human intellect.

The concept of informatics system is an effect of a dangerous simplification according to which available data is treated as information while ignoring the necessity to interpret it and then create knowledge about the object concerned on its basis. Therefore, one can say that the essence of creation of information is the border which informatics, as a tool of management (solving complex problems in the area of management), is still unable to cross.

Higher tiers of the model (mission, objectives, strategy, actions and decisions) belong to the sphere of organisation (the sphere of human activity), whereas lower ones include only components of organisation and data processing system (all its elementary operations). Management covers the whole of an organisation, defining the most significant, albeit remaining in the sphere of ideas, concepts like mission (*raison d'etre*), objectives (states which the organisation wants to achieve within a defined timeframe), actions (all activities which serve the purpose of achieving the objectives), decisions (choosing from among many possible modes of operation) and information (an abstract concept which indicates a mode of action to its holder) with respect to the necessity to choose a mode of action or make a decision. The last of the organisation components listed – i.e. information (not data, but information as such – an abstract) – remains an element of the mind of its creator as well as user and holder. Information is created in an individual manner by those who need it, for various reasons, and who use it in accordance with their needs and authorisations. The process associated with this component is totally dependent on its operator – a human being – and the possibilities to substitute it by information technique are very limited to strictly defined fragments.

An organisation is a product of accurate merger of complementary components which are able to act effectively. Information technique as a tool is of secondary importance, as it does not cause changes but offers opportunities to improve the results of those changes. Although an organisation remains a social system, it must continuously adapt to the requirements and take opportunities, including those offered by information technique. Application of information technique should serve the purpose of overhauling the information system of an organisation. Achievement of this strategic objective is aided by designing an informatics system (a technical change) and a simultaneous adaptive redesigning of the organisation (an organisational change). Any attempts to make partial changes either run a risk of failure or can be only partially successful, for they are ineffective (an informatics system – only a technical change) or inefficient (an ineptly introduced organisational change without the required tool).

A strategic organisational change must be a synchronised and coordinated change that is technical and organisational. Such a change, made possible by the potentially unmatched efficiency of information technique, must take place in order to overcome unsatisfactory competitiveness (Benker, Jürck 2016, pp. 25–32).

Although data processed does not constitute information (in the strict sense of the word), it contributes to a dramatic improvement of information efficiency. Availability of the required data, improved thanks to the information technique capabilities, enhances the associative capabilities, thus leading to further improvement of information efficiency. The ability to use information technique tools and required data stimulates further development of information behaviour and, in consequence, efficiency in utilisation of information. Although it does not provide information itself, information technique is an essential factor in its creation by the human – a member of an organisation.

In the modern-day world, it is noticed that technical (technological) changes are a necessary condition for an organisational change. From the organisation's point of view, they must be advisable and subjected to better realisation of the organisation's objectives. An organisational change is a complex process due to its area and nature – a human activity system.[3] A technical (technological) change is its component which determines the possibilities and scope. An information technique (technical) change is not an end in itself but it is to ensure that all users are provided with appropriately processed data in accordance with the requirements of the potentially most efficient organisation achieving its objectives. For example, a new data processing system designed for an existing organisation may process data for users who do not need any output data. At the same time, a non-existent user will get data which he or she is not able to use because he or she is not authorised to do so or there is no such need. In view of such a threat, adequate problem solving should be ensured, as illustrated in Figure 2.20.

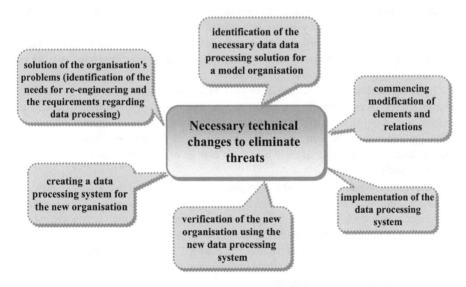

FIGURE 2.20   Necessary technical changes to eliminate threats.

Source: Own work.

A technical and organisational change thus implemented will ensure efficiency and effectiveness of an organisation but only in the conditions of synchronisation and coordination of new organisational solutions and data processing solutions subordinated to them. Subordination of all the components to the mission and objectives of an organisation, as well as synchronisation and coordination of actions, resources and tools will allow success. The new organisation arising from a strategic change will achieve the expected competitive advantage, i.e. it will meet the expectations regarding effectiveness and efficiency.

Improving data processing alone will not necessarily solve the problem of an inefficient organisation. For an inefficient organisation it is important to have its main elements and relations between them modified in the first place, and information processing comes after that. As the problem owner, the organisation is directly involved in its emergence and is often unable to determine how to solve it. It must be stressed that a complex organisational change concerns the information system (comprised of data, methods, technical means, organisation and human resources), not the informatics system understood as hardware and software (software suite). A change affecting only the area of the informatics system is pointless, for a data processing system must be based on a real organisation. The required modernisation of the information system is, in fact, an organisational change which entails a change of the system of work (Alpar et al. 2019, pp. 3–23), whereas implementation of a new information system based on the old organisation can seriously decrease its efficiency – such are outcomes of incompatibility of the organisation and data processing system. Therefore, a conclusion can be drawn that implementation of technical solutions to modify the information system (a component of a living organisation) may lead to mistuning the entire organisation. A change of the technique used in data processing to an advanced information technique should not be made as a simple computerisation but should be prepared as a complex coordinated organisational change. Only under this condition can one expect effects that the organisation desires – namely, improved operating efficiency, financial results, higher effectiveness, competitiveness, better market position, improved quality of services, increased competitive advantage.

Implementation of an information system by an organisation can bring only partial effects arising from actions related to adapting organisational solutions to potential capabilities of the information system (partial organisational changes). These partial changes will never lead to results that can be achieved through methodical systemic operation, while their cost is often higher than the cost of a comprehensive change.

An organisational change is the objective and reason behind introduction of information technique, which with time has become its most important factor. Information technique alone does not cause changes in an organisation (human activity system), although it is an important stimulus to making changes and improving the efficiency of solutions. An organisational change, if planned purposefully and deliberately, becomes a success factor for the entire organisation, contributing to its better market position and competitive advantage.

The proposed conceptual model covers the entire sphere of organisation management, including the data processing support tool for organisational units, and represents a proposal of a holistic approach – unlike partial changes. The functioning and application of the model should be seen as a condition for maintaining the necessary level of organisational integration in the context of the constant necessity of organisational changes. Practical observations confirm that there is a tendency to disintegrate the process of creation or modernisation of organisations when introducing information technique or designing systems. This is so because of unjustified separation of technical designing of organisation elements (information system or data processing system) from designing of organisations (information system). Subordination of information system design to the needs of the organisation should enhance the integrity of the entire organisation and ensure its ability to function during subsequent transformations. In the today's turbulent environment, organisational changes are still necessary and organisations must flexibly and efficiently tackle such challenges. Information technique is a tool which provides for efficient introduction of complex changes without losing cohesion and without permanent disturbances, and even with improving the efficiency and effectiveness of the organisation at the same time.

An organisation's information system is a space where organisational changes must take place continually due to the unpredictable situation in the environment. An organisation must adapt to identified conditions, which cannot be achieved only by structural changes – these must correspond to modifications of behaviours and processes. A technical change offers the necessary flexibility which provides for modifying processes in order to make them more efficient, but it does not give any guidelines regarding structural changes. Meanwhile, a systemic organisational change must ensure orientation (vision, objective), restructuring (appropriate structure) and dynamic for the organisation. A technical (technological) change alone contributes to achieving only the last of the properties listed, which is a necessary, albeit not sufficient, requirement to achieve success. For an organisation, success markers include increased competitiveness leading to an improved market position and, consequently, higher profits.

These success markers are used for defining objectives which, in the form of a common vision, can become a starting point for a process approach to the whole change within a parallel, coordinated and synchronised modernisation of the statics (structure) and dynamics (processes) in the organisation aimed to serve a specific purpose. In management, neither computerisation nor informatisation can be regarded as the ultimate objective of an organisation. All changes must serve the pursuit of the mission and objectives so that the organisation's integrity and growth could be ensured.

2.3   APPLICATIONS OF INFORMATION TECHNOLOGY IN ORGANISATIONS AND PUBLIC INSTITUTIONS

The matter of applications of information technology is one of the most important and, at the same time, broadest areas of economic informatics.

In general, information technology (IT) is associated with methods and means of information processing. IT includes computer equipment, software, database and data warehouse technologies, network infrastructure and mobile technology.

IT development has made it possible to develop global information systems and processes. Globalisation of information processes stimulates globalisation of economic processes. In turn, globalisation of economic needs requires information satisfaction of economic operators, i.e. various classes of enterprises as well as financial, banking and insurance institutions. Applied IT allows creation of appropriate interactions between managers, customers and employees meant to acquisition of information and knowledge. Putting the technology to active use affects organisational changes within economic operators and methods of communication with the environment.

The main purposes and advantages of IT use in an enterprise mentioned by authors include the ones listed in Figure 2.21.

Information technologies developed and used in practice for the purpose of supporting existing and newly established business structures, processes and systems differ greatly in terms of technological support in achieving their respective purposes of operation. In this context, unambiguous interpretation of structural areas of an enterprise is important.

Today's modern enterprises are objects with complicated structural and functional links both internal and external. They are related to the performance of specific management functions to allow enterprises to implement their strategies and achieve their objectives in the technical and economic area of business (Allweyer 2020).

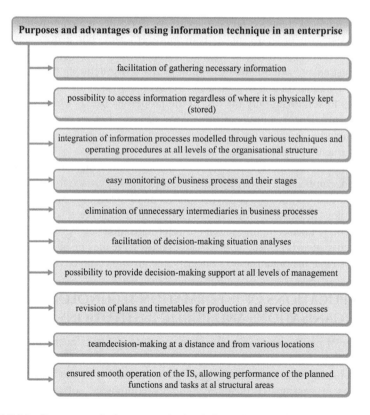

FIGURE 2.21   Purposes and advantages of using information technique in an enterprise.

Source: Own work based on: Tiemeyer 2020.

Structural areas of an enterprise (an organisation) are illustrated in the literature through a systemic approach (Figure 2.22).

Environment plays an important role in shaping the aforementioned systems. Relations of an enterprise with its environment allow the latter to produce materials and services which are useful to the environment and to implement its strategy and accomplish its objectives. Economic effects are, in turn, the resultant of the functioning of respective structures of the enterprise.

Possible applications of IT in enterprises are diverse and concern a number of areas. Figure 2.23 below shows the ones that support the functional systems enumerated above.

A synthetic review of these areas is shown in Table 2.1. Allocated to each area are IT groups which differ in terms of functional and applicational properties. To differentiate between them, relevant examples of technological solutions encountered in operations of enterprises are provided.

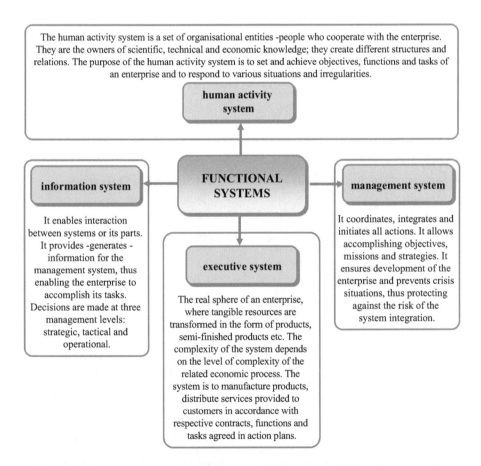

FIGURE 2.22 Objectives and advantages of using information technique in an enterprise.

Source: Own work based on: Romanowska 2016, pp. 29–35.

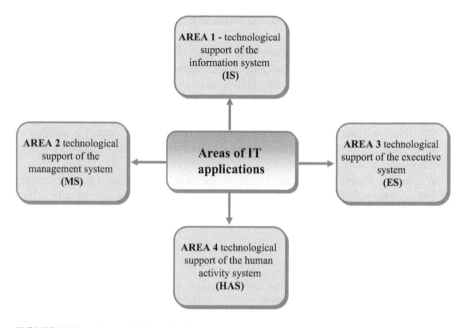

FIGURE 2.23   Areas of IT applications in an enterprise.

Source: **Own work.**

TABLE 2.1

A Systemic Structure of Areas of Technological Support of Enterprises

Areas of Technological Support	Groups of Technologies and Examples of Technological Solutions
1. Information system	• **data gathering technologies**: medium of information – magnetic tapes (MT), magnetic disks (MD), diskettes, CDs; sets of information – databases (DB), data warehouses (DW); product identification – bar codes, RFID techniques; automatic positioning – GPS and GSM • **data processing technologies:** mechanical equipment, calculator simple computer sets – PC, handheld microcomputer, printers, plotters, laptops; computer systems – hardware, software; client-server technology; analytical processing technologies – spreadsheets; analytical and statistical software; OLAP technology; complex computer sets – superservers, corporate servers • **data/information transmission technologies:** communications – telephone, telex, computer; electronic data interchange (EDI); computer networks – local (LAN), wide (WAN), Internet, Intranet, Extranet; mobile technologies – mobile telephones, handheld computers, portable computers; wireless technologies – analogue, digital and universal networks – UMTS • **data storage technologies:** memory technologies – TM, DM, diskette, CDs; database technologies

(*Continued*)

TABLE 2.1 (Continued)

Areas of Technological Support	Groups of Technologies and Examples of Technological Solutions
2. Management system	• **recording-reporting system technologies:** domain systems – material management systems (SEM), HR systems, payroll systems, financial and accounting systems, integrated systems – MRP and ERP • **informing system technologies:** information search system; data analysis system – STATISTICA module; Management Information System; MRP and ERP system modules; SCM systems, CRM, BI systems • **expert system technologies (ES):** sales programming, plan scheduling, diagnostics • **office automation system technologies:** text editors, computer graphics, EXCEL; multimedia programming; communications devices and systems, LOTUS NOTES suite; Internet technology, Microsoft Office, workflow systems
3. Executive system	• **production engineering technologies:** production planning and design suites – CAD/CAM • **production monitoring technologies:** technological operations control; production automation – machine (robot) assembly; production control and monitoring – mobile and wireless technologies
4. Human activity system	• **internal support technologies:** database, network, client-server, multimedia, call centre technologies • **informatics system technologies (MIS):** domain-specific, informing, integrated, CRM, SCM, BI, SE • **Internet technologies in business:** e-commerce, e-marketing • **external support technologies:** remote conferencing, electronic document management (EDM); work flow; EDI; analytical data processing

Source: Own work.

Area 1 concerns support of information system (IS) and covers technologies which allow operation of information systems related with data gathering, processing, transmission and storage. Secondary information media represent the basic technological solution. Computer technology introduces various hardware, software and network solutions. Information resources are organised with the use of database technologies and data warehouses. Local and wide area networks (LAN and WAN, respectively) facilitate communication between the lowest levels and the decision-making centre. Various configurations of distributed and centralised processing can be created. New hardware platforms equipped with superservers, UNIX machines and high-class corporate servers lead to increased efficiency and customised functionality responding to the needs of their direct users. Analytical processing technology, OLAP and data mining are well developed, while tools and techniques are designed to help improve sharing and exchanging information as part of the following services: www (World Wide Web), electronic mail (e-mail), news groups and IRC (Internet Relay Chat). Mobile technologies (mobile telephone and laptops) and wireless technologies (wireless and digital networks) play an active role. Dissemination of communication through the Internet and telecommunication devices introduces new reality – virtual reality. The Internet, particularly websites make it possible to access multiple sources of information. Worthy of notice are product identification technologies – bar codes and RFID (Radio Frequency Identification). These technologies ensure efficient warehouse operations (Erner, Hammer 2019, pp. 123–170).

Area 2 concerns various directions of development of management informatics systems (MIS) in the form of advanced technical, programming and networking tools designed to support the management system. Recording-reporting, informing, decision-making support, smart and office automation systems are developed here. Widespread solutions include domain-specific recording systems which cover warehouse, payroll and human resources management as well as financial and accounting systems. More advanced production and service procedures lead to the deployment of integrated management suite technologies of MRP (Material Resource Planning) and ERP (Enterprise Resources Planning). A multi-functional role is played by informing and decision-making support system technologies focused on individual applications, user learning or adaptive design. The design and dialogue basis is formed by databases (DB), model bases (MB), method bases and knowledge bases (KB). Important technological tools include graphics systems, fourth generation languages (4GL), electronic mail, software suites, BI (Business Intelligence) systems, OLAP (On-line Analytical Processing) tools and data mining. The highest level of technological advancement is shown by smart systems, including expert systems (Behringer 2017, pp. 1–35). A separate group is comprised of office automation systems. They are design to support office work and often form company communication centres (Kofler 2018, pp. 73–99). Well-known software includes text editors, computer graphics, spreadsheets, multimedia software as well as EDI (Electronic Date Interchange) and workflow systems.

Area 3 concerns utilisation of IT in the production process. Technologies used in this area include Class MRP II integrated suites which support planning, scheduling, production control and coordination (Lambert et al. 2017, pp. 43–62). Well-known suites include CAD (Computer-Aided Design) and CAM (Computer-Aided Manufacturing), whereas an important role in the production monitoring area is played by robots and mobile and wireless technologies, e.g. UMTS (Universal Mobile Telecommunications System).

Area 4 stresses the practical utilisation of IT by all organisational entities (both internal and external) involved in operations of an enterprise. These entities use all the aforementioned technologies to support information processes which take place in the technical and economic activity of their enterprise. The technologies are complemented by remote systems which provide for contacts between employees, consultations with experts, marketing and logistic presentations, remote learning, remote work, etc.

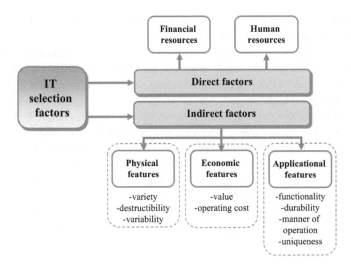

FIGURE 2.24 Factors which determine choice of IT.

Source: Own work.

The information technologies enumerated and characterised in the aforementioned structural areas indicate great possibilities of their application in the technical and economic activity of an enterprise. They provide for designing various approaches to supporting and shaping an enterprise's strategy in the turbulent environment. When adopting a specific research approach, it is necessary to choose the IT for implementation of the strategy selected.

All factors that determine the choice of a specific technology can be divided into direct and indirect factors. The structure of these factors is shown in Figure 2.24.

Direct factors include human and financial resources.

Financial resources concern the ability to incur costs of implementation of projects related to improvement of operations of an enterprise.

Human resources include research teams, among them system analysts and designers who take part in improving respective structural areas of an enterprise.

Indirect factors include physical, economic and applicational features which represent the principal characteristics that distinguish specific information technologies.

The **physical features** include variety, destructibility and variability. The **economic features** include value and operating cost. The **applicational features** include functionality, durability, manner of operation and uniqueness.

Below is a description of the aforementioned features of IT.

Variety means that information technologies are a product of scientific and technical progress. Every technology has its unique attributes: design, functionality and operating procedures. These attributes determine the universality or uniqueness of their practical application in economy.

Destructibility means that IT is subject to wear in the process of its practical use and is not resistant to faulty actions of its users.

Variability means that IT is periodically subject to certain modifications and improvements in functional, structural and applicational terms. Variability is manifested by the emergence of subsequent new versions of a given type or category of technology.

IT value can be established as the relation between entities active on the market as sellers and buyers. The value of a technology is demonstrated by the demand, utility, uniqueness and transferability of ownership rights. In general, unique technologies are characterised by a high investment value, whereas simple technologies rely on universally used methods and techniques as well as hardware/software and networking tools.

Operating cost of IT is a result of technical and software solutions used in a given technology. In simple solutions, this cost is relatively low and generally accepted by buyers of those technologies. In the case of complex or unique technologies, the cost is relatively high compared with the purchase prices. These generally include investment technologies used throughout longer periods of operation.

Functionality, as an applicational feature of IT, enables modernisation and development of information systems (IS) through changing their purposes and functions. Technologies used in this respect focus on flexibility and openness of the system as well as its internal and external integration with newly designed tools and analytical software systems. IT functionality is the fundamental factor behind innovation of enterprises. The ease of operation and clarity of parameters of a given software/hardware and network/communications tool are the main attributes of its functionality.

Durability means the ability to use IT for a long time and resistance to faulty operation or adverse operating conditions.

Manner of operation is a feature of IT which affects satisfaction of the needs of its buyers in order to complete organisational, functional, technical and technological actions planned in a given enterprise (Figure 2.25)

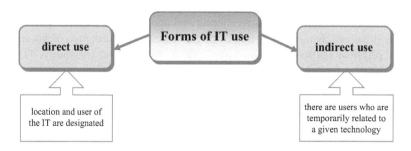

FIGURE 2.25 Forms of IT use.

Source: Own work.

The latter form of IT use is present in the case of the provision of outsourcing services.

Uniqueness is and economic feature which affects the IT value – expressed by the price given by the seller. The price level indicates the amount of costs to be incurred by the IT buyer. Unique technologies require specialised solutions to be developed. Their operation requires high informatics, engineering and analytical-designing qualifications. This group of technologies is used when the economic performance of an enterprise is favourable.

The aforementioned factors determining selection of a specific IT form a complex system with very complicated links which determine the possibilities of their application in specific structural areas of an enterprise.

Activities of contemporary enterprises are accompanied by the necessity to use information technologies designed to support information and supply (materials, power) processes and communication systems. IT development allows integration of information processes at all structural and functional levels of an enterprise. When used in practice, information technologies contribute to the symbiosis of various classes of management informatics systems with production control and service systems in the area of trade, distribution and supplies. The needs of the environment addressed at specific business entities are being satisfied to an increasingly greater extent.

The progressing market globalisation and increasing competition lead to development and use of specific informatics and telecommunications methods, techniques and tools which form the basis for various IT solutions. In turn, the rapid scientific and technical development causes that these technologies are subject to the update process – old technologies are replaced by new ones. Therefore, it is necessary to choose the right technologies. The requirements set for newly introduced technologies can normally be found in design solutions of modernising and developmental nature, where the analysis of features of respective IT groups plays an important role.

2.4   SMART ORGANISATION IN THE MODERN WORLD

The development of information processing technologies is in close relationship with tools that support management processes. In order to operate in the global economy, modern organisations must adapt their management methods and growth strategies to the new economy at the stage of digital transformation, which is gaining momentum. The recent dynamic development of teleinformatics technologies has led to dissemination of the so-called 3rd ICT platform, also known as SMAC (Social, Mobile, Analytics, Cloud), which forms a unique ecosystem of informatics solutions that allow organisations to develop their activities with lower expenditures and maximised range of influence. The constantly growing quantities of data provided by mobile devices, social media platforms, web browsers and loyalty programmes create a new model of business based on information generated by the economic environment. Appropriate processing of the said information is a necessary condition for business success.

It is agreed that a smart organisation is an organisation which bases its operating philosophy on knowledge management (Lambertz 2018). The term became popular in the 1990s, thanks to the rapid ICT development, dynamic changes in the economic environment and growing market competition. An organisation can be called smart when it learns, is able to create, acquire, organise and share knowledge and uses that knowledge to improve the effectiveness of its actions and increases its competitiveness on the global market. The idea of such an organisation is based on a systemic approach to organisation, which means treating it as a complex organism based on the existing structures and processes, with particular emphasis on the role of knowledge. In this approach – referred to as "the fifth discipline" by P. Senge – knowledge and appropriate tools make all components of an organisation and its personnel able to cooperate in achieving defined objectives (Gansmeier, Forsthofer 2019, pp. 51–68). This makes the entire organisation function as a smart organism which copes well in the competitive environment. This explains the interrelations between the methods of understanding and achieving objectives, problem solving and methods of internal and external communication shown in Figure 2.26.

The growing volume of information used in a smart organisation is accompanied by its increased importance. Peter Drucker pointed out a long time ago that the traditional production factors – land, labour and capital – are losing importance to the key resource in the creative functioning of organisations – namely, knowledge, which represents intangible resources connected with human activity which may play a key role in winning competitive advantage (Turriago-Hoyos, Thoene, Arjoon 2016). Knowledge can be treated as information embedded in the organisational context and the ability to use it effectively in the functioning of an organisation. This means that knowledge resources include data on customers, products, processes, environment, etc., in the codified form (documents, databases) and non-codified form (knowledge held by employees).

In practical terms, realisation of effective cooperation between these elements means the necessity to use advanced teleinformatics solutions which use technical, technological and organisational innovations of the recent years. They cover virtually every sphere of organisations' activities, starting from development of means of transport and equipment, to organisation and management of material flows, to development of the structures of business processes.

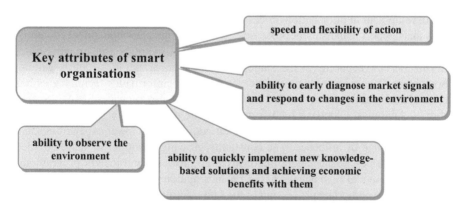

FIGURE 2.26   Key attributes of smart organisations.

Source: Own work based on: Brzeziński, Bubel 2016, pp. 85–97.

As an economic system which relies on advanced teleinformatics infrastructure in its internal organisation and communication (also external), a smart organisation is at present the essence of information society in business areas. This means in practice that informatics technology supports the fundamental structures of an organisation and the online implementation of the concept of "now economy" (Figure 2.27).

The dynamic ICT development has led to the emergence of a new technological standard in the form of SMAC systems which enable implementation of new business models based on the four pillars shown in Figure 2.28.

Over the years, there have been numerous examples which show that expectations do not meet the actual advantages in the area of utilisation of ICT solutions. This may be caused by lack of an appropriate level of integration between systems implemented. The key to SMAC-based success is to combine the four aforementioned technologies which, communicating between each other, will enable reaching the effect of synergy. None of the above four technologies will produce the full effect when deployed alone. Only the synergy generated by all SMAC elements working together will allow building competitive advantage. So far, organisations have been investing in mobility, cloud, business analytics and the use of social media in business by developing standalone and often non-cooperating solutions. Putting them together within the 3rd ICT platform has opened the way to creating new revenue-generating services that deepen the relations with customers and improve organisations' efficiency.

The development of the computing cloud and mobile technology has enabled transition from closed communication systems to social media platforms (Kubiak 2017, pp. 1–58), making a deep and permanent change in the work system and business communications. Social media channels have enabled fast development and sharing of content as well as a wider distribution of information and better cooperation and interaction with customers. Mobile technologies have allowed users to get easy access to information by means of staying online at all times. Data analyses are used for the purpose of optimising customer relations management and enhancing the efficiency of sales channels.

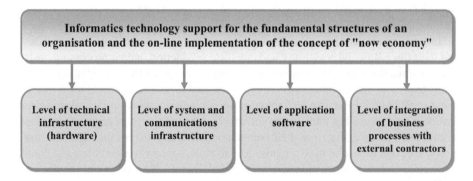

FIGURE 2.27 Informatics technology support for the fundamental structures of an organisation and the online implementation of the concept of "now economy".

Source: Own work based on: Weinstein 2018.

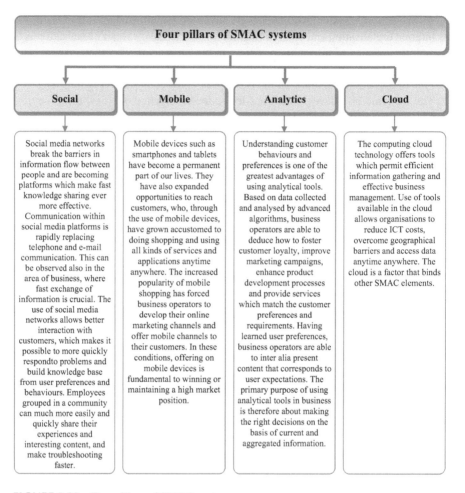

FIGURE 2.28   Four pillars of SMAC systems.

Source: Own work based on: Adamczewski et al. 2017, pp. 11–22.

In turn, the cloud is in a number of enterprises the basis for ICT systems, increasing their flexibility and scalability and entailing a reduction in data processing costs. If an organisation wants to maintain its position on the competitive market, it must be ready to provide its customers with fully customised services. Thanks to the development of SMAC, informatics technologies are no longer only support in developing business operations, but a turning point which gives advantage to organisations and allows them to stand out from their competitors. SMAC provides the right information at the right time, allowing organisations to make appropriate decisions and cooperate effectively inside, outside and within whole chains of cooperation.

The unique informatics ecosystem is normally based on advanced ERP (Enterprise Resource Planning) solutions. ERP systems, traditionally understood ERP as solutions that integrate an organisation's information infrastructure, are no longer sufficient. Their basic functionality has been augmented by Customer Relationship

Management (CRM) systems, Supplier Relationship Management (SRM) systems, Supply Chain Management (SCM) systems and Product Lifecycle Management (PLM) systems. With their capabilities, SMAC systems provide for increasing the efficiency of information support of business processes, thus ultimately leading to better market competitiveness. Even, it is possible to make a statement that these solutions are no longer a method for an organization to gain a competitive advantage – simply, they have now become a factor that decides whether an organization survives on the global market.

Modern organisations are ever more eagerly reaching for advanced SMAC solutions. In general, the growing requirements of smart organisations regarding informatics support of knowledge management arise from the fact that they operate in real time (Real Time Enterprise, RTE). This is why SMAC systems allow taking business effectiveness to a higher level (Figure 2.29).

3rd ICT platform solutions, coupled with the Internet of Things, contribute to qualitative development of Polish economy. In this respect, the use of advanced systems is becoming not only a requirement for successful competition on global markets, but a challenge to attempt to match the world's best companies.

Economic transformations and evolution of business relations lead to devaluation of traditional sources of competitive advantage such as capital, infrastructure, access to sales markets and quality of products and services offered. If they want to successfully compete on global markets, smart organisations must attach priority to organisational flexibility, ability to implement innovative business models and reorganise their processes. The vision of modern business management has entered a dynamic phase of realisation, and effective knowledge management is ultimately becoming a paradigm. It is beyond all doubts that all reserves still left in organisations should be utilised through support with advanced ICT systems, in particular SMAC-based knowledge management solutions.

The current digital transformation will affect the efficiency and activities of economic organisations and economy on the global scale. SMAC technologies offer

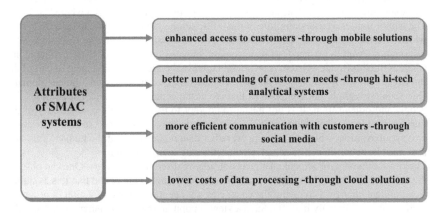

FIGURE 2.29   Attributes of SMAC systems.

Source: Own work based on: Adamczewski et al. 2017, pp. 11–22.

much greater added value when they are applied jointly. Their worth is even greater when they are integrated with the existing ICT infrastructure of an organisation and, most importantly, with business processes.

Digital transformation leaders realise that this is not just a question of selecting specific technologies, but rather their full integration aimed at harnessing the full potential of the 3rd ICT platform. Indeed, it is worth pointing out that the current implementation-related experiences show that digital transformation is not just another marketing, but a process which brings real business advantages. The development of the computing cloud and mobile technology has enabled transition from closed communication systems to social media platforms, making a deep and permanent change in the work system and business communications. Social media channels have enabled fast development and sharing of content as well as a wider distribution of information and better cooperation and interaction with customers. Mobile technologies have allowed users to get easy access to information by means of staying online at all times. Data analyses are used *inter alia* for the purpose of optimising customer relations management and enhancing the efficiency of sales channels. In turn, the Cloud is in a number of organisations the basis for ICT system infrastructure, increasing their flexibility and scalability and entailing cost reductions. If an organisation wants to consolidate its market position, it must provide its customers with fully customised services. Thanks to the development of SMAC, informatics technology is no longer only support in developing business operations, but a turning point which gives advantage to economic organisations and allows them to stand out from their competitors.

NOTES

1 Despite changes in the technical conditions and approaches to informatics, the effects anticipated in this study have materialised. Informatics is increasingly often perceived as an autonomous unit which subordinates other areas of an organisation to itself. Although it is easy to notice the results of the progressing technological integration driven by ever greater technical capabilities, this process does not guarantee organisational integration and sometimes even contributes to disintegration of the organisation as a whole.

2 The author used the basic definition of the information system as a human activity system which includes data, methods, technical means, organisation and human resources. Such a system, relevant to the needs of management, remains the subject of these deliberations, whereas the informatics system is an artefact used in the area of management (a part of the information system) which does not perform any tasks, as these remain a human domain. One should highlight the components that are at the centre of management interest – i.e. people and organisation. It is not meant to attempt to demonstrate the superiority of the management perspective but to show its primary relevance with respect to informatisation, or computerisation, which means support rather than replacement of the human. This support must be subordinated to achieving objectives of an organisation.

3 The sense of an organisational change is not fully realised in our society. One can observe that people expect the change to be made in a purely formal manner and that it is as simple as a political change. Perceiving the change as a procedural course of action (a programmatic change) is equally harmful. Such a view is popular among computer specialists who see management as technical control (well defined and structured) and do not understand the nature of human activity systems. They perceive the organisational change as a programming procedure which can be done by modifying the code.

3 Determinants Related to Threats in Information and Informatics Systems

3.1 THREATS RELATED TO INFORMATION TECHNIQUE

For a modern-day organisation, information resources represent one of the most important factors in ensuring realisation of business processes. Loss of data due to a system failure or disaster most often prevents any resumption of proper operations on the market.

The increasing share of information as a component of the final product costs and the fast pace of production processes are objective reasons which determine the necessity to employ a management informatics system in business operations, for the related processing of large quantities of information is possible only with computer-aided support. At the same time, the constant development of informatics technologies provides means to attain these objectives.

As every investment, an organisation's informatics system should be an element of increasing profits through supporting the decision-making process. The primary functional purpose of the system can be illustrated by the following phrase: delivering the right information to the right person at the right time (Figure 3.1), which translates into availability of information at the time determined by business processes.

In such a case, business operations are based on flow and use of information, and the organisation's information resources become a priority.

Problems related to ensuring information security and high level of information availability concern cases where an emergency takes place due to a system malfunction.

It is agreed that there are two distinct states of unavailability or reduced availability of system resources as shown in Figure 3.2.

Security of information held and shared has a direct impact on accomplishing the organisation's objective, including the ability to generate revenues from business activities, maintain financial liquidity and create a positive marketing image (market position).

According to research (Lenhard 2020), if an organisation loses its information resources (e.g. due to a disaster), restoring it to normal market relations is very unlikely – only ca. 6% of such enterprises return to normal operations (Figure 3.3).

There are many factors which can lead to loss of data. They are normally categorised according to their respective threat classes. Figure 3.4 shows the findings of

DOI: 10.1201/9781003271345-3

FIGURE 3.1   The primary function of an informatics system – provision of information.
Source: Own work.

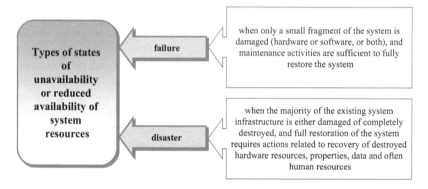

FIGURE 3.2   Types of states of unavailability or reduced availability of system resources.
Source: Own work based on: Wiegerling 2016, pp. 217–226.

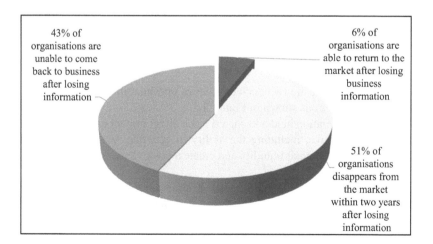

FIGURE 3.3   Enterprises after loss of information resources.
Source: Own work based on: Gadatsch, Mangiapane 2017b, pp. 17–22.

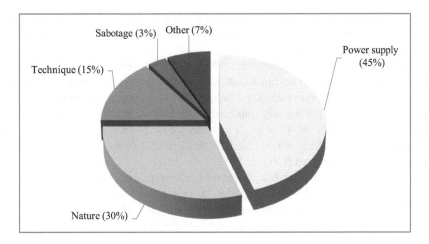

FIGURE 3.4   Main causes of loss of data.

Source: Own work based on: Gadatsch, Mangiapane 2017a, pp. 23–32.

multi-annual studies (Bühler, Schlaich, Sinner 2019, pp. 80–97) in this area, namely the percentage share of these threat classes in the overall number of data loss incidents among organisations.

When analysing causes of loss of data, one can notice that the absolute majority of incidents which lead to data loss or unauthorised modification of information are of objective nature, i.e. they can be eliminated by the system user. Therefore, all actions taken should focus on safeguards against effects of dangerous situations, i.e. they should aim at ensuring information security despite a failure or disaster (Figure 3.5).

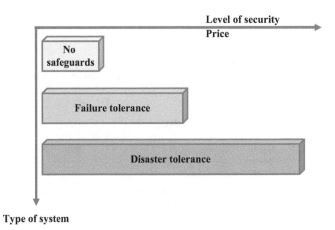

FIGURE 3.5   Levels of informatics system security against data loss in relation to the price.

Source: Own work.

At present, this is achieved by eliminating a single point of failure, i.e. by introducing redundancy of resources, as is the case with high availability servers, and by ensuring disaster tolerance.

It is not possible to build computers which will never break down or be fail-safe. However, it is possible to design a computer so that it can continuously ensure the necessary computing power despite a failure of one or more components. This type of high availability is particularly important in the case of processing large quantities of critical information, as quite often happens today. Naturally, organisational and software solutions which allow effective management of information processing resources are also required (Gruyter 2019).

In particular, high availability is required of servers, regardless of whether they are used as standalone devices, in clusters or in server farms (Cahill et al. 2019, p. 30). This is why designers equip contemporary servers with a number of high-tech solutions which ensure continuous operations in the event of a failure (Chang 2020, pp. 307–318). Such solutions are based on the concept of redundancy of resources thanks to which damaging a specific component does not affect the level of availability of the computing power provided by the sever (Figure 3.6).

This leads to an increase in the level of availability from ca. 99%, as in the case of general-purpose computers (which corresponds to ca. 4 days of downtime per year), to 99.99999% in the case of critical servers (which corresponds to several minutes of downtime per year).

A disaster can be defined as an unscheduled event which significantly affects business operations of an enterprise and is accompanied by the risk of bankruptcy due to the related loss of market value, exposure to litigation or loss of profits. Outcomes of a disaster extend well beyond loss of data (even copies thereof) – they normally involve destruction of buildings, installations and/or computer system. This takes place both in the case of a natural disaster and such human actions as terrorist attacks, infection with a computer virus or system blackout. From the information resources management perspective, the two most important parameters, shown in Figure 3.7,

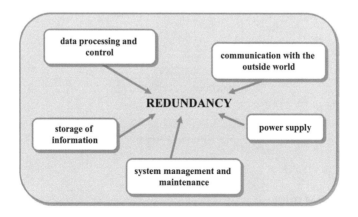

FIGURE 3.6   Critical redundancy areas.

Source: Own work based on: Pospiech 2019.

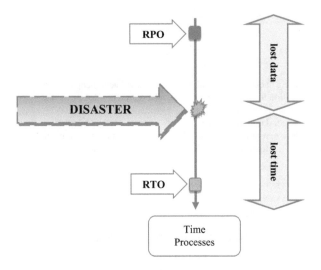

RPO (Recovery Point Objective) – time of the latest safeguard
RTO (Recovery Time Objective) – time of recovery of processes

FIGURE 3.7   Disaster and system recovery.

Source: Own work based on: Hyodo et al. 2020, pp. 1–7; Taguchi, Yoshinaga 2018, pp. 210–215.

are the Recovery Time Objective (RTO) and Recovery Point Objective (RPO) (Hyodo et al. 2020, pp. 1–7; Taguchi, Yoshinaga 2018, pp. 210–215).

The RPO defines the following element: "How big data loss can the user afford?" The recovery point is a moment in the past at which the last copy of data was made and to which we will be able to return (e.g. after a failure). This parameter may be different for different companies – some will be satisfied with a copy from a week ago, while others will need data from several seconds ago (Taguchi, Yoshinaga 2018, pp. 210–215). The RTO answers the question: "How long can the user wait for data and functions of an economic organisation to become available again?" The recovery time is the maximum time following a disaster which is necessary to restore all systems, applications and processes (Hyodo et al. 2020, pp. 1–7). When setting this parameter, one needs to reach the balance between potential losses and costs of a solution that will allow the state from before the failure to be restored as soon as possible.

When defining the RPO, one can use mechanisms offered by the two basic technologies shown in Figure 3.8.

It should be pointed out that the data recovery process from tapes or disks following a disaster can be radically shortened by application of the so-called "bare metal restore" approach. This jargon term means that in the event of a disaster, a new computer system is made available at a different location where applications and data are restored from backup media.

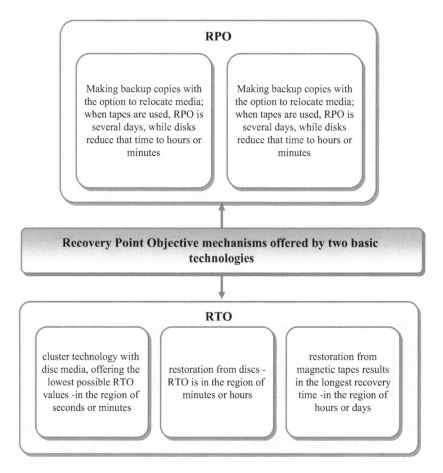

FIGURE 3.8   Recovery Point Objective mechanisms offered by two basic technologies RPO and RTO.

Source: Own work.

When managing informatics resources of an economic organisation, one is unable to plan for every possible system downtime. However, appropriate proactive measures will allow avoiding a total data loss situation in the event of a failure or disaster of the informatics infrastructure. Such measures are based on appropriate planning and preparation of resources and procedures. However, only embedding these elements (i.e. concerning mitigation of effects of failures and disasters) in everyday activities and procedures can guarantee that an enterprise is prepared for crisis situations.

Ensuring operating continuity of an organisation requires taking actions which concern both its technical sphere (informatics technologies) and organisational sphere (Figure 3.9).

Servers based on modern architecture that ensures high availability of computing power represent the first of the most important factors in the area of technology. The other element is represented by actions related to making backup copies of data and

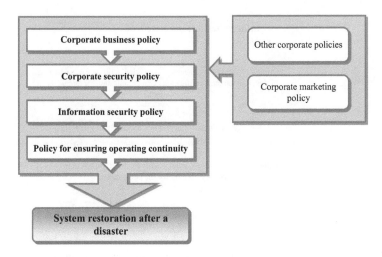

FIGURE 3.9   Hierarchy of an organisation's operating policies.

Source: Own work based on: Gadatsch, Mangiapane 2017b, pp. 17–22.

their storage at a geographically distant location, which, combined with backup services, protect against data loss in the event of a disaster. Both these factors have a significant impact on organisation and management of virtually all critical applications. It becomes necessary to carefully plan actions to be taken prior to and after a failure or disaster.

Most resources (financial, technical and organisational) are consumed by actions related to enhancing the system resistance to disasters. System restoration after a disaster is among elements of organisations' security policies. These actions are in line with business policies of organisations, the main objective of which is the fastest possible restoration of business continuity after a disaster.

3.2   INFORMATION SECURITY MANAGEMENT

As already mentioned, information is an area which can be decisive for an organisation's potential and market value. The increased value of intellectual capital of organisations which base their operations on information entails the need to establish an efficient security management system. Organisations increasingly often create information security management systems based on proven models.

Information has become the most valuable asset in the present era of development of information technologies, globalisation and consolidation. The rapid development of new information technologies and the pace of implementation of pioneering knowledge-based solutions in economy translate into new global threats for organisations which employ informatics systems.

One can venture to say that there is no organisation which has not suffered any losses related to loss of important information. Very few organisations are aware of the importance of their information and develop effective security management systems.

FIGURE 3.10   A set of the best practices in the area of informatics security.

Source: Own work based on: Friedrichsen, Wersig 2020, pp. 289–304.

Information security is not just about informatics or physical safeguards, it is also about well-trained personnel who is aware of threats. Information security is a process and, as any other process, it requires constant refinement.

The quantity and value of data stored in information systems is continually growing, as is the number of threats related to stored and processed information. In response to that increase, information security is being put on ever higher levels to ensure uninterrupted functioning of the informatics system during performance of scheduled tasks.

The authors of the book propose the following best practices in the area of informatics security (Figure 3.10)

Organisations increasingly often create information security management systems based on proven models. Informatics security can be interpreted as a set of processes aimed at achieving and maintaining the assumed level of the following attributes: confidentiality, authenticity, availability, integrity, accountability and reliability (Table 3.1).

Security management covers a set of processes aimed at achieving and maintaining a predefined level of the aforementioned attributes in the information system.

Standardisation has introduced the following basic security-related definitions:

Information Security Management System (ISMS) – a part of an organisation's overall management system based on a business risk-based approach and relating to establishment, implementation, monitoring, maintenance and enhancement of information security. (PN-ISO/IEC 27001:2014-12)

Information security policy – a documented set of rules, practices and procedures in which an organisation defines how it protects its informatics and information processing system assets. (PN-EN ISO/IEC 27001:2017-06)

Risk management – coordinated control and management actions of an organisation with respect to risks. (ISO GUIDE 73:2009 Risk management – Vocabulary, ISO 31000:2018 Risk management — Guidelines).

TABLE 3.1

Definitions of Security Attributes

Name of Attribute	Definition
Confidentiality	This attribute ensures that information is not made available or disclosed to unauthorised persons, entities or processes
Authenticity	This attribute ensures that the identity of an entity or resource is the same as declared; this applies to users, processes, systems or even organisations; authenticity is related to examining whether someone or something is what he/she/it claims to be
Availability	This attribute means being available and ready for use on demand when expected by someone or something who/which has the right to it
Data integrity	This attribute ensures that data has not been altered or destroyed in an unauthorised manner
System integrity	This attribute means that the system performs its planned functions in an undisturbed manned, free of any unauthorised manipulation (deliberate or accidental)
Integrity	Data integrity and system integrity
Accountability	This attribute ensures that actions of an entity can be clearly attributed only to that entity
Reliability	This attribute means coherent and deliberate behaviours and outcomes

Source: Own work.

A security management system is also a set of elements of a technical, procedural and behavioural nature. The respective elements of the system will be presented in the example of the risk related to interception of the password of a user of the informatics system. In such a case, the measures shown in Figure 3.11 can be taken.

A strategic approach which holistically deals with all safeguard elements is the condition for effective operations of a security management system. Disregarding any of these elements leaves a gap which, when utilised by unauthorised persons, can thwart all efforts taken to ensure security. A security management system is therefore also a set of rules and procedures which enable holistic and effective protection of an organisation's information system.

In EU Member States, British standard BS EN ISO/IEC 27002:2017 is considered the leading document in the area of security management (Figure 3.12).

One should also take note of standard ISO/IEC 27005:2018 (Figure 3.13).

In the COBIT methodology, the management of ICT processes is divided into four domains (Figure 3.14). Building on support from one of the strongest organisations (ISACA), COBIT is among the most versatile, comprehensive and universally applied standards.

Major advantages of the information security standardisation are shown in Figure 3.15.

Standardisation materials can be grouped according to the approach to the concept of security; each standard presents a different methodology and has its unique

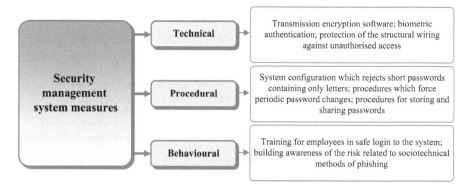

FIGURE 3.11   Security management system measures.

Source: Own work based on: Hanschke 2019.

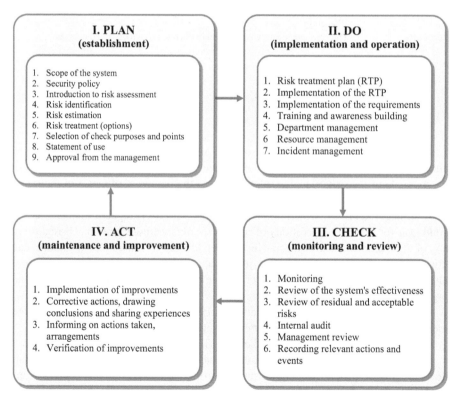

FIGURE 3.12   Information security management structure according to BS EN ISO/IEC 27002:2017.

Source: Own work.

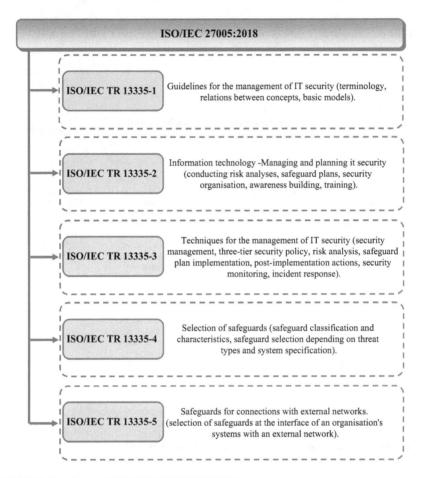

FIGURE 3.13   Standard ISO ISO/IEC 27005:2018.

Source: Own work based on: Davletkireeva, Novikova, Prasolova 2019, pp. 1–5.

advantages and disadvantages. Sometimes, a proposed solution is incomplete and does not fully cover the needs of a given organisation. When developing a security system, one should ensure – regardless of the standardisation base – a harmony between respective safeguard elements.

Security models and risk analysis play a key role in the process of developing an organisation's security system. Respective methodologies differ depending on the scale of the information system. It appears unnecessary to apply complicated and difficult-to-implement models to small information systems. Simplification of the model will reduce the cost of building a security system, which will contribute to maintaining the profitability of the entire project.

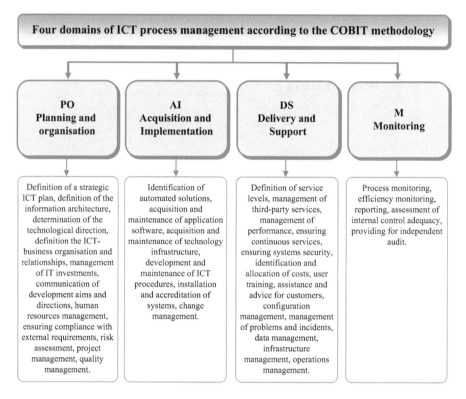

FIGURE 3.14 Four domains of ICT process management according to the COBIT methodology.

Source: Own work based on: De Haes et al. 2020, pp. 125–162.

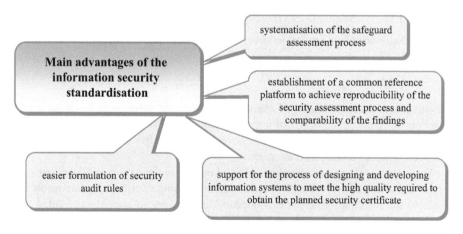

FIGURE 3.15 Main advantages of the information security standardisation.

Source: Own work based on: Andrzejewski 2019, pp. 1–9.

CERT (Computer Emergency Response Team) has developed three security models (Figures 3.16–3.18).

In order to ensure the assumed level of information security, it is recommended to conduct a periodic risk analysis – its findings will represent guidelines regarding further actions modifying the safeguard system.

Standard BS7799 puts strong emphasis on risk management (Figure 3.19).

Existing risk management strategies include (Hahn 2020, pp. 13–46):

- risk ignorance – a responsible organisation should not decide to opt for such a strategy;
- risk transfer – risk insurance – after paying a charge for the transfer of risk onto an insurance institution; but it cannot be done without hedging (risk mitigation safeguards);
- risk mitigation by means of safeguards; it requires risk estimation.

FIGURE 3.16   A model dedicated to small organisations (minimum financial expenditures).

Source: Own work based on: Huber, Hellwig, Quirchmayr 2016, pp. 162–166.

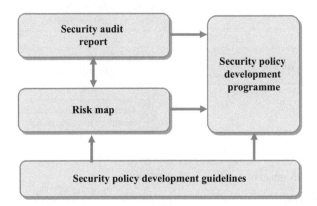

FIGURE 3.17   A model dedicated to organisations of any size (optimised financial expenditures).

Source: Own work based on: Huber, Hellwig, Quirchmayr 2016, pp. 162–166.

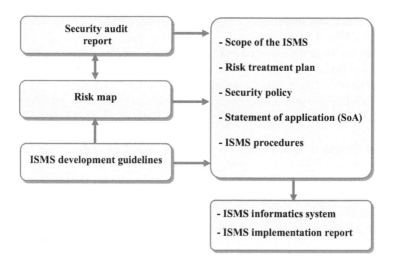

FIGURE 3.18 A model dedicated to organisations of any size (a certificate of conformity with PN-I-07799-2:2005).

Source: Own work based on: Huber, Hellwig, Quirchmayr 2016, pp. 162–166.

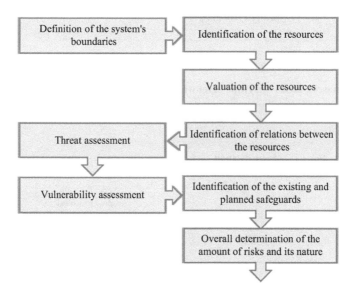

FIGURE 3.19 Conduct of a risk analysis (BS7799).

Source: Own work.

The following risk mitigation strategies, differing in terms of implementation, can be distinguished:

- application of safeguards typical of specific conditions, i.e. basic protection. Regardless of the actual risk, the whole system is treated in the same manner. No risk is examined, which normally leads to overestimation of expenditures on safeguards;
- adoption of safeguards following a simplified risk analysis. The analysis focuses on the areas which seem most vulnerable;
- adoption of safeguards based on a detailed risk analysis. The whole system is subjected to a detailed risk analysis, often with the use of specialised software;
- mixed method – based on a general risk analysis, one identifies system areas which are particularly vulnerable or strategically important to the organisation's operations, safeguards for which are selected on the basis of a detailed risk analysis. Other system areas are under the basis protection.

It is necessary to develop an effective information processing system which will be resistant to strategic threats. Actions should focus on the issues shown in Figure 3.20.

Information security management is too important to be limited only to areas related to computer technologies.

Functioning of an organisation depends on processing of various information. An information system provides its users with a tool to take deliberate actions.

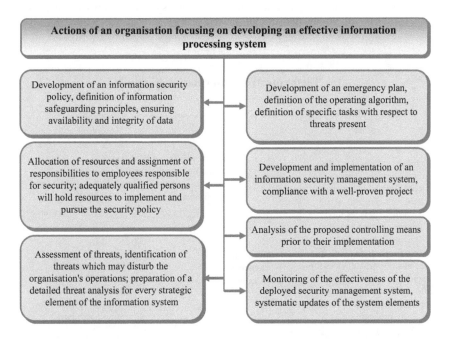

FIGURE 3.20   Actions of an organisation focusing on developing an effective information processing system.

Source: Own work.

Information represents an organisation's resources. To be useful, it must not be a set of any representation thereof, but should rather be presented according to a specific model. Requirements regarding information processing and storage by means of informatics technology differ and depend on the hardware and software deployed. Informatics systems are becoming increasingly more complex and complicated. According to an established relation, an informatics system requires more complex safeguards. Information security management in informatics systems covers a set of processes aimed at achieving and maintaining the planned security level (Hanschke, Schwarz 2019, pp. 216–223).

An information system can be defined as a multi-level structure allowing its users to process input information into output information by means of procedures and models.

In turn, an informatics system is a separate computerised part of an information system. Computerisation of information systems is an increasingly popular method of enhancing the efficiency of the management system because – despite of the initial expenditures on training, software and implementation – an informatics system provides for formalisation of the organisational structure, extended management capabilities, task automation, immediate provision of the required information and easier teamwork at multi-department enterprises.

It is worth mentioning that informatics systems – according to the authors of the book – comprise of the main elements shown in Figure 3.21.

Informatics systems are becoming increasingly more complex and complicated. According to an established relation, an informatics system requires more complex safeguards. Manufacturers of safeguards realise that and, as far as possible, try to

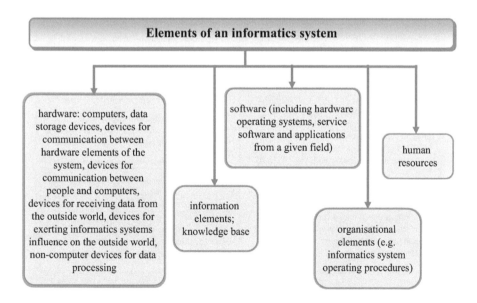

FIGURE 3.21   Elements of an informatics system.

Source: Own work.

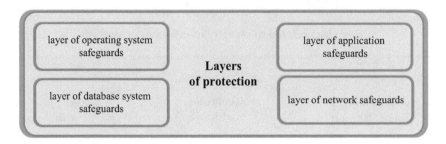

FIGURE 3.22   Layers of protection.

Source: Own work.

provide tools designed to facilitate the management and maintenance of their solutions. This involves mainly the provision of graphical and intuitive security policy editors as well as tools which support the analysis and reporting of recorded incidents. Efforts are also being made to develop a system for security policy visualisation and monitoring of the state of geographically distributed safeguard components.

Technical safeguards of an informatics system can be conventionally divided into layers of protection which, in a properly designed system, complement and cover one another (Figure 3.22).

Each of the above layers of protection meets essential tasks specific to itself. The level of security of informatics system resources depends on the state and appropriate cooperation of all layers of protection. Safeguards of different layers should be logically linked to one another so that any possible lacks in one layer could be made up by safeguards of other layers. Network safeguard layers augment other means of security deployed in the informatics system.

The safeguard architecture should be designed to ensure that respective layers of protection can cover and complement one another. In the event of a malfunction of one layer (e.g. a configuration error, a software error, safeguard shutdown), the other layers should not permit an easy attack on the protected network resources and should provide for quick identification of the irregularities.

Key risks related to security of informatics systems are shown in Figure 3.23.

Security of informatics systems represents all actions aimed at safeguarding the data stored in a computer so that it cannot be used by unauthorised persons or exposed to permanent loss.

Security of informatics systems also includes concepts, techniques and measures used for safeguarding computer systems, as well as information which provides for preventing intentional or accidental system threats.

The informatics system security aspect can be divided into operating system security, database security and network security.

Security of the information system, and of the entire computer system in which data is stored, depends on the operating system. Aided by a protection mechanism, the operating system facilitates access to files as well as access of processes and addressees to other system sources. Information on that mechanism makes it possible to establish who has what access to what files, and what authorisation he/she has to use, alter or delete files.

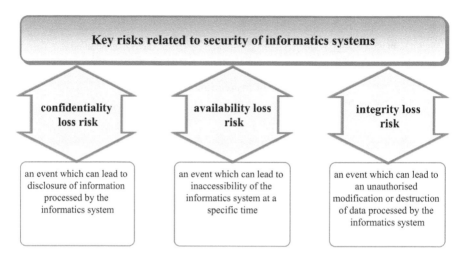

FIGURE 3.23   Key risks related to security of informatics systems.

Source: Own work.

Certain operations related to catalogues should also be subject to control. This applies to creating, deleting or altering catalogues in the system. In order to ensure protection of all files and catalogues, a system is deployed involving password and masking file names to hide them from unauthorised users (Romeike, Hager 2020, pp. 479–520).

At present, nearly all safeguards embedded in operating systems can be relatively easily bypassed – this situation is caused by *inter alia* the shared user awareness how to do it. Information on how to bypass a specific safeguard is available on a number of websites or newsgroups.

Most users have absolute trust in their systems, doubting that their personal data may ever be stolen and fall into unauthorised hands, as they are unaware of the threats to which their computers are exposed.

Computer viruses are among the most popular threats. Today, also other applications may be a source of threat. The multitude and variety of new data from the Internet, portable media and newly installed software are normally the source of unwanted ad-ware / spy-ware, which MAY greatly contribute to loss of confidentiality and, in rare cases, to physical destruction of data stored in a computer. The terms ad-ware (advertisement software) usually refers to free software which forces the user to watch advertisements on a screen in return for the ability to use it for free. Use of such applications does not entail the risk of being "under surveillance". Spyware (spying software) is a more dangerous form of "advertisement application" which contains also unauthorised elements installed without the user's knowledge. In this case, the user is exposed to action of small spying applications which collect information about him/her and create his/her profile. There are at least several thousand spy-ware applications.

The problem of inappropriate rules of handling access passwords is the simplest and most popular example, which is worth mentioning in the context of security of informatics systems. Access passwords serve the purpose of protecting information against unauthorised access. Numeric passwords and codes are often the only method used for safeguarding actions performed by users of ICT systems. Since easy-to-guess passwords, often based on dictionary vocabulary, are frequently a cause of data leaks, they are verified at the very beginning of penetration tests which are designed to simulate attacks performed by online intruders.

Passwords should be made sufficiently complicated by the use of special characters and digits. On the other hand, if a password is too complicated (and difficult to remember), there is a risk that the user will write it down on a piece of paper near the keyboard. Therefore, any requirements regarding the level of password complication should be planned with great care. This can be achieved by appropriately configuring devices and systems so that they would force the users to set passwords that are difficult to guess and to change them regularly. One should also remember about automatic account access lock in the event of repeated unsuccessful login attempts. A system which permits multiple password tests is an easy target for intruders who, depending on the resources and configuration, will be able to test hundreds of thousands of password per day.

The database security aspect is the core of the entire informatics system. The centre of the database management system is formed by the information hidden in the database. Data contained in a database is limited and either exists in an elementary form and cannot be divided into smaller portions or are complex and must be broken up with the use of the database management system functions.

Changes in databases should be of transactional nature. Such changes should be made either fully or never at all – changes in the process must not be partial. Completing a transaction is of strategic importance for the security and coherence of data stored in a database. Such data may belong to different domains. A relational database management system manages the database, as suggested by the name itself, only by means of relations (Figure 3.24).

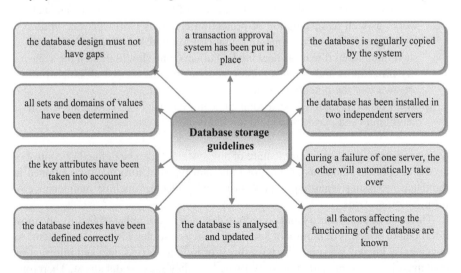

FIGURE 3.24   Database storage guidelines.

Source: Own work.

For most managers in enterprises, the necessity to protect information either does not exist or if very little. This changes in the event of limitation of access to or loss of information. The statistical likelihood of such a failure is negligible, but if it does happen, it is entails large financial, image and psychological costs. Main threats to information resources include:

Human errors: They cannot be eliminated completely. They can only be significantly reduced. This can be achieved effectively by training, building awareness of possible consequences of actions and omissions, improving the working conditions, reducing the scope of responsibilities and restricting the authorisations regarding information resources.

Natural disasters: Key systems should be replicated. Additional systems can quickly take over the responsibilities of the primary system if the latter fails. Emergency systems should be located far enough not to be affected by the disaster. Furthermore, one should ensure redundancy of hardware, data and personnel able to replace the primary personnel. Appropriate security procedures should be developed, implemented and tested for the greatest possible number of possible variants of random events.

Failures related to hardware, software or infrastructure damage: Hardware redundancy is the most popular solution. In turn, the best method of protection against data loss is by making backup copies. Furthermore, there are automated systems which monitor the hardware and software performance and which take over the tasks of the damaged element or automatically rectify defects in the event of a failure. It is also advisable to carefully test the software performance in terms of security, efficiency, universality and tolerance of various errors.

Failures related to intentional threats: In the case of malicious software, effective actions include training in safe use of third-party software and networks as well as installation of protection elements (software, encryption procedures, electronic signature, authorisation and hardware). As regards such intentional threats as hacking by humans, one should tighten the security procedures and conduct comprehensive training so that all employees are aware of the potential threat.

Indirect threats: In this case, a company can establish close cooperation with neighbours and partners to build joint anti-failure systems.

System security is an important feature of any system. It can be defined as control of access to specific functions or data, or to certain types of information contained in the database. Issues regarding data security and protection include maintenance of information systems.

The issue of data security and protection depends on a number of factors, the most important of which is definition of a security policy or strategy for a given system. As is generally known, persons who have direct or indirect access data and information contained in a system cannot be fully trusted, as they may be dishonest. Therefore, they should be forced or encouraged to comply with applicable regulations, restrictions or safeguards. All security policy rules in an organisation should be clear and precise, just as the purpose of the policy must be carefully premeditated and communicated to the system users or employees.

Human error is the greatest threat for information resources. Statistically, it is the most frequent cause of loss of time and money at companies. It is human to make errors, and everybody learns from their errors. Mistakes often arise not from bad faith but rather from fatigue, carelessness, stress, lack of experience, insufficient knowledge and many other factors that are difficult to predict. The latter include natural disasters, e.g. fires, floods, earthquakes, gale-force winds and hurricanes, torrential and sudden rains. They bring very serious consequences and most frequently lead to long downtimes or restricted usability of informatics systems.

Failures related to damage of hardware, software or infrastructure represent another group of threats to information resources. As informatics systems find application in an increasing number of new fields, their working time is becoming longer and the level of complexity higher. Both these factors lead to an increased likelihood of failure.

Intentional threats represent a separate group. They are related to malicious software, most notably viruses, and actions by malicious persons – e.g. hacking.

Unless a person who is responsible for storage and security of key data in an organisation is supervised by the top management, he/she may become a cause of losses at his/her workplace.

In order to ensure appropriate protection of data, one should establish the so-called Security Book which should include the elements shown in Figure 3.25.

Data protection and security is a key aspect in the process of maintenance of an information system at an organisation.

3.3   IT RISK MANAGEMENT

All decisions regarding the performance of informatics systems are burdened with risk. The necessity to manage risks arises from the growing and ever more unpredictable variability of threats in informatics systems. In such conditions, an organisation's information security depends on how fast its informatics services can identify new threats and then take actions to eliminate them.

IT risk management is a process whose structure depends on the exposure of the informatics system to threats and on the strategy pursued by the informatics services in this respect. The more exposed the informatics system is to threats, the more complex and varied actions must be taken to ensure information safety.

The following four stages can be distinguished in the process of IT risk management (Figure 3.26).

The first stage of the risk management process involves identification of risks. This provides for establishing the cause and nature of various types of risks which exist in separate areas of the informatics system.

The second stage involves estimation of the likelihood of defined types of risks and evaluation of probable losses. Evaluation of losses in informatics systems is a very complex task. Application of inaccurate measures can only provide for estimating which risk is greater or smaller. At this stage, the levels of respective risk types which can be accepted are also defined.

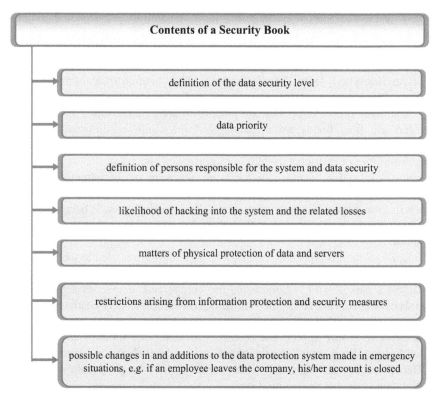

FIGURE 3.25   Contents of a Security Book.

Source: Own work based on: Poljak, Poščić, Jakšić 2017, pp. 1496–1500.

FIGURE 3.26   Stages in the process of IT risk management.

Source: Own work.

The third stage involves risk control and includes actions aimed at mitigating risks in informatics systems. The most important risk control methods include:

- risk reduction or elimination,
- risk transfer,
- risk taking.

The aforementioned risk control methods require active risk-related actions. Adopting a passive stance means avoiding the risk and may lead to compromising the security of an organisation's informatics system.

The last stage involves constant monitoring and risk checks. Actions taken here are aimed at checking how effective the risk management process is. Finding any irregularities is a signal to take corrective actions.

In order to ensure constant improvement of the whole system, respective risk management stages should be separated by feedback.

The process of risk management is not the same in all informatics systems. Certain organisations limit their risk management only to identification and analysis of threats.

Importantly, risk management in informatics systems materialises only when the management staff demonstrates a pro-active stance with respect to risks. The form and scope of the IT risk management process depends on the nature of an organisation and the significance of its informatics system to its business operations. Risk management is a decision-making and action-taking process leading to the achievement of the accepted risk level. Risk management is also a strategic skill without which organisations cannot build safe information systems.

IT risk management provides information which is necessary in the process of optimisation of risk-related losses and it also shapes the architecture of security systems.

The strategy of selecting a risk management method should ensure an appropriate level of security and identify the most critical areas of operations related to risk mitigation. First, one needs to define the criteria for selecting a risk management method for the informatics system concerned.

One can distinguish four strategies, as shown in Figure 3.27.

The above variants of risk management in informatics systems differ in terms of the level of detail of the related risk analysis. Selection of an IT risk management strategy should take into account the outcomes of any potential risk-related incidents.

Selecting the appropriate IT risk management strategy provides for planning more effective audits. It allows for identifying the areas which should be audited first.

An appropriate IT risk management strategy provides effective support for making decisions regarding:

- risk treatment strategy,
- selection of risk mitigation tools,
- assessment of risk-taking advisability,
- risk avoidance.

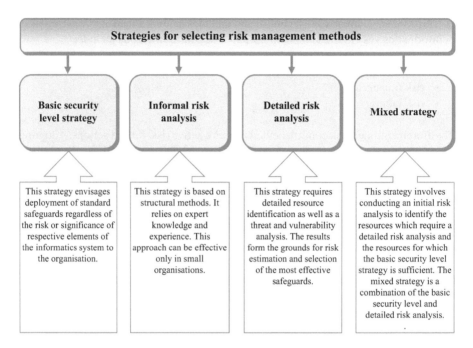

FIGURE 3.27   Four strategies for selecting risk management methods.

Source: Own work based on: Hahn 2020, pp. 13–46.

When selecting a strategy, one should also take into account the quantity of the resources necessary to conduct a risk analysis.

The selected IT risk management strategy should be described in the organisation's security policy.

Estimation of risk values in informatics systems is necessary for security-related decisions to be effective. When known, the risk value allows selecting the appropriate type of safeguards for the resource to be protected and consciously accepting a specific risk level.

Risk estimation can be done by estimating the probability and effects of a security breach incident.

Risk estimation in informatics systems is performed by means of qualitative and quantitative methods.

The risk value based on the quantitative method is expressed either using a numerical scale or directly in a currency unit as the anticipated quantity of losses related to the risk type concerned.

The advantage of expressing risk values in currency units is that it allows comparing between the anticipated losses and safeguard costs.

In the classical approach (Courtney's approach), the amount of risk is the product of the incidence of an adverse event and the amount of consequences caused by that event. In informatics systems, it is difficult to obtain data on incidence of adverse events. It was assumed that event possibility EP(i) depends on vulnerability severity level VS(i) and threat severity level TS(i). Therefore, the product of the threat severity level, which expresses the incidence of the trigger event, and the vulnerability severity level, which expresses the probability of a failure of a safeguard, is the estimation of event possibility EP(i) (Rot et al. 2011, pp. 189–203).

$$EP(i) = \frac{VS(i) \times TS(i)}{VS_{max} \times TS_{max}} \tag{3.1}$$

where:

VS(i) vulnerability severity level, expressing the probability of a failure of a safeguard

VS_{max} maximum vulnerability severity level

TS(i) threat severity level, expressing the incidence of the trigger event

TS_{max} maximum threat severity level

Risk estimation is reproducible provided that there are comparable conditions. Actions of this type allow making accurate decisions regarding safeguard selection. Further analyses and the related partial parameters will be marked with index (i), which will allow comparing scenarios and tracking the amount of risk in time.

Safeguard effectiveness SE(i + 1) is defined as:

$$SE(i+1) = EP(i) - EP(i+1) \tag{3.2}$$

By analysing subsequent values EP(i) and EP(i+1), one can evaluate the effects of the safeguards.

SE(i + 1) < 0 – increased risk, the safeguards have decreased the system security

SE(i + 1) = 0 – no risk change, the safeguards have no impact on the system security

SE(i + 1) > 0 – decreased risk, the safeguards have increased the system security

Precise risk estimation in informatics systems is difficult because it is impossible to obtain all precise data. For certain protected resources, expressing losses in a currency unit is very difficult. This applies to information such as confidentiality loss. In order to establish the value of losses caused by the loss of confidentiality, one should determine the impact of the information on the appropriate performance of a given business process and the significance of that process to the organisation's operations.

The value of information confidentiality loss can be estimated on the basis of potential losses which would take place if the protected information were disclosed, illegally altered or lost. These losses may directly affect the loss of turnover or decrease in profit.

The loss of an organisation's good image or credibility with customers is also very difficult to express in currency units.

FIGURE 3.28   Risk analysis criteria.

Source: Own work.

The qualitative method of risk analysis is based on information security criteria (Figure 3.28).

A full risk analysis can be conducted separately for each of the criteria listed.

For the purpose of a qualitative analysis, one needs to establish an information value scale, e.g. negligible, low, medium, high and very high.

The incidence rate must be established for each type of risk using a pre-defined scale which can differ from the one adopted for the information value.

Furthermore, the vulnerability must be established for each resource examined and each risk type using a conventional scale.

Each of the aforementioned scales is attributed numerical values.

$$R = W + F + V \qquad\qquad (3.3)$$

where:

R – qualitative risk value
W – information loss value
F – threat incidence
V – vulnerability of a given informatics resource to a given threat

A wider scale can be used, e.g. 1–10, to increase the accuracy of risk categorisation in informatics systems.

The economic effectiveness of risk management can be defined as seeking to optimise total costs related to informatics risk.

Majority of more expensive safeguards work more effectively. The risk cannot be reduced to zero, for there are no totally reliable devices.

At the beginning of the curve, the low cost of safeguards causes a significant increase in the level of security. However, from a certain point, an increase in the cost of a safeguard will only slightly lead to an increased security level.

In the case of an informatics system, the risk value depends on (Gleißner 2017):

- value of the protected resource,
- risk probability,
- vulnerability severity level,
- probability of a safeguard failure.

The issue of the economically effective risk management process should be viewed through the analysis of safeguard costs expressed in currency units.

The economic effectiveness of the IT risk management process can be defined as seeking to minimise the sum of risk expressed in a currency unit and the safeguard cost (Figures 3.29–3.31).

The economically optimal value of risk can be established using the marginal safeguard cost and marginal risk value.

Marginal safeguard cost (MSC)

$$\text{MSC}(i) = \text{SC}(i+1) - \text{SC}(i) \tag{3.4}$$

where: $\text{SC}(i)$ – safeguard cost

Marginal risk value expressed in a currency unit (MRVC)

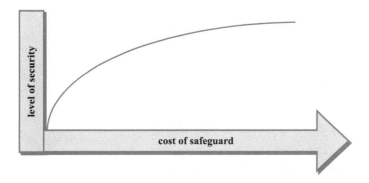

FIGURE 3.29   Relation between the security level and the cost of a safeguard.

Source: Own work.

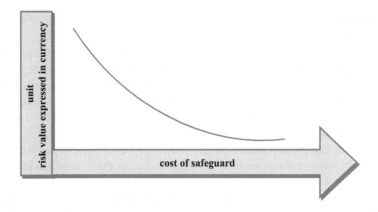

FIGURE 3.30   Relation between the risk value expressed in a currency unit and the cost of a safeguard.

Source: Own work.

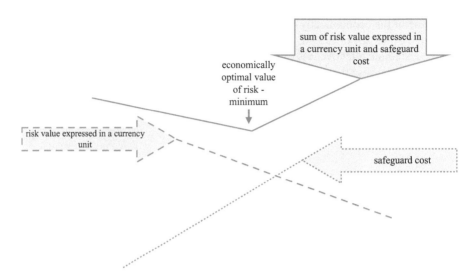

FIGURE 3.31 Safeguard cost, risk value expressed in a currency unit, sum of risk value expressed in a currency unit and safeguard cost.

Source: Own work.

$$MRVC(i) = RVC(i) - RVC(i+1) \qquad (3.5)$$

where: $RVC(i)$ – risk value expressed in currency unit

The economically optimal risk value in an informatics system is established on the basis of the following relation:

$$MSC(i) = MRVC(i) \qquad (3.6)$$

This condition is in line with the assumption regarding minimisation of the sum of the safeguard cost and risk value expressed in a currency unit.

If the marginal safeguard cost is lower than the marginal risk value expressed in a currency unit, the safeguard expenditures should be increased. Conversely, if the marginal safeguard cost is higher than the marginal risk value expressed in a currency unit, the safeguard expenditures should be reduced. The latter is the case of an informatics system which is protected too strongly in economic terms (high and unreasonable safeguard costs).

Seeking to completely reduce risks in an informatics system is economically groundless. From a certain point on, the safeguard costs grow more quickly than the reduction of risk value expressed in a currency unit.

A correctly established safeguard cost shall take into account (Madauss 2017, pp. 663–690):

- the risk-related costs after application of the planned risk mitigation or transfer measures,

- the costs of implementation and operation of the risk mitigation or transfer measures,
- the costs related to the risk management process (data gathering, risk analyses, third-party consultants, control).

In IT risk management, it must be taken into account that the risk analysis alone can generate significant costs. In order to obtain more accurate results, one should allocate more resources to the analysis, gather more data and employ qualified personnel. However, if no risk analysis has been conducted, then no risk value is known. Hence, it is not known whether the cost related to the risk analysis are reasonable. It may happen that the costs of the risk analysis are higher than losses generated by the risk analysed.

This problem can be solved by running a two-stage risk analysis. At the first stage, it can be initially estimated how detailed the second stage of the analysis should be. Such an approach provides for running an initial estimation of what resources are worth allocating to the risk analysis.

An excessively detailed IT system risk analysis may generate excessive costs, whereas a risk analysis that lacks detail may be ineffective. The problem of maintaining a balance between these variants is difficult and requires strong experience in this respect.

The same applies to risk transfer. Buying an insurance policy is justified only when it generates lower costs compared with the cost of safeguard implementation and maintenance.

An IT risk analysis can produce a set of identified risks which are categorised in terms of priority.

From a practical point of view, risk visualisation allows making more accurate decisions regarding security. A graphical presentation of a set of risk information can be important in the development of an organisation's security policy.

Forms of graphical description of risks include the so-called risk map which categorises risk areas according to their significance to the organisation.

A risk map puts respective risks in a coordinate system where the vertical axis represents risk outcome values and the horizontal line represents the probability of a given event (Figure 3.32).

Risks are placed in appropriate locations in the system of coordinates depending on their established probabilities and effects. Such a form of risk visualisation allows presenting main factors that are threats to the informatics system.

Location of a risk in one of the four quarters of the system indicates further course of risk treatment.

Creating a risk map, i.e. estimating the probability and outcomes of individual incidents, is difficult due to the lack of data based on reliable statistical studies.

When developing a risk map, one can use information from several sources (Kuzmenko 2019, pp. 50–55):

- **Experience of own informatics services**. If an organisation uses hundreds of computers, then it can be assumed that the number of incidents will be high enough to be the basis for estimating the event probability. However,

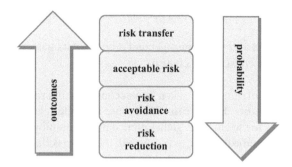

FIGURE 3.32 Risk treatment on the basis of a risk map.

Source: Own work.

the number of incidents related to natural disasters may be too low to do so, even in the case of a large organisation.

- **Manufacturer statistics**. Manufacturer statistics can be a source of data on the probability of hardware failures. The mean time between failures (MTBF) is a parameter that shows the reliability level of a given device. It is expressed in hours and allows estimating the probability of a failure of a given devices.
- **Statistics of specialised third-party institutions**. Statistics regarding fires and industrial disasters provided by the fire service can be an important source of information.
- **Exchange of data between organisations**. Information can be exchanged between organisations with similar activity profiles.
- **Delphi method**. Estimation is based on the knowledge, experience and intuition of individual experts. Results are recorded in an appropriate form and then averaged. Such an approach allows reducing the subjective factor in running a risk assessment.
- **Evaluation by third-party consultants**. This solution is useful when an organisation does not have own security specialists. Third-party consultants must first know the specificity of the informatics system concerned as well as all the conditions that affect the organisation's operations.
- **Simulation method**. Data is obtained by means of a computer simulation of real system models.

It is important for an informatics system risk map to include all risks relevant to the organisation concerned and thus be the basis for a risk analysis.

The fast development of computer technology makes it necessary to verify many views regarding informatics system security. At present, IT risk management is the foundation which allows making effective decisions regarding security. When repeated systematically, an informatics system risk analysis makes it possible to establish safeguard development guidelines and verify the effectiveness of actions taken so far. A risk analysis is the basis for establishing the economically optimal risk level in an informatics system.

In summary, it should be emphasised that imprecise and incorrect IT risk management can be the basis for a feeling of false security.

3.4 ADVANCED INFORMATICS SOLUTIONS SUPPORTING RISK MANAGEMENT IN AN ORGANISATION

Risk accompanies every process in an organisation. Failure to understand it, wrong identification of risk factors or inappropriate risk management can prevent an organisation from achieving its strategic objectives. Modern process management can be supported by informatics technologies which facilitate process modelling and execution, and ensure monitoring and supervision of process activities, thus enabling improvement of the processes. Maturity models describe the evolutionary path of an organisation, aiding its transition from the state of incoherent *ad hoc* actions regarding risk to well-structured, monitored and managed activities.

The concept of risk management is defined as making decisions and taking actions which lead to the achievement of an acceptable risk level (Figure 3.33).

Risk management is a complex process which in the broadest terms can be divided into four stages: risk identification, risk measurement, risk control and risk monitoring and checks.

Many organisations manage their risks in a reactive manner, i.e. only when an emergency takes place, or focus on selected, easily measurable risks. In more advanced solutions, individual organisation components manage risks by means of individually selected tools and applications, without communicating with other components. This attitude to risk management is referred to as silo management (Matysek et al. 2019, pp. 175–189). Most studies use the idea of integrated risk management.

Table 3.2 shows differences between the silo and integrated risk management.

The similarity of challenges and requirements faced by organisations which want to control their compliance with regulations, comprehensively manage their risks and support effective operational supervision implies a possibility to employ an approach

FIGURE 3.33 Definitions of risk management.

Source: Own work.

TABLE 3.2
Comparison between the Traditional and Integrated Approaches to Risk Management

Traditional Approach	Integrated Approach
Risks are considered in an isolated – so-called silo – manner	Holistic risk management covering all risk types present in an organisation
Zero or little link between risk management and an organisation's strategy	Strict relation between risk management and an organisation's strategy
Reluctance to take risks	Proactive approach to risks
Sporadic risk assessment	Continuous identification and evaluation of risks; verification and monitoring of the risk management process
Risks are frequently not subject to any quantification	Most risk types are subject to quantification
Zero or poor flow of information; incoherent reporting system	Good flow of information; consolidated reports
No transparently defined roles and scopes of responsibilities	Defined roles and scopes of responsibilities for risks attributed to business processes

Source: Own work.

that would integrate these aspects. The said integration of supervision (governance), risk management and compliance is referred to by the acronym GRC (Figure 3.34).

Each of the three components of the GRC concept is determined by the following four elements: strategy, processes, people and technology – depending on the accepted risk level, internal procedures (policies) and external regulations, whereas the purposes of implementing the concept are defined as promotion of ethically appropriate behaviours and improvement of the effectiveness and efficiency of actions. Such an integrated approach allows avoiding dispersion and duplication of efforts related initiatives taken in these areas, and provides for a better utilisation of the interdisciplinary nature of risk and clearer picture of the institution, particularly in the context of governance.

Together with the development of risk management, there emerged standards which include a set of best practices and allow organisations to consciously and effectively implement and run the process of integrated risk management. Below, the authors will discuss the two most popular standards: FERMA and COSO.[1]

According to FERMA, the process of risk management should be run as a sequence of the following stages (Figure 3.35).

The standard in question takes account of the fact that a risk can be linked both with opportunities (positive aspect) and threats (negative aspect). Its authors did not intend to develop a prescriptive standard with precisely defined requirements to meet, or one that would be the basis for issuing certificates of conformity – the FERMA standard is in fact a description of good practices meant to serve as a benchmark.

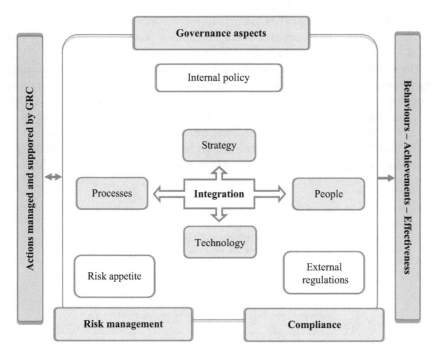

FIGURE 3.34 Integrated approach to GRC.

Source: Own work.

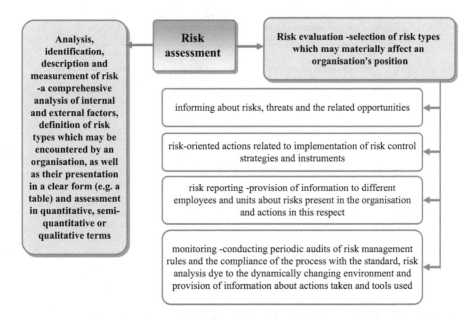

FIGURE 3.35 Stages of implementation of the risk management process according to the FERMA standard.

Source: Own work based on: Urbanowska-Sojkin et al. 2014, pp. 560–571.

The COSO standard describes risk management as a system – which distinguishes it from FERMA, which sees risk management as a process – comprised of eight linked elements (risk components), as shown in Figure 3.36.

The COSO standard implies a direct relation between objectives,[2] i.e. something that an organisation wants to achieve, and risk management components, i.e. something that is necessary to achieve the objectives at all levels of the organisation. These three perspectives of integrated risk management are presented graphically in the form of a 3D cube (the COSO Cube) on which four categories of objectives are shown in columns, eight components – in rows, and organisational units – in the third dimension. The cube illustrates an organisation's ability to embrace the whole risk

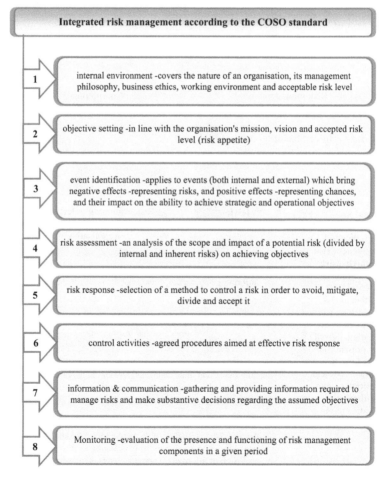

Integrated risk management according to the COSO standard

1. internal environment -covers the nature of an organisation, its management philosophy, business ethics, working environment and acceptable risk level

2. objective setting -in line with the organisation's mission, vision and accepted risk level (risk appetite)

3. event identification -applies to events (both internal and external) which bring negative effects -representing risks, and positive effects -representing chances, and their impact on the ability to achieve strategic and operational objectives

4. risk assessment -an analysis of the scope and impact of a potential risk (divided by internal and inherent risks) on achieving objectives

5. risk response -selection of a method to control a risk in order to avoid, mitigate, divide and accept it

6. control activities -agreed procedures aimed at effective risk response

7. information & communication -gathering and providing information required to manage risks and make substantive decisions regarding the assumed objectives

8. Monitoring -evaluation of the presence and functioning of risk management components in a given period

FIGURE 3.36 Integrated risk management according to the COSO standard.

Source: Own work based on: Fox 2018, pp. 4–7.

management or to focus on a specific category of objectives, component, organisational unit or any set thereof.

The FERMA and COSO standards have a similar structure. One can notice more similarities than differences between them, which shows the trend to unify the principles, techniques and criteria.

The subject of an organisation's maturity appeared in the field of management sciences in the 1970s in the context of the performance analysis of companies and institutions, alongside such concepts as efficiency and effectiveness. An analysis of the literature shows that a number of maturity models have been created, of which the process and design maturity models are the most dominant.

Despite a huge popularity of this approach, it was not before 2009 that a formal definition of the maturity model was coined. According to this definition, the model presents – in quantitative or qualitative terms – the stages of the model element's growing ability to accomplish assigned tasks in order to assess them in reference to the defined areas (Huszlak, Skrzypek 2019, pp. 209–215). Therefore, the maturity models describe a sequence of subsequent level (degrees) of maturity, illustrating the desired or logical path of transition from the initial state to full maturity, most often from complete immaturity, characterised as *ad hoc*, lack of organisation and chaos (level 1), to reproducibility (level 2), standardisation (level 3), conscious management (level 4), to continuous improvement and excellence as the expression of the highest maturity (level 5).

The maturity models can run three functions (Figures 3.37).

Based on the literature and observations of business practice, it is proposed to distinguish the following levels of an organisation's maturity in terms of risk management (Figure 3.38).

One can distinguish the following process-related transition relations between subsequent level of the proposed risk management maturity model:

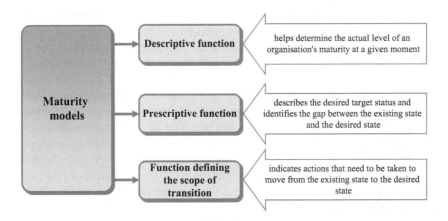

FIGURE 3.37   Maturity models.

Source: Own work based on: Nogalski, Niewiadomski 2019: pp. 15176–15176.

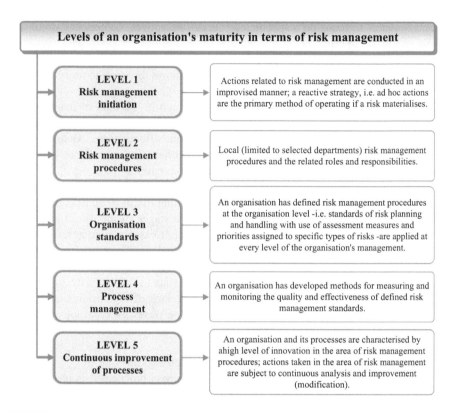

FIGURE 3.38   Levels of an organisation's maturity in terms of risk management.

Source: Own work based on: Buchholz, Knorre 2019. pp. 177–198.

- level 1 → level 2 – awareness of processes; documentation and comprehension of their structure,
- level 2 → level 3 – establishment of process metrics, process measurement and implementation of the process management system, emergence of the process owner (more generally, assignment of process roles to employees),
- level 3 → levels 4 and 5 – process-focused management (process orientation).

The third maturity level is a breakthrough one, as it involves an organisation's shift in risk management from the functional approach (silo) towards the process approach.

Deployment of informatics technologies is among key factors required for a successful implementation of the risk management system and process[3] in an organisation. Furthermore, an organisation's readiness to reach for ever more high-tech informatics solutions allows it – on meeting several applicable procedural, organisational and staff requirements – to achieve the aforementioned successive risk management maturity levels.

It is proposed to divide the analysed informatics solutions into basic and advanced ones, with informatics support of risk management in the basic variant being sufficient at levels 2 and 3 of the maturity model, and the advanced variant required at levels 4 and 5.

In a more detailed solution, the scope of capabilities of informatics support of risk management processes will be presented by reference of the existing informatics tools to the framework structure represented by the 3D COSO Cube from the COSO standard.

First, one needs to look at solutions related to the management of risk situated in integrated informatics system of the ERP and CRM class designed to support overall business processes of an organisation. The SAP system has been made the point of reference. In this system, risk management support if provided in accordance with the GRC concept, mentioned in the first point of this paper, through four modules: SAP GRC Access Control, SAP GRC Process Control, SAP Risk Management and SAP Policy Management.[4] As shown in Figure 3.39, this solution support risk components specified as items 4–8 of the COSO standard.

On the basis of an analysis of the current software offering on the market, it is possible to present a more universal proposal regarding comprehensive risk management support. The set is comprised of five components (see Figure 3.40) from two suppliers.[5]

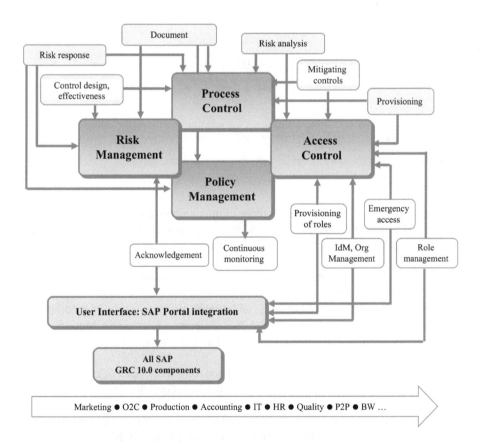

FIGURE 3.39   GRC concept in the SAP system.

Source: Own work based on: Friedl, Pedell 2020, pp. 189–217.

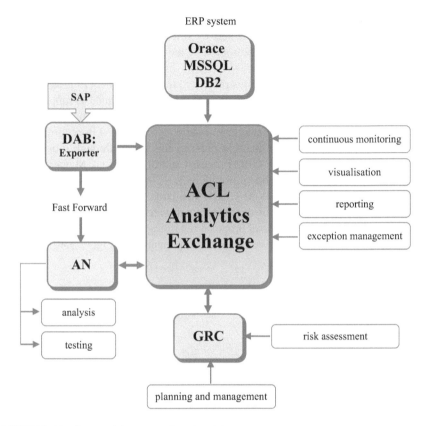

FIGURE 3.40 Proposal for comprehensive risk management support.

Source: Own work.

The ACL product family includes three solutions which could provide support for business risk identification, examination and mitigation in the areas of governance, risk management and compliance. The said support would cover[6]:

- in the basic variant: data analysis (with the ACL Analytics module) to detect irregular transactions from the perspective of business norms, internal audit standards or legal requirements, and continuous monitoring of a company's key operating areas with the ACL Enterprise Continuous Monitoring (ECM) module, complemented by the ACL Analytics Exchange technology as an early warning system,
- in the advanced variant: integration of activities in the area of governance, risk management and compliance with the ACL GRC module.

In the case of the proposed solution, its basic variant supports risk components specified as items 6 (control activities) and 8 (monitoring) of the COSO standard, while deployment of the advanced variant expands that support to components from items 4, 5 and 7.

Risk management involves identification and control – by means of neutralisation of threats and taking opportunities – of the risk types that can affect the achievement of a company's strategic objectives. Implementation of a risk management system can be aided by maturity models which provide hints about the course of action that increases the probability of success. An outline of such a maturity model is presented above. This model can be a diagnostic tool for assessing an organisation's readiness to use more or less advanced informatics solutions that support risk management.

3.5   PROBLEMS OF PERSONAL AND SOCIAL THREATS ARISING FROM UTILISATION OF INFORMATION TECHNOLOGIES IN THE MODERN WORLD

Problems regarding personal and social threats arising from the presence and inappropriate utilisation of information technologies are the subject of research of various scientific disciplines. In order to enable researchers of this field to support each another in their studies, the terminology convention and basic theoretical assumptions must be unified.

From the systemic perspective, the human environment includes sets of components which – due to their nature – can be grouped in subsystems. One can distinguish natural, social, technical and information components. Interactions between them are manifested in the form of the environment which, from a person's subjective point of view, offers the most advantageous conditions, and each of the components co-contributes to achieving the expected quality of life, which affects human well-being either positively or negatively. Indeed, the quality of the world determines the quality of life. The human anthroposphere encompasses all results of human work which have been created thanks to humans and which are meant to support humans in performing their functions. The anthroposphere is a component of the biosphere in which the humans operate. This area is normally under strong anthropopressure.

Here, the authors are interested in the information component which meets the description of the concept of the human information environment. It is referred to as **the human anthropoinfosphere** (infosphere or **anthropoinfosphere**). For humans, it is a unique kind of layer (an enclosing lampshade) which is subject to special rights and in which information dis/integration of people and the society takes place (Babik 2017).

We live in the times of civilisational transformation, the essence of which is reconstruction of the axiological model of the lives of humans and communities. The nature and scope of these transformations depends on changes which take place in key technologies for the present wave of the civilisational development. These technologies are systems of information technologies. Indeed, it should be emphasised that they include all technologies related to search for and acquisition of information as well as its gathering, sorting, segregating, storing, processing, transmitting and erasing. In each of these processes we are discovering ever new information technologies, and each of them offers us new products – information works – created with the use of increasingly more efficient and productive new informatics hardware which uses new methods (most frequently new software). Competencies required of users of new equipment to use information are changing, as are professional competencies of employees of various professions.

Just as important are those changes which manifest themselves in connection with the changing scope of use of information technologies and the extent of their social impact. Indeed, technological development is always of multidirectional nature, sometimes also negative. Therefore, the arrival of a new computer programme, operating system or security system is followed by the creation of methods and development of software for gaining illegal access to these novelties, which – according to their authors – are reliable and excellently protected.

Such a pace of changes brings risks which should earn more and more attention from the contemporary pedagogy (including informatics didactics) and psychology, and in particular they should be subject of regular studies.

We are interested in risks which arise from the omnipresence of information technologies and devices, as well as risks which may emerge in the future, which are related to the vision of our further development or the place of the human in the technicised world. We are interested in the results brought by the dazzling pace of computerisation, miniaturisation, development of microelectronics and all other advanced technologies of today.

The consequences of their spontaneous development may be very dangerous to many aspects of the human life and the surrounding world. The risks which arise from the aforementioned phenomena, most importantly from computer hardware and the Internet, encompass both personal and social threats. The first group includes threats to the human corporeality (the so-called physical threats), threats to mental life (phenomena concerning cognitive processes) and threats to spiritual life (including moral threat and various addictions). Among social threats, we can distinguish ones that concern phenomena analysed both in the local and global scale. They include threats concerning culture, including life style changes, expansion of consumerism, language transformations (dissemination of a simplified language code). Pathologies of various kinds are growing rapidly. There are new threats such as Internet crime or cyber terrorism (Macdonald, Jarvis, Lavis, 2019, pp. 1–26).

Interesting problems can be seen in this context. What consequences will be brought by these cumulated changes taking place at the same place and time, and manifested in the changed environment of human life and work? When and to what extent can these changes be considered advantageous? Can these changes be considered as having a positive impact on the quality of the environment, as an improvement of this environment? Are there any doubts, threats or dangers behind those dynamic change processes?

The pace of changes in information technologies is very high. We feel it in our everyday lives. The social and economic consequences are very significant.

However, it is not information itself which constitutes a threat, but unreasonable and irresponsible selection and use of information (Figure 3.41).

The human has involuntarily become addicted to the latest information technologies. It is only about addictions which today are the subject of studies by doctors, psychologists and sociologists and involve habitual sitting at a computer and playing video games, web browsing and communicating with other, most often unknown, people, but a total merger with all professional, and increasingly often private,

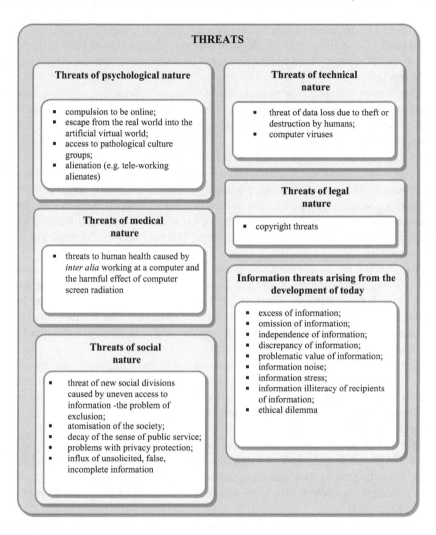

FIGURE 3.41   Threats.

Source: Own work.

activities. Employees of institutions, enterprises, hospitals, schools and universities start their every day at work from switching on their computers. The main threats arising from the use of computers in conflict with occupational health principles include eye problems, wrist disorders and problems with the spine.

Intensive use of computer equipment may generate various threats after some time (normally several years). These threats can be divided into several groups.

This is not only about the risk of human illnesses, but also about certain changes of social nature such as threats concerning ethics, including such phenomena as increased plagiarism and informal borrowing, as well as decay of independent thinking and in-depth consideration.

Abuse of information media, especially television and computes, entails a numerous hazards. Most noticeable are **physical threats**, which are quite easy to diagnose but, up until recently, could hardly be treated as occupational diseases due to weak legal regulations.

This type of threats concerns primarily the human corporeality, and their content depends mainly from our understanding of this corporeality. The human body is an expression of the mystery of the human, not the mystery of the body. Our bodily behaviours express who we are, what value we believe in, how we understand the meaning of life and who we want to be for other people.

In the case of disturbed development, it is possible that a person's sense of identity will become reduced almost entirely to the awareness at the bodily level. In the case of appropriate development, the significance of the bodily sphere becomes weaker as a person discovers other dimensions of his or her reality. Then, emotional and moral sensitivity, the ability to think and the internal freedom become increasingly more important.

The concern for health means responsible nutrition and adjusting one's activity and working life to their sex and age, as well as an appropriate life style which ensures the balance between effort, rest and sleep. This means concern for **the body ecology** – so that not only air, land and water are clean, but also our most important environment, our corporeality, is free of any physical, chemical or mental poisons (Martínková 2017, pp. 101–112).

Behavioural addictions disturb also somatic health, exposing it to many disorders and diseases. Most importantly, a person suffering from a behavioural addiction has serious problems with refraining from a specific activity, even despite evident harm this brings. Overcoming one's behavioural compulsions often requires help from other people and specialists.

A behavioural addiction (or addictive behaviour) is defined here as a recurring habit which increases the risk of a diseases and/or related personal and social problems. Addictive behaviours are often subjectively felt as the loss of control – they emerge despite conscious efforts to suppress or limit them (Vanderschuren et al. 2017, pp. 77–84).

Considered from the perspective of a syndrome, these physiological effects are termed the Internet Addition Syndrome (IAS) (Figure 3.42).

At work, we can feel all these symptoms only after a long time or after we leave the computer because our brain focuses strongly on what is going on the screen and is unable to interpret any warning signals at the right time. These signals are suppressed until they become unbearable.

Threats to mental life are most noticeable in mental addictions from the Internet (Figure 3.43).

The Internet is a tool which is successfully used by children and youth in the process of education. Reasons for which youths use the Internet include their openness and curiosity. For them, the Internet is interesting and unknown. One never knows what they can encounter in the web. People are encouraged to browse the web by the content of websites - it takes no time to find a website with information from many fields of knowledge. Also, Internet users appreciate the ease of website navigation as well as the time factor. A web user does not have to rush anywhere, as the web gives

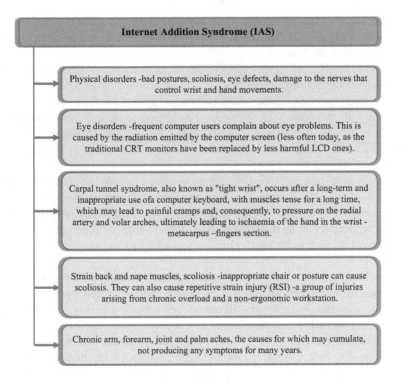

FIGURE 3.42   Internet Addition Syndrome (IAS).

Source: Own work based on: Starcevic, Aboujaoude 2017, pp. 7–13.

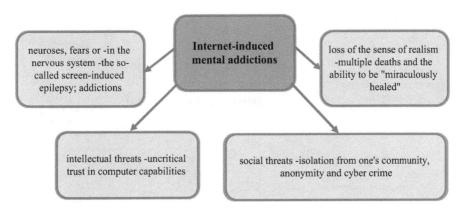

FIGURE 3.43   Internet-induced mental addictions.

Source: Own work based on: Wölfling, Müller, Dreier 2020, pp. 317–320.

time and does not hasten anyone to do anything, and information contained in the Internet are available 24 hours a day, which is why young people often choose to learn and play in the Internet.

The main intellectual threats concern disorders in the development and functioning of the human cognitive processes.

The primary source of these threats is the rapid increase in the volume of information leading to redundancy of information and information overload – the information shock and uncritical trust in the capabilities of a machine. In psychology, a good platform for describing the phenomenon of information shock is provided by **the concepts of stress**.

The excess of data and speed of its transmission – coupled with human cognitive limits arising from the functional properties of attention and memory – create a subjective sense of confusion, chaos, helplessness and even threat. All these feeling together are referred to as **the information stress**, a form of the cognitive stress.

The most addictive Internet contents, according to the authors, are shown in Figure 3.44.

In addition, one can distinguish **contact with the content which is particularly dangerous for children and youth**, such as brutal violence, xenophobia and racism. A specific content is considered dangerous when contact with it may have a harmful effect on the mentality and development of a child. While some of the aforementioned contents are illegal, e.g. child pornography, others can be present in the Internet legally – e.g. scenes of brutal violence. Contact with them may be ransom and completely unintentional. A child may encounter it when browsing for some

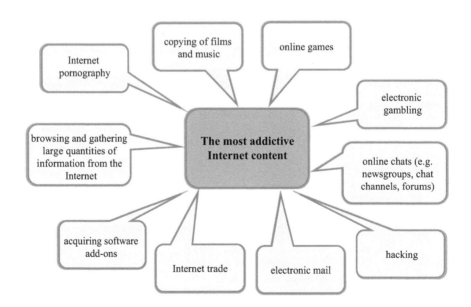

FIGURE 3.44   The most addictive Internet content.

Source: Own work.

information by means of a search engine (and by clicking a random link), or by downloading a wrong file.

Every Internet user is exposed to contact with contents they wish they would not see. These include:

- **promotional materials** – the so-called spam sent to individual users; they can include advertisements, links or other electronic materials. Spam account for as much as 50% of correspondence circulating in the Internet; most of it is not dangerous.
- **dangerous files** (viruses, trojans) which are harmful to our computers and software.
- Main **types of dangerous content** include:
- pornographic and violent content;
- racist and xenophobic content;
- crime-inciting content;
- content promoting fascist or other totalitarian systems of state;
- content inciting to prostitution or gambling;
- content promoting drugs and other stimulants – most often by highlighting their allegedly therapeutic values or by arguing that they open the human to a new reality (e.g. spiritual one);
- content with elements of psychological manipulation (e.g. promoting religious groups which are considered cults, encouraging to join a cult; content which promotes anorexia and bulimia as a style of life but not a serious disease; content which encourages suicides, etc.).

A great majority of psychologists believe that frequent contacts of young people with pornography have a deep, multidimensional and harmful effect on them. Pornographic content is a source of experiences which surpass the youth's adaptation abilities and which provide models for pathological behaviours. They shape a distorted and negative picture of the world and interpersonal relations, and consolidate the false picture of femininity and masculinity. A contact with pornography may lead to erotisation of a child's psyche as well as to stresses, psychomotor hyperactivity and symptoms of neurosis and depression (Wölfling et al. 2017, pp. 422–430).

Other threats and examples of dangerous content which may encountered by children and youth browsing the Internet include (Müller 2017, pp. 9–15):

- cyber-bullying – violent behaviour which involves insulting, ridiculing, blackmailing or dissemination of discrediting materials in the web with the use of information and communication technologies (messengers, chats, websites, blogs);
- grooming – seduction of children by adults through the Internet. To establish a close contact with a child, "cyber hunters" use mainly online messengers and chats;
- content promoting religious movements considered to be cults;
- content promoting anorexia and bulimia as a style of life, not a serious disease;

- content encouraging suicides or self-harm;
- content promoting drugs and other stimulants – most often by highlighting their allegedly therapeutic values or by arguing that they open the human to a new spiritual reality.

Information overload takes place when there is abundance of information, e.g. one is in multiple chat rooms or discussion groups simultaneously. **Information overload** means compulsion to get information (Persson 2018, pp. 78–106).

The Internet offers a possibility to experiment with one's identity. We can amazingly manipulate our own identity, e.g. by assuming a different gender or age. Identity experiments represent an important part of human development, and identity crises which we come through, particularly in youth, provide a valuable experience in our mental development. If we do not try everything, we will not know what we like best. After we have come to terms with everything, we again assume a new identity. This state is accompanied by a deeper sense of "me" (Kral 2004, pp. 273–280). Whatever we say about ourselves in the web can so easily be made more colourful or falsified that this environment becomes a tempting place for making experiments. The fact that we can tell lies there and normally get away with it is another characteristic feature of the Internet. In the text environment, we are unable to demonstrate our high social status.

On the one hand, the Internet is a very good means to maintain and establish contacts, but on the other it poses a threat to people who use it inappropriately. A young person may is exposed to many dangers which are worth knowing more about in order for us to be able to counter them at the right time.

Moral threats arise from an easy and uncontrollable access to information, negative attitudes and schematic behaviours. Threats are multidimensional. Moral threats involve, most importantly, an easy and uncontrollable access of children and youth to information about undesired content. It occurs that there are no truly effective filters which could prevent reaching morally reprehensible websites.

Threats arising from the universal deployment of information technologies have not been subject to any deeper scientific studies yet. They are connected with anonymity and lack of barriers when at a computer screen and online. This is how some people behave online – by way of the principle of contradiction of their normal lives.

Digital exclusion is a serious social problem, much more serious than digital divide alone, whether from the local or global perspective. Using new technologies is now becoming a new dimension of differentiation which makes the existing differences even deeper. The more valuable the possibility and ability to use the Internet, the more problematic the barriers related to online access. Indeed, while access to the World Wide Web brings various advantages, and increasingly often becomes necessary to fully function within the society, the lack of that access may lead to the social and economic exclusion.

Among main problems connected with widespread access to new technologies is the significant disparity concerning this access both nationally and globally. Studies into geography of the Internet show these differences clearly. Computers, Internet and mobile phones are much more often used by wealthier, better educated and younger people living in big cities. This relation can be observed in Poland as well as in other countries. The situation is improving with every year.

In English, this phenomenon is called "digital divide", which has mane translation in Polish. The term that is closest to the English original is *cyfrowy podział*. It is sometime also referred to as *cyfrowe wykluczenie* (digital exclusion), which to a greater extent emphasises the consequences of inequality in access and ability to use digital technologies.

The digital divide is defined as "inequalities in access to the Internet, intensity of its use, knowledge of methods of searching for information, quality of connection and social support in using the Internet, as well as inequalities in the ability to assess the quality of information and diversity of web uses" (Mihelj, Leguina, Downey 2019, pp. 1465–1485).

Dimensions of the digital divide are shown in Figure 3.45.

As illiteracy in the past excluded people socially, the **digital illiteracy** may have similar consequences. The digital gap in the society is growing, with the division between people proficient in information and informatics technologies and people who are digitally incompetent.

This gives rise to the information gap between people who by their education (or certain personality features) are better equipped to use new media. The society is

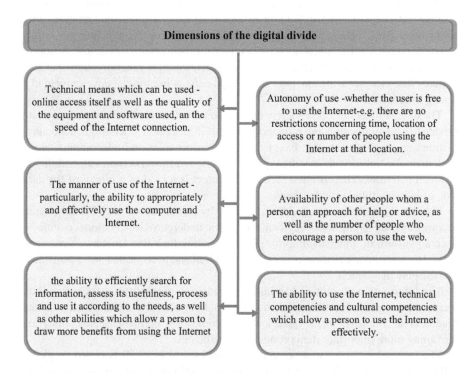

FIGURE 3.45   Dimensions of the digital divide.

Source: Own work based on: Vartanova, Gladkova 2019, pp. 193–213.

becoming more diversified rather than unified. The distance between comprehension of the technical environment and technical ignorance is becoming greater.

The Internet has revolutionised many fields of human life. It allows universal communication and facilitates contacts while eliminating the space constraints and ensuring real time communication. It has become necessary as a tool of work and entertainment. It makes it easier to learn and develop one's interests. The Internet is no longer a matter of choice - it is practically the necessity. On its own, the Internet is neither good nor bad. It is just a helpful tool, like a car which makes transport easier and faster. However, its use is accompanied by a certain risk. It is difficult to give a clear estimate of the scale of threats, for only some incidents related to cyber-tormentors are reported to law enforcement agencies. Understanding the essence of these threats and knowledge of address details of institutions which provide help to the victims of cybercrime make us stronger in the fight against potential hazards.

New addictions include addictions from gambling, shopping, work, sex and food. An exceptional increase in these kinds of addictions has been observed in recent years.

A person is considered to be addicted to the Internet when a computer is enough for him or her to live a happy life. Such persons communicate with other people and excite about things through the web. They have the impression of participation in the political, social and cultural life. At present, it is evident that excessive use of the Internet has a negative impact both on an individual's social sphere and relations with loved ones. Such people are ready to sacrifice everything for the Internet – they resign from personal contacts with others, neglect their families and, just as importantly, lead a passive life in terms of physical effort, which is generally known to lead to many diseases and ailments, poor fitness and deficits in physical development of a young Internet user.

The danger of a controlled society means, first of all, intrusion of information into private life, centralisation and monopolisation of information, alienation due to automation and employment cuts. Every functional informatics and telecommunication system can be linked with specific types of threats, and shows certain vulnerability to criminal activities. The criminal face of computers is a kind of a mirror of the dark side of human attitudes and actions.

"Modern" national culture has been replaced by global culture, with US dominance accompanied by strong local, regional and ethnic undercurrents. "National culture" – once a platform of understanding for people speaking the same language – ceases to exist. The high culture content is being homogenised and transformed into a post-modernistic play of symbols.

The information revolution has initiated transformation of the mass culture into locally supervised education adopted to local labour markets where actual sills and readiness to improve one's qualifications (somewhat permanent education) are becoming more important than ratings and certificates.

The Internet is a vast area populated by millions of users. It is called "a global village". It is a civilisation, a metaculture unlike anything else in the "real world". In fact, the Internet is more than a culture – it is a community. It is joined by people from all over the world, coming from completely different backgrounds. It represents widespread consumerism, a style of life based on pleasure and temporary satisfaction, also referred to as "an arranged style of life" (Jabłońska 2019).

It comes at the price of disintegration of traditional communities which are replaced by "cyberspace", or rather by global culture. Mindsets, ways of action, experiences and awareness are being radically redefined. In front of our eyes, the web, a computer, or perhaps ICT technologies, have begun replacing traditional sources of power and wealth.

In the era of globalisation, the division of the world has become even stronger and deeper. This has happened *inter alia* because of major differences and disproportions in the development of informatics and information technologies. The "digital divide" affects economic development and somehow in advance determines whether progress can enter specific parts of the world. Developing countries are poorly or very poorly equipped with modern information and communication technologies and the related technical infrastructure. The lack of this "flywheel" and driving force of the globalised economy puts those countries in a losing position in competition with the rich. Where these technologies are already in place, they are being improved and modernised. Thanks to this, the progress is gaining momentum in every field, and constant economic growth comes together with growing wealth of the society and polarisation of societies in the global scale. The poorest part of the world is bound to remain on the margin of the processes of technological development and, consequently, on the margin of the creation of the face and shape of the modern civilisation. That poorest part is not that small – suffice it to say that there is a high share of people who have not made single phone call yet.

The modern-day civilisation is "wrapped" by the network of the Internet, together with all its accompanying infrastructure. Thanks to this, it takes us a fraction of a second to learn about events which only a dozen years ago would need several hours to reach us. People no longer write traditional letters and send electronic correspondence instead. E-mail boxes have become miniature archives and sources of access to virtually every one of us, to every institution, company, etc. Few people think about threats arising from this state of things. Almost complete loss of privacy is the first of these threats.

Considering that we store our greatest private and professional secrets on computer discs and other memory media, they become available and thus are no longer secrets. Every device working online, every computer, is a potential prey for hackers – Internet thieves.

How is "traditional" violence different from cyber-bullying?

Unlike the "traditional" form of violence, cyber-bullying is characterised by (Casas, Ortega-Ruiz, Monks 2020, pp. 71–84):

- a high level of anonymity. In the web, a perpetrator can remain unidentified (of course, anonymity in the Internet is only apparent – when a serious breach of rules or law is committed, the owner of the service or the police track the perpetrator down);
- physical or social force is less important than the ability to use the potential offered by electronic media. That potential includes: the speed of dissemination of materials used against the victim and the general availability of the web;

- the speed at which materials damaging the victim are disseminated is dangerous. Their widespread availability online and difficulty in removing them make this type of violence very severe;
- victims of cyber-bullying are constantly exposed to attack. It can take place anytime and anywhere, and its timing is very difficult to predict. Children and youth are most vulnerable to it;
- such behaviours are subject to little social control. It even happens that the parents or teachers cannot notice the problem. It is often the case due to little knowledge of and experience in electronic media. At the same time, this problem shows no signs, e.g. bruises or scratches like in the case of traditional violence.

Primary **forms of cyber-bullying** include (Meter, Bauman 2018, pp. 303–326):

- verbal violence online;
- making films and photos against the person's will;
- publishing and distributing ridiculing or discrediting information, photos, films online without consent of the persons concerned;
- posing as someone else online against that person's will.

Notice should be taken of the typology of electronic aggression (Chaux et al. 2016, pp. 157–165):

- **flaming** – aggressive discussion between online communication users, e.g. in chat rooms or newsgroups. These discussions are public and can concern a large number of people;
- **harassment** – a form of flaming which is different in that this type of aggression involves only two people. It involves regular sending unpleasant, aggressive or ridiculing messages via online communication channels (e.g. mobile phones, online messenger). It is agreed that harassment can take place also during online games;
- identity theft – impersonating the victim in cyberspace. Such actions are taken after obtaining the password to the victim's profile, electronic mail box or messenger. The perpetrator impersonates the victim and can be offensive also towards other people, e.g. by ridiculing them or by sending insulting messages;
- outing – the sharing of private information of another person (photos, films, text records). Outing leads to disclosure of the information to people who originally had no access to it. Normally the victim knows and trusts the perpetrator, thanks to which the latter can come into possession of the said information, which he/she then steals from a mobile phone or computer;
- stalking – cyberstalking of another person and flooding him/her with unwanted comments (e.g. online or on a mobile phone). This type of aggression takes place between people who used to be on good terms with each other, e.g. a girlfriend and a boyfriend;
- happy slapping – attacking and provoking another person while recording it. The recording is subsequently disseminated in the Internet and shared

among friends. Such a situation can end in beating the perpetrator and damaging his/her equipment.

- humiliation – uploading insulting texts, images or films about another person. These materials can be fabricated and false. They are placed online deliberately, not accidentally. The perpetrator knows what reaction his/her action is going to evoke;
- exclusion – intentional blocking another person in Internet contacts. It may take form of not accepting someone among friends in a social media portal or removing him/her from contacts in a messenger. The victim is ignored in the online social life.
- "technical" aggression – directed not against the victim, but the computer equipment, software and IT infrastructure (e.g. website) he/she is using. It may involve sending viruses, hacking or blocking certain services (e.g. e-mail box).

Results of electronic (informatics) aggression, not necessarily prolonged, are as follows (Song et al. 2019, pp. 167–178):

- compromising information, photos or films can rapidly spread across the Internet, and their erasure is often virtually impossible;
- the victim is constantly exposed to attacks – anywhere anytime;
- a relatively low level of social control of these types of behaviours – a situation where a child/teenager is harmed through electronic media is often difficult for parents or teachers to notice, particularly when they have poor knowledge of and experience in using electronic media;
- the perpetrator's advantage is not "force" understood in physical or social terms, but the ability to use the potential offered electronic media.

Acts of cyber-bullying often cause irritation, fear and embarrassment in their victims, who often feel abandoned with their problems (Chandrashekhar, Muktha, Anjana 2016, pp. 95–102):

- nearly 50% of children and youth do not inform anyone of their negative experiences; only one child in ten talks about it with their parent or teacher;
- they often encounter views or advice which ignore the harassment they are experiencing.

Cyber-harassment is most often less dangerous than hazards in the real world, but they are very exhausting. Although most cases of cyber-harassment begin and end online, some of them do migrate to the real world. Then, they can produce very dangerous situations. The phenomenon of seducing children by adults through the Internet is termed "grooming" in the English-language literature. It was noticed as a problem in the 1990s and its scale has been growing with the development of messaging services and growing population of children who use the Internet. At present, it is recorded more and more often. To establish a close contact with a child/teenager, "cyber hunters" use mainly online messengers and chats. The Internet has become an ideal "hunting ground" for many criminals – from ordinary fraudsters to paedophiles.

Many Internet users provide their real name and other data in their profiles. Meanwhile, profiles can be found in the web by means of searching software, which allows users to find other people interested in music by a specific band or in a specific sport, but also to find children or teenagers of specific sex born in a specific year, as well as their addresses of residence, schools which they attend, their telephone numbers, etc.

Aggressors sometimes take a long time to "groom" their victims, i.e. to win their favours and trust. They find a person of interest in the real world by using any means of searching for people. They try to convince children/youth to talk about sex, which may be an introduction to further cornering and molesting of the youngest users. An adult, often posing to be a peer of the victim, gradually wins his/her trust, obtains his/her personal data, photos, and sometimes becomes "a good friend". He/she convinces the child to watch pornography and gradually insists on a meeting in the real world. When the meeting takes place, the child is usually sexually abused and often falls victim to the pornographic industry. To keep everything in secret, the aggressor threatens the victim by telephone or traditional mail, or provides contact details of "his/her victim" to others in the Internet and encourages them to harass him/her. And what about online flirting, popular among teenagers? An initially innocent and casual play of words in the internet becomes an opportunity for a meeting and abuse in the real life.

While some people talk eagerly, others simply watch and listen to what is being said and who is saying it. Such people are called "lurkers". Since they do not do anything to attract attention, nobody notices them, including network admins. People upload many pieces of information and simply forget to click the privacy option or share more information than necessary. Our data can be found in cyberspace in *inter alia* competition and application forms we fill in, user profiles we share, etc. – and fraudsters/thieves can use it for their purposes.

There are many more threats connected with the Internet, not just the most important ones mentioned above, like the possibility of formation of a controlled society or a society completely addicted to technology. There are also more down-to-earth threats connected directly with our use of the web such as information rush which increasingly often takes the form of information noise, or threats related to access to disturbing, socially undesirable or even illegal content. Other problems include anonymity in the Internet and the "intoxicating" effect of the Internet on certain users.

The following terms are connected with computer crime (Kizza 2017, pp. 339–353):

Cracker – a person who cracks computer safeguards. Two main categories of cracker activities can be distinguished: cracking safeguards in closed software and cracking server safeguards.

Carding – a type of computer crime which involves illegal acquisition, gathering, selling and using payment card or numbers thereof.

Phreaking – involves breaking safeguards in order to reach or use telephone networks or BBSs without paying any charge. It comes from the so-called tech-hacking, i.e. an activity involving minor modifications in various devices, e.g. computers, lift control systems or drink vending machines.

Bankring – involves finding and breaking legal and technical safeguards related to banking operations, both in the real world and the Internet, and utilising contradictions in bank regulations to achieve personal or financial gains.

Phishing (spoofing) – in the computer industry, fraudulent acquisition of confidential personal information, such as passwords or credit card details, by posing to be a trustworthy person who urgently needs the information. This type of attack is based on social engineering.

Depending on the ethics used, the following types of hackers can be distinguished:

- **black hats** – hackers operating either on the border of law or illegally. They either do not publish the vulnerabilities they find, utilising them for illegal purposes, or publish them right away in the form of ready programmes (the so-called exploits) which can be used by people of inferior skills. Some people challenge the use of the word "hacker" in this case, imposing to use the word "cracker" instead.
- **white hats** – hackers who either operate legally or try not to cause any damage. They normally publish the vulnerabilities they find in the form in which they can easily be patched by the software developers, but are very difficult to be used to harm anyone. Security auditors can often be found among them.
- **grey hats** – hackers/crackers who used methods of both the above groups.
- **plagiarism** – theft of intellectual property.

One should also mention cyberterrorism, which is deliberate activity of groups or other enemy forces targeted against information, computer systems, software and data, leading to civilian losses. According to another definition, cyberterrorism involves actions that block, destroy or distort information which is processed, stored and transmitted in ICT systems, including also destruction of such systems.

Cyberterrorism has become a component of international terrorism. There is no need to send troops to effectively paralyse a city or even the whole country. Cyberterrorism will soon represent a more serious threat to individual countries than any other form of aggression. By mid-1990s, the illegal practice of codebreaking had taken criminal proportions. Threats to national and international security have increased significantly.

In the today's world of threats and risks, the term of responsibility is gaining on importance. In the today's IT culture, responsibility (El Emary, Brzozowska, Bubel 2020; Reinhold 2016, pp. 253–256):

- is becoming dependent on knowledge, information and technique, not only from the sensitivity of operating entities;
- must be based on trust not only to transmitted and received information, but also means of information transmission and processing; trust to the computer as a carrier of information and means of its processing is the basis for computer-aided decision- making;

- Decentralisation of bonds and globalisation of relations characteristic of the information society is manifested by the fact that *inter alia* these bonds take a networking character; depending on the network type, consequences of actions are no longer effects of cause and effect relationships; there are many unintentional outcomes, hence there is no clear relation between the subject of action and the subject of responsibility.

NOTES

1 Matters of risk assessment are present also in the International Standards on Auditing developed by the International Federation of Accountants (IFAC), and in the International Standards for the Professional Practice of Internal Auditing developed by the Institute of Internal Auditors (IIA).
2 The framework structure of risk management described in COSO focuses on achieving an organisation's objectives in four categories: strategic, operations, reporting and compliance.
3 Here, the risk management system means a set of interrelated elements designed to manage risks. It is composed of persons directly involved in execution of its tasks as well as IT tools, organisational solutions, information resources, decision-making structures, etc. The risk management process is a sequence of actions aimed at achieving a predefined and planned result.
4 Support for governance aspects is handled by the Policy Management module; risk management is done through the Access Control and Risk Management modules, and compliance is based on the Process Control module. The Access Control is the basic version of the SAP solution.
5 These companies are: ACL (http://www.acl.com) i DAB (http://www.dab-europe.com).
6 The offer presented here is complemented by two solutions related to the integrated ERP class environment - they would operate in two areas: extraction and download of data from the integrated system (module dab:Exporter) and data analysis using predefined analytical tests (module dab:FastForward).

4 How Information Technology Is Changing E-business on the Way to the Digital Economy

4.1 E-COMMERCE BUSINESS MODELS AND GLOBAL TRENDS IN THEIR DEVELOPMENT

The scientific maturity of any discipline is demonstrated by its methodological maturity, which is built of un-ambiguity and awareness of the nomenclature used.

The issue of key information technology skills requires detailed consideration, mainly due to its methodological convention. The following terms require clarification: technology, information technology, skills, key skills, information technology skills.

4.1.1 E-COMMERCE BASIC DEFINITIONS AND FEATURES

Significant amounts of information and the inability to quickly process and control it in manual mode created the need for special software. Thus, emerged a new information technology market for managing financial flows and electronic commerce (E-commerce). The rapid development of financial management technologies has created modern business proposals such as digital and cryptocurrencies, crowdfunding, peer-to-peer (P2P) lending, mobile banking, online investment and new payment systems (Impact of technology on the financial sector https://www.kemplittle.com/news/impact-of-technology-on-the-financial-sector/).

Social networks opened access to the personal data of consumers and provided an opportunity for financial institutions to predict their behaviour. This also opened up the possibilities for financial institutions to use consumer data for pricing, targeted placement, and sale of goods and services.

At the same time, new IT creates a challenge for regulators, who should monitor how this or that technology affects the financial sector. An example is the cryptocurrency market that created chaos until the middle of 2018 and led to significant losses for participants in the currency exchange market.

When starting to consider the business models of e-commerce (EC) and global trends in its development, it is necessary to pay attention to the basic definitions and features of EC.

DOI: 10.1201/9781003271345-4

EC has become a buzzword for business over the past years. Increased awareness about the information and communication technologies has led to simplifying business procedures and increased business efficiency. EC provides a way to exchange information between individuals, companies and countries, but most important of all between computers. It is combining a range of processes, such as Electronic Data Interchange (EDI), electronic mail (e-mail), World Wide Web (WWW) and Internet applications. EC comprises core business processes of buying and selling goods, services and information over the Internet. EC information on the Internet is huge and still growing. There are many sectors where EC is witnessing rapid growth in the global market (Turban et al. 2008, p. 550).

EC is any form of business in which the interaction between the parties occurs through electronic means.

EC is a form of business for buying, selling, transferring or exchanging products, services or information with the WWW. The main forms of EC are based on its main features as digitalisation and virtualisation:

- The product, process and delivery agent can be digital or physical
- The companies that are engaged only in EC are called virtual organisations or pure-play
- Click and mortar organisations – organisations are those that conduct some EC activities, yet their business is primarily done in the physical world
- Pure vs. Partial EC depends on the degree of digitalisation involved
- EC can involve five actors – a seller, a buyer, a banker, a delivery agent and a service agent

The following categories can be classified as EC subjects:

1. Customers
2. Financial institutions
3. Business organisations
4. Internet providers
5. State

The objects of EC include traditionally goods, works and services, and information product, which acts in the following forms:

- "physical" goods with order and payment through the seller's website
- Electronic products
- Financial services in real time
- Information services
- Telecommunication services
- Database management
- Rental of software products

Categories of goods and their features of demand and supply on the Internet are presented in Table 4.1.

In general, the development of the EC market today is quite dynamic.

The three main classes of EC subjects are the following: financial institutions, business organisations and customers.

Financial institutions are banks where EC entities have accounts. Communication with banks is necessary for sellers in any case. Moreover, sellers depend on offers from banks and settlement centres. The seller is forced to accept the proposed payment scheme. However, if these payment schemes do not provide a direct connection with Internet shops with EDI systems, then making payments via the Internet is impossible.

TABLE 4.1

Features of the Demand and Supply of Goods in the Internet Environment

Category of Goods by the Elasticity of Demand	Description	Features of the Internet Offer
Goods with inelastic demand by price:	The goods whose consumption remains stable when the price changes: Essentials (medicines, shoes, electricity and other energy sources) Goods, the cost of which is insignificant for the family budget (pencils, toothbrushes) Hard-to-replace goods (bread, light bulbs, gasoline, drugs)	Low to medium marketability. The main reason for the low efficiency of online sales is the lack of a consumer habit of purchasing such goods via the Internet.
	Products with unique characteristics or brands for which the buyer is willing to spend additional efforts on purchasing: luxury items: jewellery, delicacies	The Internet is highly effective in the sale of this type of goods. Also, it allows sellers to expand their sales market through its global presence.
Goods with cross-elasticity of demand:	Goods that the buyer compares with each other in the selection process according to a wide range of characteristics	The Internet is highly effective in the sale of this type of goods since it allows you to provide the maximum information about the product and conduct a comparative analysis for a wide range of characteristics, and also has a low cost of sale.
Goods with elastic demand by price:	Goods that the buyer does not think about purchasing, regardless of whether he knows about their existence or not: Pre-selection goods Passive demand goods	The Internet can be effectively used to promote this category of goods, but it will require significant marketing efforts.

Source: Own work.

The tools that an organisation can use to realise EC capabilities can be divided into four groups of business programmes, the Internet shop itself, the gateway to the electronic data exchange system, and the payment server.

Communication with financial institutions is carried out through various payment systems.

Business organisations – any organisation that interacts through the Internet. They either sell or buy goods or services through the Internet, carrying out trading operations.

When the customer buys something for himself or herself, this market sector is called the retail EC sector. Trading companies, working in this market, offer for sale a wide range of products from different suppliers.

In traditional business, it is difficult or even impossible to simultaneously manage several different projects from the same place, e.g. the sale of food and the sale of cars. The Internet can open as many stores as necessary, and each of them will carry out a separate task; the opportunity to compete on equal terms with giant corporations and at the same time be successful.

Since electronic stores are built on a single model, a small company or even a private entrepreneur can create a store that looks and acts just like a huge supermarket and will provide a high level of service for customers.

4.1.2 E-COMMERCE SECTORS AND THEIR FEATURES

EC has certain differences that depend on the types of interaction between participants and are associated with the specifics of doing business. By objects and subjects of activity, the following sectors of EC are distinguished (Figure 4.1):

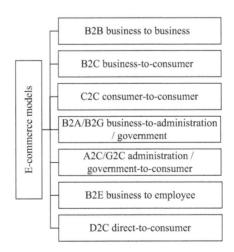

FIGURE 4.1 E-commerce models.

Source: Own work.

B2B – Between different types of business or business-to-business. Sellers and buyers are business organisations. This model represents most of EC operations.

B2C – Between business and consumer or business-to-consumer. Sellers, organisations and buyers are individuals.

C2C – Between consumers or consumer-to-consumer. Individuals sell products or services to other individuals.

B2A/B2G – Between business and government bodies or business-to-administration/government.

A2C or G2C – Between the state and consumers or administration/government-to-consumer.

B2E – Business to an employee. The organisation uses EC internally to provide information and services to its employees (take training classes, buy discount insurance, travel packages, events tickets, etc.)

D2C – Connect the producer with the consumer directly bypassing intermediary trading platforms or direct-to-consumer (D2C). This model is based on elements of blockchain technology and was first used in the cryptocurrency market.

4.1.3 BUSINESS-TO-BUSINESS

Companies following the business-to-business (B2B) business model sell or buy products to intermediate organisations who then buy or sell the product to the final customer. As an example, Amazon places an order from a company's website and after receiving the consignment, sells the end product to the final customer who comes to buy the product at one of its retail outlets (Figure 4.2).

The B2B sector or "business-to-business" is a category of EC, where companies operate from selecting a supplier or product, ordering goods from suppliers, receiving invoices and ending with payments and other transactions using the web. This model dominates EC. The tasks of B2B systems include:

1. Organisation of interaction between enterprises – quickly and conveniently
2. Building secure, reliable channels of information exchange between firms
3. Coordination of activities of enterprises and their joint development based on information exchange

The B2B model is a category of EC, where companies operate starting from selecting a supplier or product, ordering goods from suppliers, receiving invoices and ending with payments and other transactions using the web. This model dominates EC. The tasks of B2B systems include:

FIGURE 4.2 B2B sector.

Source: Own work.

1. Organisation of quick and convenient interaction between enterprises.
2. Building secure, reliable channels of information exchange between business organisations.
3. Coordination of activities of enterprises and their joint development based on information exchange.
   - Interaction can be associated with trade, technology exchange, experience, investment activities, etc.

Classification of B2B systems is possible by the set of proposed functions:

1. Corporate website
2. Online store
3. Services procurement supplies
4. Information site
5. Brokerage sites
6. Electronic trading platforms (ETPs)

The B2B model is the most promising in EC.

4.1.4 BUSINESS-TO-CONSUMER/CONSUMER-TO-BUSINESS

The B2C sector or "business-to-consumer" is a category of EC that is the equivalent of retail and is represented by various types of e-shops.

A website following the B2C business model sells its products to a customer using intermediaries' services. A customer can view the products shown on the intermediary website. He can choose a product and order. The website will then send a notification to the retailer via e-mail, and the business organisation will dispatch the product/goods to the customer (Figure 4.4).

An example is Alibaba places an order from a producer and after receiving the consignment, sells the end product to the final customer who comes to buy the product at the Alibaba website.

In this model, a consumer uses a website showing multiple business organisations and can place an estimate of the amount he/she wants to spend for a particular service. For example, the comparison of prices on the cars provided by various distributors via websites. A business organisation that fulfils the consumer's requirement within the specified budget approaches the customer and provides its services.

The automotive market is very promising in this segment. In many ways, the success of B2C is associated with the development of telecommunications since it allows direct sales with a minimum number of intermediaries. B2C telecommunication

FIGURE 4.3 B2C sector.

Source: Own work.

solutions are one of the links in the chain of business processes of an enterprise using Internet technologies and tools to facilitate interaction with customers.

Depending on the volume of functions performed, the B2C EC system can be classified into one of the types:

- Showcase sites
- Internet trading systems
- Electronic storefronts
- Electronic malls

B2B EC is much larger in volume than B2C EC. However, B2C EC is more complex and involves many more buyers. It may be single stores as well as big malls.

4.1.5 CONSUMER-TO-CONSUMER

The C2C sector or "consumer-consumer" is a form of EC that involves the sale of goods and services between consumers. A consumer sells directly to another consumer. In this case, the site acts as an intermediary between the buyer and the seller (Figure 4.4).

This model allows people who are experiencing certain restrictions to conclude deals at any convenient time. As a result, overhead costs are reduced, which in turn saves money. A website following the C2C business model helps consumers to sell their assets like residential property, cars, motorcycles, etc. or rent a room by publishing their information on the website. The website may or may not charge the consumer for its services. Another consumer may opt to buy the product of the first customer by viewing the post/advertisement on the website.

4.1.6 BUSINESS-TO-GOVERNMENT

B2G or B2A model is a variant of the B2B model. B2G sector or "business state" is economic interaction between a legal entity and a state or municipal institution. The B2G relationship involves only two participants: business and government (Figure 4.5).

FIGURE 4.4   C2C sector.

Source: Own work.

FIGURE 4.5   B2G sector.

Source: Own work.

The B2A sector or "business administration" is a category of EC that covers all types of transactions between companies and government organisations.

Governments use B2G/B2A websites to trade and exchange information with various business organisations to support auctions, tenders and application submission functionalities. Such websites are accredited by the government and provide a medium for businesses to submit application forms to the government.

Besides, this type of EC is in the stage of rapid development in areas such as taxes and payments.

4.1.7 GOVERNMENT-TO-CITIZEN

C2G model or "consumer-to-state" determines the interaction of consumers with the administration.

Governments use G2C model websites to approach citizens in general. Such websites support auctions of vehicles, machinery or any other material. Such a website also provides services like registration for birth, marriage or death certificates. The main objective of G2C websites is to reduce the average time for fulfilling citizens' requests for various government services.

4.1.8 DIRECT-TO-CONSUMER (D2C)

EC models are growing and changing. Until recently, few people thought that online shopping could successfully compete with ordinary commerce. Assortment optimisation with artificial intelligence, smart pricing, virtual and augmented reality technologies, the use of blockchain for supply chain management, user data security and payments don't sound like science fiction anymore. To purchase goods and services, the buyer can easily access needed producers via the web. As usual, intermediaries get money to provide information and consulting. Amazon and eBay have become giants of the marketplace and have established a de facto monopoly on the EC market. Small-and medium-sized retailers have found themselves in a disadvantageous situation. In practice, Amazon's commission reaches 15%. Besides, the platform's rules are causing retailers to lose control of their sales. Amazon is also known for striving to restrict direct contact between consumers and sellers and may disable a store page without any explanation.

Therefore, the key issue is disintermediation. With ever-growing anti-Amazon sentiment, the antitrust issues are getting louder, and merchants are beginning to question the wisdom of working with Amazon. Many top brands will avoid or limit their relationships with Amazon in the future.

At this time of change, large intermediary marketplaces are being replaced by free micro markets. Changing the commercial ecosystem of the Internet is one of the missions assigned to the blockchain-based E-commerce platform (BBEP). The introduction of the BBEP platforms created a new EC model. This decentralised model will allow the seller and the buyer to interact directly. It will also lower the available business entry threshold and increase the number of players in the market. This EC model is called D2C. It aims to connect the producer with the consumer directly bypassing intermediary trading platforms (Figure 4.6).

FIGURE 4.6 D2C sector.

Source: Own work.

The producers following the D2C business model sell their products directly to a customer. Customers can view the products shown on the website. They can choose a product and order. The website will then send a notification to the producer via e-mail, and the producer dispatches the product/goods to the customer.

The model D2Cs gets products to market quickly, allowing capitalising on trends as they come, having complete control over its brand's products as well as its reputation.

Big-name brands such as luggage manufacturer Away and office supplies manufacturer Quill have already leapt with D2C marketing and D2C selling campaigns, and we're anticipating that more manufacturers will do the same beyond. The customers also have benefited from going to the D2C route. They can contact directly with the producer and get products quickly.

4.1.9 Global Trends in the E-commerce Development

The development of EC sectors is ongoing and has a global scale because there are many things that EC has up on in-person retail. One of them is the ability to shop from anywhere. In 2019, the global EC market has already crossed the US$2 trillion thresholds, and China is number one in EC. Globally, the online's share of total retail sales is now 16.4%, with EC accounting for more than three-quarters of overall retail growth. 40% of the world's Internet users have purchased products online, which amounts to more than 1 billion online buyers. The data predicts that by the end of 2020, global EC sales will reach $4.2 trillion. And these numbers are only predicted to go up as we continue into the 1920s (Meyer, 2020).

Moreover, mobile commerce has been constantly on the rise. In 2019, Statista estimated that by the end of 2021, 73% of EC sales will take place on a mobile device.

Tech giants and newly emerged EC businesses do their best to improve user experience and facilitate mobile payments, including using e-wallets. China's leading third-party online payment solutions WeChat and Alipay each have over 1 billion users. This leadership is based on a growing number of mobile Internet users.

In addition, more and more mobile users are using progressive web apps (PWA). PWAs can give mobile shoppers a native app-like experience with features like the ability to work offline and allow push notifications. They can give EC brands another way to improve the customer journey for online shoppers using mobile devices (https://www.growcode.com/blog/ecommerce-trends/).

If we analyse the global trends in the development of EC (Figure 4.7), then we can conclude the positive dynamics over the next years.

The EC market is steadily growing each year, and new EC trends are emerging at an overwhelming pace. Businesses can use a variety of tools and technologies to

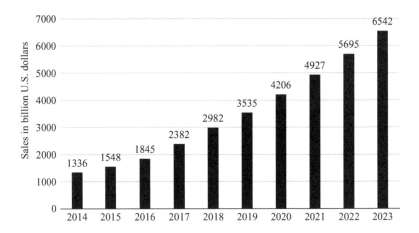

FIGURE 4.7   The retail E-commerce sales 2014–2023 (in billion US dollars).

Source: Statista 2019 (https://www.statista.com/), Meyer 2020.

support their EC activities. The main technological trends that find overall global EC market for the last years are the following:

1. Mobile Shopping and Mobile Payments
2. PWA for EC
3. More ways to pay
4. Blockchain technology
5. A new level of logistics
6. Growing B2B
7. Headless EC
8. Voice Commerce
9. Chatbots improve the shopping experience
10. Artificial Intelligence (AI) and Machine Learning
11. Personalisation
12. The Rise of Virtual Reality
13. Augmented reality
14. Big data plays a big part in creating personalised experiences
15. EC Conversion Optimisation
16. Customers respond to video
17. Digital strategy optimisation for conversion
18. A focus on D2C

4.1.10   Mobile Shopping and Mobile Payments

With the advent of smartphones, mobile commerce is growing steadily. The size of the mobile payment market has been on the rise of 15% since 2016 and is expected to grow faster. Statista estimated that by the end of 2021, 73% of EC sales would take place on a mobile device (Ogonowski, 2019). EC businesses do their best to optimise apps and mobile-friendly websites so that their clients receive the best mobile experience possible. They do their best to improve user experience and facilitate mobile payments, including using e-wallets. China is the leader – both WeChat and Alipay have over 1 billion users each.

4.1.11 PWA for E-commerce

Another response to ever-increasing mobile users is the use of PWAs or progressive web apps. A progressive web app is a mobile website that has the look and feel of a native mobile app. PWAs can give mobile shoppers a native app-like experience with features like the ability to work offline and allow push notifications. They can give EC brands another way to improve the customer journey for online shoppers using mobile devices (Saltis, 2020a).

Twitter and Gmail have already used PWA technology, and now it bleeds over into many popular EC websites, as well.

For example, AliExpress uses of PWAs in EC to great success.

4.1.12 A New Level of Logistics

Another area of blockchain technology implementation is supply management. Rational organisation and efficient supply management are key aspects of any activity in the trade sector. The dynamic growth of the EC market has posed new complex logistics problems for the business that are difficult to solve with old tools.

The blockchain advantages, such as openness and the inability to manipulate data, can play great value in supply chain management. This technology allows businesses to create solutions for tracking deliveries at all stages of the movement. The facility can be monitored and its history checked at any stage of the logistics cycle. This allows the manufacturer to reduce costs, eliminate the corruption component and abolish the mediation in transactions.

One of the examples illustrating the blockchain possibilities in logistics is the VeChain project. It works as follows. On the VeChain network platform, a personal identifier is assigned to the product, which is sent to the blockchain and simultaneously placed on the product itself using an NFC chip, RFID tag or QR code. These devices allow them to track the goods at any stage of their movement. By comparing the information on the identifier with the manufacturer's database, the seller can verify the product for authenticity. This completely solves the problem of counterfeit goods.

4.1.13 Headless and API-driven E-commerce

Headless EC is allowing the presentation layer of a website to be decoupled from the EC functionality. Thanks to that, services can provide a more personalised customer experience and be richer in content.

Headless EC refers to the use of EC platforms that do not require a pre-designed storefront and are therefore described as being "headless." Data is retrieved from the backend via an API and is separate from the frontend. This gives retailers full creative control over their storefronts across a variety of channels, including desktop, mobile and social media.

This can allow retailers to use a CMS, DXP, PWA, or any other existing or custom frontends to complete their tech stack. This can have powerful implications for what the store can accomplish with content marketing, SEO and digital experience on their storefront.

Every year may see increased adoption of headless – particularly new headless frontend solutions like more IoTs and PWAs. It will also likely to be considered by a wider market including smaller businesses and B2B use cases (Meyer, 2020).

4.1.14 VOICE COMMERCE

There will be a growing volume of voice searches. Voice assistants like Apple's Siri, Amazon's Alexa and Google's Assistants are getting more and more popular to do everything from checking the weather to buying products online. Now only 11% of smart speakers' owners in the United States use them to buy products. Voice technology still needs more development and improvement. OC&C Strategy Consultants forecast that by 2022 the number of US buyers will grow to 55%. Voice shopping is expected to grow to 40 billion by 2022. Amazon's Echo, Google's Home and Apple's HomePod will drive the industry forward. The projected growth in Voice Commerce suggests that businesses will be aware of this trend (Meyer, 2020; Saltis, 2020a).

4.1.15 AI AND MACHINE LEARNING

AI helps shops learn about shoppers. The prevalence of AI and machine learning will increase, as retailers target new ways to enhance personalisation and improve customer service, which is why all online businesses should invest in this development.

Today, the most successful EC players are those who invest in Big Data and AI tools. AI can:

- Help businesses learn about their customers and supply them with the personalised experiences they are demanding
- Help companies connect customer data with real-time insights to improve the shopping experience
- Automate tasks such as customer support through chatbots to help customers 24/7 or generate timely offers
- Optimised pricing and discounting and demand forecasting
- Optimisation of product catalogues using AI

The greatest prospects for AI technology are opening up precisely in the field of EC. Chatbots are a form of AI to improve the shopping experience. Chatbots are great helpers for online shoppers that help customers find the right products, analyse consumer preferences and offer interesting alternatives. They improve the personalisation of the shopping experience, create effective interactions with users and provide them with only the information customers need.

The global chatbot market has attained a massive 24.3% compound annual growth rate, and 45% of end users consider chatbots their primary choice for customer service inquiries. By 2025, the global chatbot market is expected to generate revenues of over 1000 million dollars. Besides, EC represents a big slice of this.

The study found that more than 60% of customers report preferring having websites, apps or chatbots to provide a personalised approach. The cheery chatbot who can serve the role of the brick-and-mortar greeter and salesperson is at the crux of personalisation.

Nowadays, chatbots entail making a technology understand repetitive human habits and help shops learn about shoppers. This is the helpful in-store associate who can offer product recommendations and personalised guidance based on the shopper's needs or requests.

We can also observe growing willingness among users to share their personal information in exchange for tailored recommendations and offers. Chatbots will become more prevalent, using previous data to help anticipate new products that users like. All this stimulates sales and income 24/7 (https://www.sellbrite.com/blog/ecommerce-trends-2020/) (Meyer, 2020).

Chatbots allow stores to communicate with thousands of customers while giving them the feeling of personal attention and thoughtful recommendations based on their responses.

One of the major reasons for this is because of the faster response time.

Experts see chatbots becoming increasingly personalised to improve customer experience.

Another example of AI technology in modern EC is product catalogues optimisation. AI allows online stores to set competitive prices for a particular product and optimise the catalogue. AI algorithms are capable of analysing trends and identifying non-competitive products. They can automatically rank the assortment by removing or moving unpopular positions on the site and replacing them with more offers that are profitable. A dynamic pricing approach helps retailers to be competitive and offer the best price to consumers.

Today, major players in the EC market use AI algorithms to analyse and process huge amounts of data. Of course, big data plays a big part in creating personalised experiences. However, not all personalisation is created equal, and different experts have different visions for where EC personalisation will go in the next years. Some also consider personalisation to be a double-edged sword because data and privacy are being raised as concerns for some consumers.

4.1.16 THE RISE OF VIRTUAL REALITY

VR, also known as computer-simulated reality, makes us feel as if we have entered a simulated environment. Virtual reality will create an even more personalised shopping experience for customers.

The availability of devices, the development of 3D scanning and the technology itself have allowed VR to expand its scope. Many industries benefit from VR/AR technologies. Retail and EC are one of them.

For example, users can "visit" virtual showrooms and with the help of VR equipment "try on" clothes from different collections, to evaluate the things themselves, and how a person looks at them in different conditions: at work, in a restaurant, in a gym, etc. VR-dressing room application has been created to emulate a virtual dressing room for smartphones and tablets. Shortly, brands such as Zara, H&M and Bershka are planning to rely on VR (https://10ecommercetrends.com/).

4.1.17 Augmented Reality Enhances the Reality of Online Shopping

Augmented reality enhances the reality of online shopping. If VR is trying to isolate us from the real world, then with AR technology the opposite is true. Augmented Reality has become a major game changer, helping online shoppers visualise the products that they are interested in, whether it is a clothing item or furniture. A good example is the IKEA Place application, which allows you to place virtual furniture from a catalogue into a real interior. It also has a "visual search" function: by pointing the camera at any piece of furniture in the house, the device recognises it and suggests which IKEA product it most resembles.

This helps online shoppers overcome the hurdle of not being able to see the product firsthand, bringing comparison shopping to a completely new level.

In 2019, Gartner predicted that 100 million consumers would shop using AR by 2020 (https://10ecommercetrends.com/) (Meyer, 2020).

4.1.18 B2B Is Growing

The global B2B market in EC is moving solidly upward currently and likely into the future. Global retail EC sales for B2B are expected to reach $1.1 trillion in 2021, according to data from Statista.

As more B2B businesses move online and existing online businesses hone their offerings, one factor to take into account is the changing expectations of B2B buyers.

Nowadays, audiences prefer a simpler, more self-serve user experience that allows them to research and get the information they need without talking to salespeople.

B2B EC brands are working to meet these needs by beginning to understand the value of servicing their customers online. By automating these tasks through their EC site, teams are moving away from spending the bulk of their time on processing order entries from e-mail spreadsheets or hard copy forms to engaging with customers, providing them with excellent customer experience and establishing ongoing client relationships (https://10ecommercetrends.com/) (Meyer, 2020).

4.1.19 A focus on Direct-to-Consumer (D2C)

Despite the dominance of the B2B sector, the manufacturing landscape is changing. New trends in EC development allow buyer easy access to needed producer via the web without intermediaries' services.

The companies use the D2C model to thrive in their respective industries. There are many benefits of selling D2C, such as:

- Earning higher margins
- The ability to forge a closer and deeper relationship with customers and gain a better understanding of the customer
- The ability to get products to market quickly, allowing to capitalise on trends as they come
- Having complete control over products and the brand's reputation

Another advantage of selling D2C is the potential of selling through its online store on a headless commerce platform (Saltis, 2020b).

More CPG brands choose D2C because they can get a better understanding of their customer, have more control over their brand and get more freedom to innovate. Moreover, D2C can benefit manufacturers to help to improve brand awareness and boost leads and sales for retailers. Online sales may be accounting for 18% of total sales by 2022, and more and more brands will shift to a D2C fulfilment model.

4.1.20 NEW WAYS TO PAY

We talked about the expectation around payment options for mobile devices, but customers are also expecting more and better payment options full stop.

For example, when shopping from an overseas business they may expect to be able to buy goods using their preferred local payment provider (Meyer, 2020).

Additionally, customers are used to the ease of shopping in big online retailers. They save the customers' billing and shipping information to make for a fast and easy checkout experience without a lot of data entry. EC websites are increasingly using payment options like Apple Pay, PayPal and other financing options that enable a frictionless checkout.

Modern translation systems, despite their efficiency, are far from perfect. Existing payment systems provide a commission for using their platform. It averages 2–3% of the cost of any transaction.

Blockchain technology can be considered an alternative to traditional payment systems.

Using blockchain technology for EC payments brings the most obvious benefits.

Blockchain enables fast, secure and cheap transfers. This has been successfully proven by projects such as Request Network or ECoinmerce. As this technology spreads to eCommerce, financial transactions may become cheaper, and large players will lose their right to monopoly on the payment system market. Any EC business model will be able to function with minimal transaction fees. As far as security standards are concerned, the bitcoin (BTC) story was a good test of the strength of this system.

A report from the World Economic Forum (WEF) defines blockchain technology or distributed ledger technology (DLT): it is a technological protocol that allows data to be exchanged directly between various contracting parties within a network without the need for intermediaries.

The use of encryption ensures that users can only modify the parts of the block-chain that they "own". It is assumed that they have private keys, without which writing to the file is impossible. Also, encryption ensures that copies of the distributed blockchain are synchronised for all users. Blockchain technology is built from the ground up to be secure at the database level. Satoshi Nakamoto proposed the block-chain concept in 2008. With further development, blockchain has been defined as a separate technology that can be used outside of cryptocurrency.

Today, this technology has been successfully implemented in the idea of a decentralised market in projects such as OpenBazaar and Can Ya.

The use of various e-business models leads to the emergence of new forms of doing business.

For example, the P2P economy is an IT-facilitated P2P model for commercial or non-commercial sharing of underutilised goods and service capacity through an intermediary without transfer of ownership (Schlagwein, Daniel; Schoder, Detlef; Spindeldreher, Kai (2019). P2P economy is an alternative term for the sharing economy. The sharing economy is an economic activity of acquiring, providing or sharing access to goods and services that is often facilitated by a community-based online platform (https://www.investopedia.com/terms/s/sharing-economy.asp#:~:text=The%20sharing%20economy%20is%20an,%2Dbased%20on%2Dline%20platform). The sharing economy is an all-encompassing term that refers to a host of online economic transactions that may even include B2B interactions. Other platforms that have joined the sharing economy include:

- Co-working Platforms: Companies that provide shared open workspaces for freelancers, entrepreneurs and work-from-home employees in major metropolitan areas.
- Peer-to-Peer Lending Platforms: Companies that allow individuals to lend money to other individuals at rates cheaper than those offered through traditional credit lending entities.
- Fashion Platforms: Sites that allow for individuals to sell or rent their clothes.
- Freelancing Platforms: Sites that offer to match freelance workers across a wide spectrum ranging from traditional freelance work to repair services.

Initiatives, usually based on the concept of book-lending libraries, in which goods and services are provided free (or sometimes for a modest subscription). This type of "share" economy is in the true ethos of a shared economy, which is not intended for any one person to make an income, or a profit.

Spurred primarily with the growth of Uber and Airbnb, it is expected that the sharing economy would grow from $14 billion in 2014 to a forecasted $335 billion by 2025.

Technology has been the biggest driver behind the sharing economy's growth. "These apps have brought underutilized resources online and efficiently matched them to demand," says Ming Hu, professor of business operations and analytics at Rotman School of Management at the University of Toronto (Simon Lovick, 2020).

4.2   FEATURES OF E-COMMERCE IN SMALL- AND MEDIUM-SIZED BUSINESSES

EC is associated with the buying and selling of information, goods and services over the Internet. However, it also used to transfer information within the organisation via the Intranet to improve decision-making and eliminate duplication at various stages of its development.

The main EC models for small and medium enterprises are:

- Corporate website
- Online direct marketing – manufacturers or retailers sell directly to customers
- Online auction
- Online store
- Internet exchange
- Electronic trading systems
- Membership

A corporate website is an information page with information about a company, project, products, types of activities, proposals for cooperation, which performs the following main functions:

- Providing clients and partners with corporate information about the company
- Attracting additional clients and partners
- Establishing two-way communication with visitors to the resource
- Shaping the company's image

The results of using this business model are the uninterrupted operation of the site, reducing the cost of providing information to clients and the ability to compose a portrait of site visitors.

Online direct marketing works by the D2C model's rules – manufacturers or retailers sell directly to customers.

An online auction is a trade showcase where users can sell any product. The income of this auction consists of transaction fees and advertising revenue.

The main online auction functions are the following:

- Provision services, both for the participant-seller and for the participant-buyer
- Sale of goods and services
- Collecting information about demand

There are the following types of electronic auctions:

1. Reverse auctions – a service through which the buyer posts request (RFQ) for the purchase of certain goods, and sellers submit a bid.
2. Forward auctions – a service where sellers place items, buyers bid continuously.

Forward auctions result in higher prices over time, whereas reverse auction results in lower prices over time.

An online store is a showcase of an online or traditional business, which hosts an offer of goods and services with a limited or complete set of functions for making sales; an online store can be part of a corporate website.

An e-shop is an Internet address at which an enterprise advertises and sells goods or services to other network users.

An electronic store is a combination of two components: computer data and electronic arrangement of this data for running a business on the Internet.

All information in the Internet store (the enterprise logo, information about the company, product catalogue, etc.) always appears on the screen, is created on the computer owned by the seller or the enterprise and stored on it. The computer on which the store is recorded is part of the Internet. Therefore, it is open to any user of the network who wishes to visit it.

The Internet stores provide the movement of goods and services, familiarize them with potential buyers who have access to the Internet and perform the same functions as ordinary types of advertising. However, the electronic store does not stop its activities after the interest in it disappears as it happens with advertising. It will work regardless of anything, offering its services as much time as the seller plans, without limiting the viewing time. Electronic stores also offer interactive means of communication with the buyer, based on multimedia technologies, including order processing.

The acquisition of goods and services in the EC system is as follows. The company installs a constantly running computer – a server with Internet access and special software called a "virtual store." A potential client sees on the screen an advertisement with several options. Choosing one of them leads to a page with information on the screen and the client has the opportunity to view the goods, receive additional information and place an order.

The advantages and disadvantages that the online store provides to customers and sellers are presented in Table 4.2.

The benefits of EC for organisations are the following:

• Makes national and international markets more accessible
• Lowering costs of processing, distributing and retrieving information

The main benefit to customers is access to a vast number of products and services 24 hours, 7 days a week, 365 days a year without a break.

Benefits to Society include the ability to easily and conveniently deliver information, services and products to people in cities, rural areas and developing countries.

The limitations of EC are technological and non-technological. Technological limitations:

• Lack of generally accepted safety standards
• Insufficient telecommunications bandwidth
• Expensive accessibility

Non-technological limitations:

• The perception that EC is insecure
• Unresolved Legal issues

TABLE 4.2

Advantages and Disadvantages That the Online Store Provides to Customers and Sellers

Players	Advantages	Disadvantages
Customers	• Search for goods • View the seller's price list • A detailed review of the characteristics, a description of the features • Selection of goods in the shopping cart • A list of invoices for payment • View the history of orders and payment • Saving time (the ability to select and purchase goods and services without leaving home) • The relative anonymity of the purchase • Immediate delivery and support when purchasing an electronic product • Obtaining new previously unavailable services in the field of entertainment, consulting, training, etc. • Obtaining additional information about the required goods	• The inability to get acquainted with goods' properties before purchasing • The threat of credit card fraud • Problems due to inadequate quality • Difficulties in assessing the quality of services provided • The intrusiveness of e-mail advertising (SPAM)
Sellers	• Increase in sales for the creation of additional outlets • An increase in the number of buyers without an increase in retail space • Reducing sales costs • Competitiveness • International trade – it is possible to sell goods throughout the world without opening regular stores in each country • The ability to work on the Internet 24 hours, 7 days a week, 365 days a year without a break • May have several unrelated projects • Ability to automatically identify and register IP addresses of potential customers • Facilitating interaction with customers and partners	• Additional costs for the system implementation • The threat of damage by hackers • Ability to steal programmes when trading through the network

Source: Own work based on: Davydov, Rudetskaya 2015.

Results of using this e-business model are the following:

- Increase in sales of goods and services
- The ability to analyse consumer demand for products
- Reduction of implementation costs
- The opportunity to get a client portrait
- Increasing the base of potential customers
- Lack of a critical mass of sellers and buyers

4.2.1 ELECTRONIC EXCHANGE TO IMPROVE B2B ACTIVITY

Another promising EC business model is the e-exchange model. Electronic exchange is essential for boosting the activity of the B2B sector. An Internet exchange is a trading platform that allows businesses to organise barter models of commodity trading and use clearing systems. Functionally, it is similar to real exchanges and is used to trade consumer goods such as grain, paper, metal, etc. It can be single-industry or multi-industry.

The Internet exchange performs the following functions:

- Information support for participants
- Organisation of trade in goods
- Organisation of payment and delivery processes
- Attracting additional participants
- Establishing two-way communication with exchange participants

ETPs allow organising a full-fledged Internet trade with the provision of the necessary set of services to participants.

The classification of trading floors is presented as follows.
ETPs

- Independent trading marketplace
- Private marketplace
- Industry-sponsored marketplace

Depending on the specialisation:

- Vertical (industry)
- Horizontal (functional)

Depending on the method of creation:

- Buyer-driven
- Supplier-driven
- Third party-driven

Independent marketplaces were typically set up by Internet companies to serve specific industries or product groups. They offered participants a solution to the problems of finding trading partners, a single place to do business, virtual business relationship management and the ability to analyse prices in the market.

Large firms create private trading platforms to maximise the possibilities of Internet technologies for deepening integration with their partners. These sites combine the existing internal information systems of the participants to improve the operation of the entire supply chain and reduce the costs of transactions between them.

Industry marketplaces have enabled industrial enterprises to take advantage of e-business and drive the development of EC in their sector. Typically, ETPs specialise in a specific industry or product (vertical) or a specific business process (horizontal). Attempts to work across the board are ineffective.

Vertical ETPs serve vertical markets (mechanical engineering, rolled metal products, oil products). They provide industry-specific information and take into account the specifics of industry relationships.

The following factors contribute to the success of such ETPs:

- increased fragmentation among sellers and buyers
- the decrease in the efficiency of the existing supply systems
- in-depth knowledge of the specifics of the market
- creation of main catalogues and convenient search systems
- the presence of accompanying verticals balancing the client base

Horizontal ETPs are focused on performing certain functions or automating a certain process (logistics, insurance, payments) for various industries.

The following factors contribute to their success with ETP:

- the level of process standardisation
- deep knowledge of the process and experience in its automation, supplementing automation with deep information content
- the ability to adapt the process to the specific requirements of various industries

4.2.2 Mechanical Trading System as Example of B2C activity

The Internet has created the global availability of information. Also, the financial statements for most corporations are published for public use on the WWW. The access to this public information makes it easier for more investors to have the information they need to make smart, well-background decisions for investing. Since investors can be better educated about investing, more investors have entered the market. This way information technology enhances investment growth.

Online Stock Trading is one of the most demanding EC utilities. The ability to offer market access at a competitive price is a key advantage of online stockbroking companies, and now this is rapidly growing.

- Bond markets provide financing through the issuance of bonds and enable the subsequent trading thereof
- Commodity markets facilitate the trading of commodities

- Money markets, which provide short-term debt financing and investment
- Derivatives markets provide instruments for the management of financial risk
- Futures and forward markets provide standardised forward contracts for trading products at some date
- Foreign exchange markets facilitate the trading of foreign exchange
- The cryptocurrency market facilitates the trading of digital assets and financial technologies
- Spot market
- Interbank lending market

The success of exchange trading depends on the speed of processing requests and the use of integrated flow processing systems.

There are large numbers of users who use the Internet for some form of financial guidance.

Participating in the market is not only easier but also cheaper. Since the information is out there for everyone to see, more and more people are becoming their investors, cutting out the broker. Cutting out the intermediary allows the investor to keep the percentage of the money he used to pay the broker.

Key developments can be received through new networks. Through the Internet, an investor can find large amounts of information on the Stock Market and many corporations. New technology also allows investors to be able to buy and sell stock and bonds online. The investor can maintain online brokerage accounts. An investor can do this either by keeping up with their accounts daily or by putting a low or high cap on each stock. An investor can also get information on particular stocks and the history of these stocks. Moreover, an investor can receive online advice from a broker if needed.

However, there are negative aspects of the information technology age for investors; i.e. distorted facts, wrong information or information that has been cooked, changed or distorted in the corporations' favour. And the more information there is out there, the harder it is to find the information users need because they have to trudge through all the excessive information.

Many software applications are available from brokerage firms and independent vendors claiming varied functions to assist traders. Most brokerages offer trading software, armed with a variety of trade, research, stock screening and analysis functions, to individual clients when they open a brokerage account.

Much of the software is complimentary; some of it may cost extra, as part of a premium package; a lot of it, invariably, claims that it contains "the best stock charts" or "the best free trading platform." Fact: There is no single best stock chart or best stock screener software. There are too many markets, trading strategies and personal preferences for that. One of the most widely used trading software is MetaStock.

The Mechanical Trading System (MTS) has the following work model (Figure 4.8). MTS (https://www.pdsnet.co.za/) automatically generates orders for the purchase or sale of securities based on data on the course of exchange trading. The MTS is located on the user's computer and consists of two parts: SmartTrade, external trading, and analytical system. As an external system, MetaStock, Omega Research 2000 and WealthLab can be used.

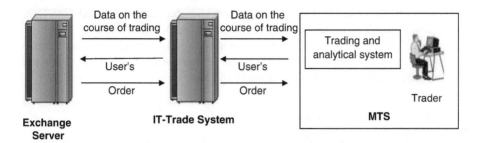

FIGURE 4.8 MTS work model.

Source: Own work.

MetaStock is a product of Equis International (a division of Reuters). MetaStock first hit the market in 1984. It has since gained tremendous popularity among traders all over the world.

It contains all the tools that users need to develop, test and implement advanced trading systems based on technical analysis.

MetaStock offers more than 300 technical indicators, built-in drawing tools like Fibonacci retracement to complement technical indicators, integrated news, fundamental data with screening and filtering criteria and global market coverage across multiple assets: equities, derivatives, forex, futures and commodities.

The software contains powerful analysis tools to help make informed decisions about what to buy and sell and when to execute to make the most money possible. MetaStock Daily Charts and Refinitiv DataLink is the perfect solution for end-of-day traders, who do their analysis after the markets close.

MetaStock Daily Charts contains powerful analysis tools so users can make informed decisions about what to buy and sell, and when to execute resulting in the most profitable trades.

MetaStock Daily Charts comes with many out-of-the-box trading solutions that are reliable and easy to use. It has the tools needed for superior market analysis and financial success to trade stocks, options, mutual funds, futures, commodities, FOREX, bonds or indices.

MetaStock Real Time is specifically designed for real-time traders who use intra-day data to transact in real time throughout the trading day.

MetaStock Real Time comes with many out-of-the-box trading solutions that are reliable and easy to use. And if the user wants to take analysis to the next level, MetaStock Real Time gives the ability to customise these solutions to the user's particular trading style.

4.2.3 ANALYSE TRADING SIGNALS

The MetaStock FORECASTER offers new ways to analyse trading signals and provides insight into future performance. This tool could paint a more probable, easy-to-read picture of the future. The image is based on proprietary technology that uses any of 69 event recognizers or custom templates. A picture that helps users more precisely set profit targets and stops. That's what users get with the MetaStock FORECASTER, the latest Power Tool available exclusively in MetaStock. The FORECASTER plots a "probability cloud" based on user selection of any of 67 event recognisers or his custom pattern. It uses advanced mathematics to examine the price action after these events determine the probable performance of future events.

4.2.4 METASTOCK EXPLORER

MetaStock Explorer uses built-in criteria to scan multiple securities to find those that match the user's strategy. The Explorer includes a new exploration results interface to view scan results as well as a good amount of detail on stocks after the scan has been processed. Multiple charts can be opened at once, and multiple scans can run at the same time. The user may also keep the Explorer open while viewing his charts.

4.2.5 ENHANCED SYSTEM TESTER

With the Enhanced System Tester, it is possible to create, back-test, compare and perfect user strategies before risking any of the money in the markets (Figure 4.9). System testing helps answer the question, "If I had traded this security using these trading rules, how much money would I have made or lost?" The surest way to increase user confidence in a trading system is to test it historically. The Enhanced System Tester lets you take a group of stocks and compare them to a group of trading

FIGURE 4.9   The Enhanced System Tester.

Source: Own work based on: MetaStock Professional.

systems to find the best scenario. Designed to simulate real trading scenarios, the Enhanced System Tester allows you to change variables such as entry, exit, order sizes, commissions and more. This tool gives incredible customisation, comprehensive results and detailed reports.

4.2.6 CHARTING

MetaStock gives nine of the most widely used price charting styles: bars, line, candlesticks, point and figure, Kagi, Renko, three-line break, equivalent volume and candle volume (Figure 4.10). As well as this, Page Layouts help you save time and stay organised. It allows saving all of the on-screen charts together like pages in a book. Therefore, whenever the user opens his layout, the same securities appear. Templates also save time by applying the same set of indicators and studies to different securities. Built-in toolbars let easily refresh data, change periodicity, rescale the Y-Axis, zoom in & out, choose "previous" or "next security" in the open folder, and choose a security to open. The Object-Oriented Interface allows clicking on an object and getting an instant menu for that item. The Click and Pick/Drag and Drop features let drag price plots, indicators, text and lines from one chart to another.

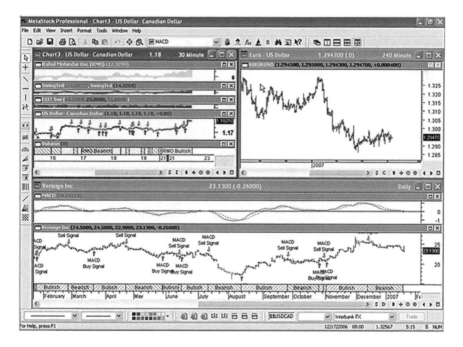

FIGURE 4.10 Charting.

Source: Own work based on: MetaStock Professional.

4.2.7 THE EXPERT ADVISOR

The MetaStock Expert Advisor gives the input of industry professionals when and where the user needs it. It displays the industry's most popular systems and charting styles with the click of a mouse (Figure 4.11). If a user needs more info, the commentary screen will specify information about the security he is charting. User can even create his system using the easy-to-learn MetaStock formula language. Expert Alerts keep the user in touch with current trading conditions. Expert Commentary shows in detail how the user's expert assesses the chart user is viewing. Is it a buy, sell or hold situation? If so… Why? User gets insight gained through years of research and real-world trading. Expert Symbols and Trends – Buy and sell arrows, text or any other symbols in the MetaStock palette automatically flag special conditions, according to own criteria.

4.2.8 INDICATOR BUILDER

MetaStock includes over 150 a comprehensive collection of indicators and line studies. MetaStock's comprehensive collection of indicators and line studies over 150 are included. MetaStock's built-in indicator interpretations even help you understand how to trade each indicator (Figure 4.12). For advanced users, the Indicator Builder lets them write its indicators. Standard indicators use a fixed look-back period, which makes them less responsive to prevailing market conditions. MetaStock incorporates

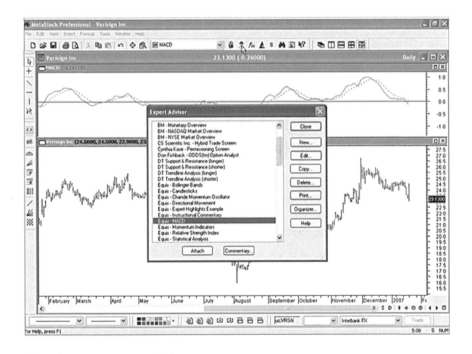

FIGURE 4.11   The Expert Advisor.

Source: Own work based on: MetaStock Professional.

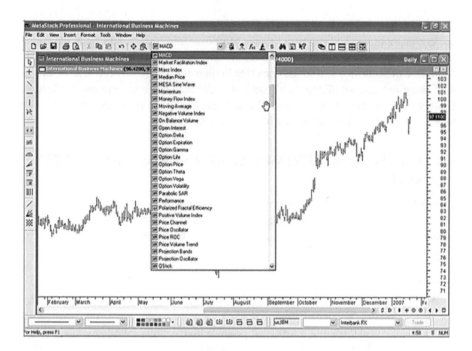

FIGURE 4.12 Indicator builder.

Source: Own work based on: MetaStock Professional.

42 Adaptive Indicators with dynamic look-back functionality based on volatility, cycle or a combination of both. This method provides the most responsive and accurate results. MetaStock knows that many clients have their ideas about what makes a great system. The MetaStock formula language is easy to learn and allows us to create just about any system user can think of.

MetaStock is satisfied with all trader needs. It's easy to use package, no matter what kind of securities you trade. This is the tool that is allowed to fine-tune the trading approach. Advantages of MetaStock are the following:

- The quick and easy workflow in the new Explorer.
- Easy to find your past scan results data in the Exploration Results Report window.
- Workflow increases even more when using multiple monitors.
- Creates a list with favourite scans in them.
- Creates a list of favourite backtesting scans and runs them all against data for maximum results.
- The system by default stores the past 20 used indicators.
- Local data for charts can now be edited.
- Scans for candlestick patterns.
- New Sector Stat templates and Indicators.
- The dynamic tool makes drawing Support and Resistance lines far easier.

MetaStock has real tools to find winning securities. There are thousands of stocks, currencies, options and futures out there. Moreover, there are hundreds of indicators and systems that might want to use to trade them. Users can use their criteria to scan a universe of securities to find the ones that fit their strategy. Users can scan results as well as a good amount of detail on stocks after the scan has been processed. Multiple charts can be opened at once, and multiple scans can run at the same time. The user may also keep the Explorer open while viewing his charts

4.3 THE TYPES OF SETTLEMENTS: ADVANTAGES AND SECURITY RULES

The ability to pay and get paid is critical for every business. However, business payments are inherently complex and getting more so every day, making it difficult for organisations to create a business payment strategy that helps them to be successful (Turban et al. 2008, p. 550).

The types of settlements for different sectors of EC are different and presented in Table 4.3.

While physical cash isn't yet endangered in most places, the experience of a few countries, notably Sweden, China and even to some extent the United Kingdom, shows that a world with much less cash usage is increasingly possible (Figure 4.13). That is why the BIS, sometimes called the central bank for central banks, published a report sketching out possible designs for a P2Pcentral bank digital currency (John Detrixhe, 2020) (Figure 4.13).

TABLE 4.3

The Types of Settlements for Different Sectors of E-Commerce

E-commerce Sector	Types of Settlements
B2B sector	• Traditional cashless payments • Client-bank systems • Traditional payments by check • Corporate plastic cards
B2C sector	• Traditional cash • Payments with plastic cards • All online payment systems • Internet banking • Mobile banking and SMS banking
Sector C2C	• Traditional cash • IPR based on digital cash • IPRs based on virtual accounts
Sectors B2A, C2A, B2G, C2G	• Traditional cashless payments • Client-bank systems (B2A, C2A) • IPR based on plastic cards
Sectors B2I, C21,121	• Traditional cashless payments • Client-bank systems

Source: Own work.

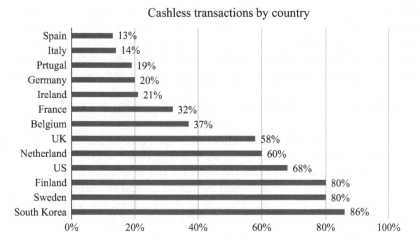

Cashless transactions by country

FIGURE 4.13   Cashless transactions by country in 2019.

Source: Detrixhe 2020, Quartz.

Electronic Money (EM) and Internet payment methods can be divided into several types depending on the methods of functioning, according to the security level, and according to the payment method.

An authentication system is a much more secure option for using a credit card on the Internet. This system uses a special protocol for secure exchange of information with authenticated digital certificates and digital signatures of the client and the merchant. This excludes the refusal to fulfil the terms of the agreement and the substitution of identity.

Internet clearing systems. The main idea of Internet clearing systems is that the client does not have to open his personal and financial data to the seller every time he makes a purchase. Instead, he only tells him his ID or his name in this system. The supplier then requests the system and receives a confirmation or denial of the payment. The system guarantees payment to the supplier, while the client transmits his data once using well-secured protocols. Money is deposited in the system in any way available to the client. The client can pay by card immediately after registration. Besides, the system issues digital certificates confirming the identity of the customer and the merchant, and the customer and supplier "data exchange" protocol uses these certificates and the digital signature.

EM or Plastic card uses encryption technologies in exchange transactions. Plastic cards provide a relatively secure payment option. The transaction on the Internet takes place using encryption technologies. It is almost impossible to intercept information during a transaction and under the protection of communication session protocols. But it can be done from the merchant's server. Also, there is a possibility of forgery or substitution of identity by both the seller and the buyer since there is no signature.

Smart card: The technological pinnacle of the e-money is systems based on smart card technology. A smart card is a small computer with its processor, memory, software, and information input/output system. The smart card is used as a regular debit card, called an electronic wallet, which records the information about the withdrawal of money and information about the customer. E-money based on smart cards can provide the necessary level of confidentiality and anonymity. Also, they work in offline mode and do not require communication with the centre to confirm payment.

There are two types of EM according to the storing method:

- Systems that store electronic money (e-money) on smart cards. To perform settlements, this system requires special devices for recording the EM on a smart card and transferring the EM from one smart card to another. The devices that allow viewing information about the EM stored on a smart card is called "electronic wallet." Depending on the system, the "electronic wallet" can perform the function of transferring digital notes from one smart card to another and perform the calculation procedure directly.
- Systems that provide for the storage of EM as files on a standard storage device (hard disk, floppy disk, etc.). To work with these systems, buyers and sellers do not need any special hardware other than personal computers.

EM is money, which exists in banking computer systems and is available for transactions through electronic systems. Its value is backed by fiat currency and it can be exchanged into physical form; however, its uses are often more convenient electronically (https://www.investopedia.com/terms/e/electronic-money.asp).

E-money is used for purchases and transactions globally. While it can be exchanged for fiat currency, it is much more conveniently monitored and utilised through electronic banking systems and electronic processing.

E-money can be held in various accounts. Most individuals and businesses store their money with banks, which provide electronic records of the cash on deposit. Other forms of stored value EM include digital wallets such as PayPal and Square or prepaid cards that allow users to deposit fiat currency for EM (https://www.investopedia.com/terms/e/electronic-money.asp).

The primary means for EM transactions is through payment-processing networks. In the United States, American Express, Visa and MasterCard are the primary payment-processing networks facilitating the transactions of EM across the nation.

Digital wallets are also available following similar transaction protocols. EM is also easily transacted through EC allowing consumers to shop and purchase all types of goods and services online.

The value of EM is established by its fiat currency that makes it different from emerging cryptocurrencies. EM is backed by the central bank system.

Below is a payment scheme using EM (Figure 4.14).

So, in general, EM is understood as the media of information on monetary value involved in operations to pay for purchased goods and provided services. The specific type of EM depends on the carrier of this information. It can be plastic or magnetic cards, mobile devices and other electronic media.

EM is also a claim on a private bank or other financial institution such as bank deposits (https://www.investopedia.com/terms/e/electronic-money.asp).

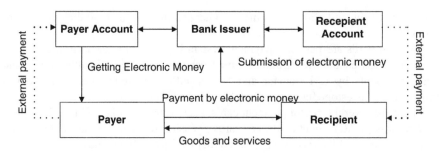

FIGURE 4.14 Make payments with electronic money.

Source: Own work.

Applied EM tools today are payment cards, flashcards, mobile devices. The most widely used are payment cards Visa, MasterCard and American Express.

4.3.1 E-commerce Payment Systems: Advantages and Security Rules

EC systems give users a variety of privileges. But using them, you should also remember the safety rules. There are the following types of EC payment systems:

- Electronic checks (e-checks)
- Electronic bank cards
- Internet banking
- Electronic wallets
- Virtual accounts

An e-check is an electronic document containing all the details required for a traditional check, except for the signature. E-check is signed with the digital signature.
Benefits of using an e-check:

- It can be transferred via the Internet from the user's computer to the seller's computer and vice versa
- The use of a digital signature allows for mutual authentication of the seller and the buyer
- The payer can close his details with the bank's public key, which will make them inaccessible to the store
- Payment authorisation is carried out without involving processing centres
- It is impossible to create a check without the payer's private key

E-check disadvantages:

- Need to install special software to be able to sign checks with your digital signature
- Preliminary registration in the system is required
- Only banks that have an agreement with the Payment System can participate in the settlements.

Electronic credit card allows customers to charge online payment to their credit card account.

Payment cards are part of a payment system issued by the bank, to a customer. Payment cards enable the cardholder to access the funds in its bank accounts and make payments by EM transfer and access automated teller machines (ATMs) (https://www.investopedia.com/terms/e/electronic-money.asp).

There are several types of payment cards, such as bank cards, ATM cards, money access cards (MAC), client cards, key cards or cash cards. But the most common are credit cards and debit cards. A bank card or debit card combined the two functions of ATM cards and debit cards. These cards can be used to perform banking tasks at ATMs and make point-of-sale transactions with a PIN.

Edward Bellamy put the idea of a credit card forward as early as the 19th century. But for the first time, credit card cards began to be used in commercial enterprises in the United States only in the 1920s of the last century. Finding the material that would be most suitable for a credit card has dragged on for decades. Only in the 1960s was found an acceptable solution found. This was a plastic card with magnetic tape. In 1975, Frenchman Roland Mareno invented and patented an electronic card. A few more years passed. SWIFT (France) developed and patented a smart card. Since then, electronic means of payment have been constantly improved.

The simplest type of plastic card is a magnetic card. It has a magnetic tape for 100 bytes of information about the number of the card or bank's current account, the holder's name and the due date of the card. There is no financial information on magnetic tape. There are two modes for magnetic cards. In the online mode, the device reads information from a magnetic card and transmits it to a bank where the message is processed, and then the purchase amount is debited from the owner's account. At the same time, it is checked if the card is not stolen and there is enough money in the holder's account. In the offline mode, purchase information is not transmitted but stored in the trading terminal.

The functioning of banking self-service systems based on plastic cards is provided by ATMs and trading terminals. ATMs are designed to issue cash by plastic cards. Trading terminals provide payment in the store using plastic cards.

More complex is a smart card with an integrated microcircuit containing a memory and a device for recording and reading information. The memory varies over a wide range but on average does not exceed 256 bytes. Such cards have more features compared to magnetic, but their price is higher. Smart cards are the most promising types of plastic cards. This type of card should be replacing credit cards with magnetic tape and even cash in the future. Smart cards have a built-in microprocessor, random access memory, and permanent memory and can have a data protection system. These cards fulfil various financial purposes; the most often is used as electronic wallets.

According to the settlement types, credit cards and debit cards are allocated.

Credit electronic payment systems are analogues of conventional credit card systems. The difference is that all transactions are conducted via the Internet and, as a result, there is a need for additional security and authentication tools. The general scheme of payments in such a system is shown in Figure 4.15.

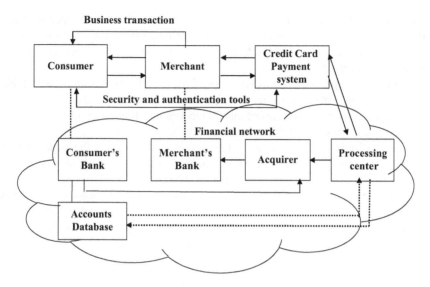

FIGURE 4.15 Credit card payments scheme.

Source: Own work.

The credit scheme provides for a zero initial balance on the credit of the account. A credit card is linked to a credit limit created by the issuer of the credit card for the cardholder. All operations with the card are paid by the bank, but in the future, the card user will have to pay off his debt to the bank.

The cardholder can either repay the full outstanding balance or a lesser amount by the payment due date. The amount paid cannot be less than the "minimum payment," either a fixed amount or a percentage of the outstanding balance. Interest is charged on the portion of the balance not paid off by the due date. The rate of interest and method of calculating the charge vary between credit cards, even for different types of cards issued by the same company. Many credit cards can also be used to take cash advances through ATMs, which also attract interest charges, usually calculated from the date of cash withdrawal. Some merchants charge a fee for purchases by credit card, as they will be charged a fee by the card issuer.

At first, magnetic plastic cards as electronic wallets were used in the form of credit cards to arrange payment for goods purchased on credit and received services. Credit cards mainly contain information about the card itself (a unique card number that identifies it and consists of the issuer's number and additional service characters); the expiration date of its validity; the full name of the cardholder; and sometimes a sample of his signature on the back as well as specific data (payment limit, service code, etc.).

The name of the holder, card number and date of issue, as a rule, are printed in a convex font.

The owner of the IPC uses it as a card of automated banking machines (ATMs) to receive cash. In many countries, ATMs operate 24 hours per day, but there are restrictions either on a one-time amount or on the amount that can be received within 1 day. The cash amount issued by the card is withdrawn from the client's account in the bank that owns the ATM (the ATM is connected to the bank's server; the loan amount is monitored).

Plastic cards in particular are used as electronic wallets. An electronic wallet, like a credit card, must provide the client with payments for services and goods as well as receive cash. There are two main options for electronic wallets: individual, or personalised, and anonymous. The difference between them is as follows.

A personalised electronic wallet contains the individual data of the owner, including the number of his current account, the number of the service agreement, etc. An anonymous electronic wallet does not contain such data.

A personalised e-wallet is issued by the issuing bank or its branch based on an individual agreement concluded with the client. The issuance of an anonymous e-wallet is much simpler because the contract with the client is not concluded; only his consent to follow the rules for using the wallet is enough. Moreover, the bank prepares an anonymous electronic wallet with a zero balance and a primary PIN code in advance. Moreover, the client can purchase an anonymous electronic wallet at the issuing bank or even from a bank agent.

The primary personal identification code of the client is established by the bank and informs its client when the contract is concluded. The client, having received the EG, can change this code.

Downloading (depositing money) an electronic wallet is always performed in the bank terminal or on special equipment in the online mode of the issuing bank's server with a mandatory requirement of the PIN code.

Using an electronic wallet is beneficial to all participants in the system.

First, the owner of the electronic wallet has the opportunity to keep a little cash with him, and therefore, he risks less if he loses money or is robbed. Besides, it saves time on payments for goods and services.

Second, trade and service enterprises reduce the expenses of working with cash. At the same time, the risk of an unpaid loan is reduced due to a lack of money in the cardholder's account.

For the bank issuer, an electronic wallet is a means of attracting funds, equivalent to attracting deposits from individuals. Also, e-bank has the potential to provide profitable wallet loading services.

A debit card, like an electronic wallet, is a multipurpose subscription card. Therefore, the characteristic of an individual electronic wallet is largely related to a debit card. The main differences between a debit card and an electronic wallet are the following:

- The transaction is debited from the cardholder's account. The operation is not carried out if the amount exceeds the balance on the account.
- Each debit card has its account in the issuing bank, which reflects all operations performed.
- The debit card is used for medium and large payments, so some of the payments can be performed online. The use of a debit card for payments in small amounts is not excluded.

- During all operations with a debit card, a personal identification code is mainly used.
- Interest is accrued on account balances.

When a cardholder uses a debit card, funds are withdrawn directly from his bank account or the balance on the card. Some cards are used only for online purchases and have no physical card.

Debit cards are used worldwide and have overtaken the use of cheques and cash. Moreover, debit cards are used widely for telephone and Internet purchases. Debit cards allow withdrawal cash, acting as the ATM card, and as a cheque guarantee card. Merchants can also offer "cashback"/"cashout" facilities to customers, where a customer can withdraw cash along with their purchase. Merchants do not charge a fee for purchases by a debit card.

The advantage of a debit card over an electronic wallet includes security and a guaranteed refund in case of loss of a card. The disadvantage of a debit card is the higher cost per transaction compared to an electronic wallet.

A payment card is intended for managing a client's current account. It is also a reusable and multipurpose card. The payment card does not contain data on the balance in the current account. All operations with payment cards can only be carried out online.

The guarantor of operations with a payment card is the bank. Therefore, after authorisation by the payment card and confirmation of purchase, the required amount is withdrawn from the current account and transferred to a temporary account, and then does not participate in operations.

A payment card, like a debit card, is designed for medium and large payments; therefore, operations with it are performed online using a PIN code.

The right to issue a payment card can only be the bank that maintains a customer's current account.

The benefits of using a payment card are the same as using an electronic wallet. But the risk of un-payment due to the absence of account or funds is reduced for merchants. The funds managed by the payment card are individualised in the bank. Therefore, the processing centre generates a debit payment document for each transaction and sends it to the bank, where the client's current account is. The bank also stores the general database of all issued payment cards.

The bank issues cards in the same way as debit cards. Downloading a payment card comes down to placing client funds in his current account.

When paying for a payment or service performed online, the balance on the client's account is also checked. The client can also receive cash on the payment card in any amount not exceeding the balance on the current account. All operations can be blocked if the payment card is lost.

4.3.2 Mobile Digital Wallets

Several EM systems use contactless payment transfers to facilitate easy payment and give the payee more confidence in not letting go of their electronic wallet during the transaction.

Mondex and National Westminster Bank provided the first "electronic purse" in 1994 to residents of Swindon.

Mobipay in Spain used simple short message service facilities of feature phones intended for pay-as-you-go services including taxis and prepay phone recharges via a BBVA current bank account debit.

In January 2010, Venmo (https://venmo.com/about/fees/) was launched as a mobile payment system through SMS. It can be linked to your bank account, credit/debit card or have a loaded value to limit the amount of loss in case of a security breach. Credit cards and non-major debit cards incur a 3% processing fee (https://www.cnet.com/news/this-day-in-tech-google-wallet-launches/; Easytrip, O2 launch mobile toll payments service in the Republic of Ireland). In 2011, Google Wallet was released in the United States to make it easy to carry all users' credit/debit cards on their phones (https://www.o2.co.uk/money).

In 2014, Apple Pay released an update to work on iPhone 6 and Apple Watch very similar to Google Wallet, but for Apple devices only (https://www.theverge.com/2014/9/9/6127587/apple-watch-works-with-apple-pay-to-replace-your-credit-cards).

In a normal trading operation, there are two participants: the seller and the buyer. There are already three participants in the e-money system: seller, buyer and bank. Moreover, as a rule, the bank is primarily responsible for the operation of the entire EM system. The Bank issues EM and ensures the operation of electronic machines for depositing money and their reception from merchants. Bank provides outlets with special equipment – cash settlement terminals that can accept EM. The Bank is responsible for the activities of all elements of the system as a whole, for their interaction and the implementation of relevant payments.

The bank is directly involved in settlements for the purchase of EM used. The money circulation when using EM, in general, can be divided into the following stages (Figure 4.16):

- Payment for the goods by the owner of the electronic wallet.
- Entering by the bank of the payment into the seller's account.

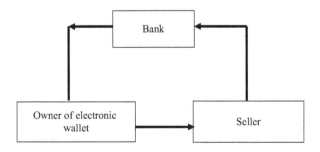

FIGURE 4.16 Money circulation scheme in electronic money system.

Source: Own work.

The main elements of the EM system are the following:

1. Magnetic plastic cards are carriers of cost information. They are a direct expression of money.
2. Cash settlement terminals in retail outlets are used for settlements with buyers – owners of EM.
3. Bank machines for loading amount onto magnetic plastic cards.
4. Merchant's card, where information about all operations that were performed from an electronic wallet at a given outlet for a certain time is concentrated.
5. A system for processing banking information, in particular, settlement (processing) centres.

Each of the elements of the system has certain functions. Therefore, the cash settlement terminal in retail outlets performs the following basic operations:

- Provides a connection with customer card and merchant card;
- Shows the buyer the current amount of money;
- Reflects the purchase price;
- Allows the holder of EM to express consent to purchase and enter his PIN code;
- Prints and issues a paper document (receipt, invoice) about the purchase;
- Maintains a merchant's transaction journal, which is sent to the bank.

The cash settlement terminal cannot deposit money on the card. However, it accepts the sale if the amount of money is sufficient to purchase.

The EM system can be nationwide, and then it includes numerous banks and clearinghouses. The government created the system mainly based on one bank so that it can be tested before being distributed nationwide.

If the EM system consists of many banks and many outlets, the problem of mutual settlements between banks arises if the owner of EM makes purchases at a point of sale that does not have a current account with the issuing bank. This problem is similar to the problem of settlements between customers served by different banks.

The scheme of interaction participants with the payment system using plastic cards is shown in Figure 4.17.

Figure 4.17 indicates the following processes:

1 – registration and issuance of the card to the client
2 – provision of a card for registration of the purchase or payment for services
3-4 – authorisation request
5-6 – authorisation results
7-8 – check transfer for purchased/sold goods
9-11 – settlements of the issuing bank with the acquiring bank for the transactions carried out

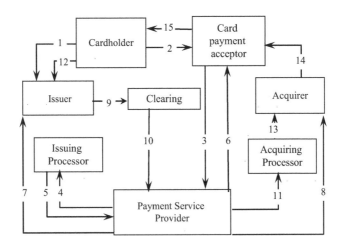

FIGURE 4.17 Scheme of interaction between participants in the card project.

Source: Own work based on: Sytnyk 2008.

12 – settlements of the cardholder with the issuing bank
13-14 – transfer of funds for purchased goods to the Bank acquirer account
15 – transfer of goods and a check to the payment acceptor

4.3.3 SMART CARDS AND THEIR USE

As practice shows, the most complete function of cash is performed by smart cards. This card not only stores data but also operates on them, processes them under the given rules. These functions are provided by a card-integrated microcircuit. Thus, the smart card has a processor, memory, input/output and operating system.

A smart card is a small computer. Characteristics of a smart card are the following: clock frequency – about 3 MHz, RAM capacity – 256 bytes; the amount of permanent memory is about 10 KB.

A card with the microcircuit can store the cash limit, take into account expenses and determine the balance and the size of the actual balance without having to go to the bank. The limit amount is set in the bank and recorded on a smart card. The number of current expenses and the current balance are determined at the merchant on settlement terminals.

The payment terminals, in contact with the smart card, activate the corresponding fields in it and change the cash balance, as well as "read" the customer's identifier, his bank account number, the purchase amount and payer bank identifier. Based on these data, a merchant's card is formed and then connected with the bank, and money is credited to the merchant's account.

The general technology for using a smart card in electronic payment systems is almost the same as magnetic plastic cards. The settlements scheme using smart cards is shown in Figure 4.18.

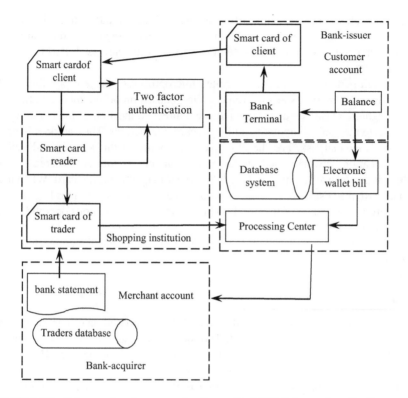

FIGURE 4.18   Scheme of settlements using Smart Card (SC) "electronic wallet."

Source: Own work based on: Sytnyk 2008.

The buyer presents their purchases and a smart card to the cashier. The terminal read card and the buyer authenticate with the PIN. The card is checked if it is valid and whether there is an amount on it to pay for the purchase.

If not, then there is a "return" of the goods – the purchase is postponed. Otherwise, a smart card is debited and a cash register is credited. All this is done in a matter of seconds, without any connection with the bank. Funds are sent via communication channels to the seller's bank account.

A smart card contains EM that helps to solve problems associated with cash. At the same time, the amount of cash is reduced. Thus, EM leads to a reduction in the amount of cash used and the release of the money.

Reducing the cash is beneficial to everyone: banks, and retailers, and most customers. Electronic money is first of all reliable, weakening the threat of robbery and theft. Also, when used, financial authorities can organise and control the entire range of financial transactions.

The smart card has physical and technical parameters under the requirements of the specifications of the World Organization of Standards: length 85.6 mm, width 53.9 mm and thickness no more than 0.76 mm. As well as there are operational characteristics: shelf life – at least 10 years; read/write cycle – at least 10,000 times. There are also established requirements regarding the stability of cards to environmental influences (temperature, acidity, etc.) as well as their transformation (twisting).

The high parameters and the integrated microprocessor make it possible to efficiently use smart cards as an electronic wallet focused on offline mode. At the same time, magnetic plastic card systems require a direct connection of the equipment of the outlet to the bank computer to authorise card transactions. They work only online to reduce financial risk. For the effective functioning of this system, a developed communication network based on dedicated channels is required. To create such a system, it needs investments for the US $ 150 per magnetic plastic card. When using a smart card, the cost is approximately $ 50 per card. This is three times less since the smart card is focused on offline mode. This ensures the autonomous operation of the equipment in retail outlets.

To make payments via the Internet, an electronic store must be connected to one or more Internet payment systems.

4.3.4 E-MONEY ADVANTAGES

E-money is most correctly compared with cash, as the circulation of non-cash money is necessarily personified, and the details of both parties are known. It is sufficient to know the requisites of the recipient of funds in the case of payments by EM.

E-money has the following advantages over cash:

Your crypts are only on your computer in the electronic wallet and no one and under no circumstances will be able to do anything with them.

No control by the banks or the state. As a consequence, the inability to control cryptocurrency by various state structures.

Open cryptocurrency code – BTC uses the same algorithms that are used in Internet banking. The only difference in Internet banking is the disclosure of information about end users. In the BTC network, all information about the transaction is shared (how many, when), but there is no data about the recipient or the sender of the coins (there is no access to the personal information of the purse holders).

Absence of inflation – the number of coins in this system grows with a certain speed, laid in such a way that it coincides with the speed of gold mining on the planet.

There is no main server responsible for all transactions in the P2Pcryptocurrency network. Information is exchanged between 2–3 or more client programmes. Neither banks, nor taxation, nor the state can control the exchange of money between users' wallets.

Unlimited possibilities of transactions – each of the purse owners can pay to anyone, anywhere and for anything. Transactions cannot be checked or disabled so that transfers can be made anywhere in the world, no matter where the other user with the BTC wallet is.

The commission in this system is lower than in any other. They constitute 0.1% of the transaction amount. Interest is in the purse of the "earners" BTC.

Excellent divisibility and consistency – no payment is required when making a payment.

High portability – the amount of the sum not related to the dimensional or weighted amounts of money, as is the case with cash.

It is not necessary to physically recalculate money; this function is transferred to a storage tool or payment instrument.

Easier than in the case of cash, organise physical protection of EM. The moment of payment is fixed by the electronic system and reduced the human factor impact. Security is provided by cryptographic and electronic means.

Despite widespread use in World, there are still a large number of countries such as China and India that have some problems to overcome regarding credit card security. Thus, the smart card systems can be widely implemented in regions where there are no reliable telecommunication facilities, criminal structures are active and the population has low credit reliability.

Over the years, plastic cards have become one of the most common forms of payment for EC transactions. It would be difficult for an online retailer to operate without supporting credit and debit cards due to their widespread use. Increased security measures include the use of the card verification number (CVN). It detects fraud by comparing the verification number printed on the signature strip on the back of the card with the information on file with the cardholder's issuing bank. Also, online merchants have to comply with stringent rules stipulated by the credit and debit card issuers (Visa and MasterCard); this means that merchants must have security protocols and procedures in place to ensure transactions are more secure. This can also include having a certificate from an authorised certification authority (CA) that provides Public Key Infrastructure (PKI) for securing credit and debit card transactions.

American Express, Visa and MasterCard credit payment card security rely on the physical security of the plastic card as well as the privacy of the credit card number. Therefore, the person other than the card owner should not access the card or its number, to avoid security being potentially compromised. It is now common practice to only ship to confirmed addresses as a security measure to minimise fraudulent purchases. Some merchants will accept a credit card number for in-store purchases, whereupon access to the number allows easy fraud, but many require the card itself to be present and require a signature (for magnetic stripe cards).

A lost or stolen card should be cancelled, and if this is done quickly, will greatly limit the fraud. Banks can require a cardholder's security PIN to be entered for in-person purchases with the card.

The goal of credit card companies is to reduce fraud to manageable levels. This implies that fraud prevention measures will be used only if their cost is lower than the potential gains from fraud reduction, whereas high-cost low-return measures will not be used.

Internet fraud may be by claiming a chargeback that is not justified ("friendly fraud") or carried out by the use of credit card information which can be stolen in many ways, the simplest being copying information from retailers, either online or offline. Despite efforts to improve security for remote purchases using credit cards, security breaches are usually the result of poor practice by merchants. For example, a website that safely uses TLS to encrypt card data from a client may then e-mail the data, unencrypted, from the webserver to the merchant or the merchant may store unencrypted details in a way that allows them to be accessed over the Internet or by a rogue employee; unencrypted card details are always a security risk. Even encrypted data may be cracked.

Controlled payment numbers (also known as virtual credit cards or disposable credit cards) are another option for protecting against credit card fraud where the presentation of a physical card is not required, as in telephone and online purchasing. These are one-time use numbers that function as a payment card and are linked to the user's real account, but do not reveal details, and cannot be used for subsequent unauthorised transactions. They can be valid for a relatively short time and limited to the actual amount of the purchase or a limit set by the use

The Joint Committee of the European Supervisory Authorities has identified IT-related operational risks as key risks to the stability of the European financial system.

The key message for firms is that the impact of technology on the financial sector is increasingly a central focus for regulators. The firms should look at their business models, strategies and structure to ensure they can identify and manage the root causes of technological risk.

4.3.5 Safety Rules, When Using the Card

Rule number 1. Never write down the PIN code on a plastic card.
Rule number 2. Block the card or financial phone number in case of theft or loss.
Rule number 3. Warn the bank if you intend to use the card abroad.

ATM use:

Rule number 4. Use the card at a reliable ATM, while:
• When entering the PIN code, cover the keyboard with your hand;
• Use the withdrawal service without a card.
• Rule number 5. In the case of payment in supermarkets:
• Use contactless payment PayPass, Google Pay, Apple Pay;
• Do not hand the card into the hands of the cashier in the calculations.
Rule No. 6. If significant expenses are planned abroad, the bank recommends issuing a smart card, which will be replenished for expenses.

4.3.6 Internet Banking Services and Rules

The bank services market has high competition. To be able to survive and grow banks are going for the latest technologies that can help in developing more flexible structures that can respond quickly to the dynamics of a fast-changing market scenario.

The middle and late 1990s were the top of financial reforms, deregulation globalisation coupled with the rapid revolution in communication technologies and evolution of the novel concept of convergence of communication technologies, Internet, mobile/cell phones, etc. Technology has continuously played an important role in the working of banking institutions and the services provided by them.

Information Technology enables sophisticated product development, better market infrastructure, implementation of reliable techniques for control of risks and helps the financial intermediaries to reach geographically distant markets. The Internet has significantly influenced the delivery channels of banks, and it emerged as an important medium for the delivery of banking products and services.

The customers can view the accounts, get account statements, transfer funds, and purchase goods and services online. The smart cards, i.e. cards with microprocessor chips have added a new dimension to the scenario. With the introduction of "Cyber Cash", the exchange of cash takes place entirely through "Cyber-books". Collection of utility and regular bills has become easy. The upgradeability and flexibility of Internet technology gave opportunities for the banks to reach out to their customers. The shift from traditional banking to e-banking is changing customers' expectations.

E-banking made its debut in the United Kingdom and the United States in the 1920s. It became prominently popular during 1960, through electronic funds transfer and credit cards. The concept of web-based banking came into existence in Europe and the United States at the beginning of 1980.

The electronics revolution has made it possible to provide ease and flexibility in banking operations to the benefit of the customer. E-banking has made the customer say goodbye to huge account registers and large paper bank accounts. The e-banks, which may be called easy banks, offer the following services to their customers:

- Credit Cards/Debit Cards
- ATM
- Electronic Funds Transfer (EFT)
- Accounts
- Mobile Banking
- Telephone Banking
- Internet Banking

Internet banking is the general name for the technology of a bank's business day that allows access and operations on accounts and at any time and from any computer with Internet access. Modern Internet banking models are based on the interaction through the bank's website, through an intermediary web-server, via e-mail banking. There is no need to install the client part of the system software because a browser is used to perform operations.

There are two levels of interaction between the bank and the client:

1. Informational
   - Viewing the current account balance
   - Account statements
   - Provision of information on banking products (deposits, loans, etc.)
   - Applications for opening deposits, obtaining loans, bank cards, etc.
2. Transactional (or settlement)
   - Internal transfers to bank accounts
   - Transfers to accounts in other banks

- Money conversion
- Sending financial payment documents
- Paying a loan, utility bills
- Converting currency
- Opening deposits
- Operations with securities
- Additional services, etc.

Internet banking allows a client to work with any bank documents without visiting a bank, to carry out transactions with payments in any world currencies and makes it possible to track the status of an account in any part of the world.

A large number of banks provide Internet banking services.

Advantages of the Internet banking system are the following:

For a client of a credit institution:

- Ability to open an account in any bank and ability to simultaneously manage different accounts in different banks
- Managing funds in real time and most importantly, 24 hours a day, 7 days a week
- Competitiveness of services provided through the Internet banking system
- Access to the account from any computer from anywhere in the world that has Internet access
- Cash withdrawal from any branch/ATM
- Online purchase of goods and services including online payment for the same
- Tracking operations with plastic cards as well as transferring money and using the services of Internet shops
- Convenience acts as a tremendous psychological benefit all the time

For a credit institution:

- An effective tool of promotion of various schemes of the bank, a marketing tool indeed
- The ability of a credit institution to work 24 hours and real-time operations
- Inter-branch communication is immediate thereby reducing chances of fraud and misappropriation
- The innovative scheme addresses competition and present the bank as technology-driven in the banking sector market
- Wider customer base reach
- Maintenance of the Internet banking system is cheaper than maintaining an extensive network of branches and highly qualified personnel
- There is no need to work with cash
- Offers more competitive services and attractive prices
- Automatic tracking of risks arising from transactions with customers

- Reduces customer visits to the branch and thereby human intervention
- Integrated customer data paves way for individualised services

Banks have three goals developing these technologies:

- Maintain and expand own market share in the services
- Reduce operating costs
- Get new sources of income

The Internet banking system is recognised as promising and there is no doubt about its need, this is only a matter of time.

4.3.7 INTERNET BANKING VULNERABILITIES AND SECURITY

The system of interbank electronic payments is being improved and developed. The degree of data security increases and the reliability of the system increases, cryptography software systems are replaced by hardware protection. Means of cross-protection of electronic payments are created and implemented the application of an "electronic signature" on a document.

However, the development of the Internet and consumer-friendly electronic technologies, as well as the provision by the banks of new types of services on a competitive basis, is associated not only with benefits but also with risks. Risks must be considered in conjunction with the factors since only knowing the information on these factors can be created as an advanced risk management system. The division into financial factors and factors of non-financial risks makes it possible to assess the state of the system from two sides: internal – it depends entirely on the activities of participants in the payment system, and external, which does not depend on the behaviour of counterparties of the payment system. This is extremely important for developing methods and mechanisms for risk management.

The risks of payment systems and banking risks are similar to each other and have both financial and non-financial nature. Financial risks should be associated with the purchasing power of money and with the investment of capital. This approach leads to the appropriateness of classifying the liquidity risk and inflation risk as a financial category. Therefore, credit risk, risk of liquidity and systemic risk have financial nature. The legal risk and operational risk are non-financial.

Credit risk is the risk when the participant in an operation who must pay out the funds will not be able to settle its obligations on time due to his full or partial insolvency.

The risk of liquidity shortage arises from the risk that the transaction participant or intermediary who must pay the funds may face difficulties in covering his negative position and failing to fully meet their obligations on time.

Systemic risk – this type of risk is determined by the fact that when one participant in the system fails to timely settle the obligations, the consequence of this may be a failure to fulfil obligations by other participants, thus triggering a chain reaction, sometimes also called the "domino effect."

Legal risk – the non-financial risks associated with the payment system and includes an imperfect legal framework, forgery of financial documents, theft, fraud and errors.

Operational risk arises from the possibility of violations of data processing systems since the activity of the centralised payment systems increasingly depends on the security, safety and security of the operation of data processing and transmission systems. The increase in automation of operations leads to increased dependence on technology support and a higher degree of vulnerability in cases of technical violations.

When making mutual settlements in payment systems, two systems are distinguished: gross and on a pure basis. Risks in the net settlement system: credit risk; hidden costs; the concentration of demand for funds at the end of the payment-processing cycle increases the liquidity risk.

Risks in gross settlement systems: liquidity risk; risk of blocking system; credit risk.

The risks associated with Internet banking, with varying degrees of impact include credit, interest, stock, currency, operational, strategic, reputation, legal, as well as liquidity risk, phishing, attacks from all kinds of "computer scammers."

In the case of Internet phishing attacks, the client can be misled about the fact that he is dealing with a bank known to him. Phishing uses specific false e-mail messages simulating a message from a credit institution to mislead customers of credit institutions and, at the very least, to entice their personal registration data, through which access to their accounts and financial resources is made. According to statistics, about 5% of clients come across this.

Risk "associated with the use of third-party technology." These risks arise when the party with whom the web connection is established may adversely affect the customers of the credit institution. The client may misinterpret the received information in hyperlinks as bank products or services.

Therefore, the list of the risk management areas includes (Melnyk, Brukhanova 2010; Donlea 2015; Saraswat 2015; Jaffe, Tippins, Wesley 2000):

- Asset risk relating to returns
- Asset liquidity risks
- Inadequate pricing
- Regulatory risks
- Reputation risks
- Operational risks
- Strategic risks
- Marketing risks

The description of the risk management process is (https://www.metastock.com/):

- Identify and analyse loss exposure
- Measure potential loss exposure
- Select a mitigation technique
- Implement the chosen technique
- Monitor and make necessary changes

It is better to work with your own account only from a home PC or personal device when using the Internet banking service. Even a work terminal is a potential source of data leakage. Work in the system requires certain computer security settings, including anti-virus and anti-spyware programs. The payment made should be displayed by the Internet banking system with a delay of no more than an hour. Otherwise, the user should call the bank.

Rules, safety when using online banking services are the following:

Rule 1. Never provide information about your cards to third parties, even if they contact you on behalf of the bank.

Rule 2. Set a password. Modern phones and tablets allow restricting access to the device with a password, PIN, graphic key, etc.

Rule 3. Do not pass the smartphone to strangers. If your phone or tablet falls into the hands of an attacker, he will be able to use your SMS banking, receive one-time passwords to log into your Internet bank account and confirm payments.

Rule 4. Protect your smartphone and tablet from viruses. In order not to infect your phone with viruses:

- Do not hack into the operating system of your smartphone and do not conduct banking operations via the Internet on a device with a broken operating system
- Do not visit unfamiliar sites
- Do not click on suspicious links
- Install software only from trusted sources
- When installing applications from the App Store or Play Market, carefully read the permissions that applications request;
- Make sure that anti-virus software is installed and updated on mobile phones on time.

Rule 5. When selling goods on the Internet, to receive a transfer to the card for the sale of goods, enter only the card number.

The buyer's requirements to provide other data (CVV2 code, card validity period, balance or card type) for transferring money to the seller's card should be suspicious.

Rule number 6. Do not leave your financial phone number on the Internet.

For those doing business, the bank recommends having a separate contract phone number for negotiations with counterparties.

Do not use the financial number when contacting the public. This can lead to the theft of the SIM card by scammers through re-issuance in the offices of the mobile operator.

Rule 7. When making purchases over the Internet from unknown persons, the bank recommends the use of cash on delivery.

Rule 8. When paying at verified sites of Internet giants, use an Internet card in your calculations.

4.3.8 DIGITAL AND VIRTUAL MONEY SYSTEM IS AN ALTERNATIVE TO C2C AND D2C MODELS

Money performs five basic functions: measures of value, means of circulation, means of payment, means of accumulating value and world money. They perform each of these functions in one of the forms. For example, money circulation is the movement of money in cash and non-cash form during servicing the circulation of goods and services.

Cash is functions as means of payment and accumulation.

Non-cash money exists as a record on accounts in credit and financial institutions. Long time, these records were mainly kept on paper and were directly perceived and processed by humans. If the information is stored not on paper but the computer and is also perceived and processed by electronic devices, this is the so-called EM.

Most of the traditional money supply is bank money held on computers. This is also considered digital currency. One could argue that our increasingly cashless society means that all currencies are becoming digital, but they are not presented to us as such (Chaum, 1982).

In conclusion, we summarise the classification of EM systems. Nowadays, monetary systems can be generalised into two large groups: centralised and decentralised.

The centralised EM is under the control of banks and the government. In the centralised money system, currency can be exchanged electronically using debit and credit cards. These types of money systems are the following: Smart Cards, Magnetic Plastic Cards, EM and Wallets, Digital Currency and Mobile Digital Wallets. All these tools are electronic carriers of financial information.

Decentralised monetary systems are dependent on the behaviour of the currency market and characterised by high exchange rate volatility. These money systems are digital and represent Virtual Currencies, Cryptocurrency and Cryptocurrency Wallets.

Virtual currency is a type of decentralised digital currency that is only available in electronic form. It is stored and transacted only through designated software, mobile or computer applications, or through dedicated digital wallets, and the transactions occur over the Internet through secure, dedicated networks. Unlike fiat currency, virtual currency is not issued by a bank. This lack of regulation means virtual currencies are susceptible to price swings (Table 4.4).

4.3.9 DECENTRALISED ELECTRONIC MONEY SYSTEMS

According to the Bank for International Settlements' November 2015 "Digital currencies" report, it is an asset represented in digital form and having some monetary characteristics (https://www.fujitsu.com/es/about/resources/case-studies/mobipay_en.html). Digital currency can be denominated to a sovereign currency and issued by the issuer responsible to redeem digital money for cash. In that case, digital currency represents EM. Digital currency denominated in its units of value or with decentralised or automatic issuance will be considered as a virtual currency.

Digital currency is a type of currency available in digital form (in contrast to physicals, such as banknotes and coins). It exhibits properties similar to physical

TABLE 4.4

Centralised and Decentralised Electronic Money Systems

Centralised Money Systems			Decentralised Money Systems	
Electronic Money/ Wallets	Smart/Magnetic Plastic Cards	Digital Currency	Virtual Currencies/ Cryptocurrency	Cryptocurrency Wallets
PayPal	Visa	EasyPay	Bitcoin and its	bitcoin wallet
Google Pay	Mastercard	QIWI	forks	eCash
WebMoney	Payoneer Mondex	RBK	Etc…	
Apple Pay	Octopus	Money		
Microsoft Wallet	Chipknip			
Samsung Pay				
Alipay				
Mobikwik				
Paytm				
Etc…				

Source: Own work.

currencies but can allow for instantaneous transactions and borderless transfer-of-ownership. Examples include virtual currencies and cryptocurrencies (https://www.bis.org/cpmi/publ/d137.pdf) and central bank-issued money accounted for in a computer database (including digital base money). Like traditional money, these currencies may be used to buy physical goods and services but may also be restricted to certain communities such as for use inside an online game or social network (Al-Laham, Al-Tarawneh, Abdallat (2009).

Digital currency is a money balance recorded electronically on a stored-value card or other devices. Digital money is exchanged using technologies such as smartphones, credit cards and the Internet.

Digital money can either be centralised, and controlled over the money supply, or decentralised, where the control over the money supply can come from various sources.

4.3.10 DIFFERENCE BETWEEN DIGITAL, VIRTUAL AND CRYPTOCURRENCIES

Digital currency is the overall superset that includes virtual currency, which in turn includes cryptocurrencies. Compared to virtual currency, a digital currency covers a larger group that represents monetary assets in digital form.

Digital currency can be regulated or unregulated. In the former case, it can be denominated to a sovereign currency – i.e. a country's central bank can issue a digital form of its fiat currency notes. On the other hand, a virtual currency often remains unregulated and hence constitutes a type of digital currency.

Cryptocurrencies such as BTC and Ethereum (ETH) are considered a part of the virtual currency group. A cryptocurrency uses cryptography technology that keeps the transactions secure and authentic and helps to manage and control the creation of new currency units. Such cryptocurrencies exist and are transacted over dedicated

blockchain-based networks that are open to the common public (https://thenextweb.
com/hardfork/2019/02/19/the-differences-between-cryptocurrencies-virtual-and-
digital-currencies/; https://www.investopedia.com/terms/v/virtual-currency.asp).

4.3.11 VIRTUAL CURRENCY

According to the European Central Bank's 2015 "Virtual currency schemes – a further analysis" report, virtual currency is a digital representation of value, not issued
by a central bank, credit institution or e-money institution, which, in some circumstances, can be used as an alternative to money (https://www.ecb.europa.eu/pub/pdf/
other/virtualcurrencyschemes201210en.pdf). The virtual currency was defined as a
type of unregulated, digital money, which is issued and usually controlled by its
developers, and used and accepted among the members of a specific virtual community (https://www.fdic.gov/news/news/financial/2009/fil09066.pdf). Virtual currencies are mostly used for P2P payments and are finding increasing use for the
purchase of goods and services.

The US Department of Treasury in 2013 defined it more tersely as "a medium of
exchange that operates like a currency in some environments but does not have all the
attributes of real currency" (https://www.treasury.gov/about/organizational-struc-
ture/ig/Audit%20Reports%20and%20Testimonies/OIG-16-006.pdf). The key attribute a virtual currency does not have according to these definitions is the status as a
legal tender.

All virtual currencies are digital, and they exist online only. But not all digital currencies are virtual because they exist outside a specific virtual environment.

Virtual Currency may be represented in terms of tokens and maybe unregulated
without a legal tender such as coins or banknotes. For example, all FarmVille players
have access to the in-game virtual currency coins with which they can purchase items
for their farm. Virtual currency though is only valid within the specified community.
You cannot take your FarmVille coins and use them to buy a hamburger from
McDonald's, therefore, it has no real-world value.

Virtual currency is currency held within the blockchain network that is not controlled by a centralised banking authority.

Virtual currency is different from digital currency since the digital currency is
simply currency issued by a bank in digital form.

Virtual currency is unregulated and therefore experiences dramatic price movements since the only real force behind trading is consumer sentiment.

4.3.12 CRYPTOCURRENCY

A cryptocurrency is a type of digital asset that relies on cryptography for chain-
ing together digital signatures of asset transfers, P2Pnetworking and decentralisation. In some cases, a proof-of-work or proof-of-stake scheme is used to
create and manage the currency. http://theconversation.com/from-your-wallet-
to-google-wallet-your-digital-payment-options-14540

https://web.archive.org/web/20131224084601/http:/motherboard.vice.com/blog/
beyond-bitcoin-a-guide-to-the-most-promising-cryptocurrencies

https://eur-lex.europa.eu/legal-content/en/ALL/?uri=CELEX:32009L0110
https://www.ecb.europa.eu/pub/pdf/other/virtualcurrencyschemes201210en.pdf
Cryptocurrencies allow EM systems to be decentralised. The first and most popular system is BTC, a P2Pelectronic monetary system based on cryptography.

As such, BTC is a digital currency but also a type of virtual currency. BTC and its alternatives are based on cryptographic algorithms, so these kinds of virtual currencies are also called cryptocurrencies.

4.3.13 Types of Cryptocurrencies and Their Classification

The list of cryptocurrencies can be divided into five parts:

1. Recognised cryptocurrency
2. Cryptocurrency with a large market share
3. Alternative cryptocurrencies (mainly Forks)
4. Forkom (with minimal modifications)
5. Clones. They have no prospects. They differ from the fork in the absence of innovations.

The most popular cryptocurrencies in the world in 2021 were:

- Bitcoin (BTC)
- Ethereum (ETH)
- Solana (SOL)
- Cardano (ADA)
- Dogecoin (DOGE)
- Yearn.finance (YFI)
- Polygon (MATIC)

Unfortunately, now there are more and more speculative cryptocurrencies. This is because only a few dozen people possess 80% of cryptocurrencies.

Recognised cryptocurrencies

BTC, Bitcoin – The first successful cryptocurrency. It is highly popular; however, more than 95% of BTC is concentrated in an extremely narrow circle of people. The problem is also by the fact that the generation of BTCs is possible on special equipment, which leads to an extremely uneven distribution of coins. This not only increases the risk of speculation but also reduces the reliability of the network.

A decentralised P2Pnetwork regulates transactions and BTC emissions. BTC uses a single database distributed across the network, including in a decentralised P2Pnetwork that uses an electronic digital signature and is supported by a proof-of-work protocol to ensure the security and legitimacy of the funds put into circulation.

Even though formally for the use of BTC does not need the identification of the user, the currency is not completely anonymous. All information about BTC transactions is stored in a chain of blocks called a blockchain. Each block contains a header and a list of transactions. The header consists of several properties, among which is the hash of the previous block. Thus, the entire blockchain stores all transactions for the entire time BTC runs.

In the current versions of the BTC programme, the chain of file blocks is completed by every client, which makes the system completely decentralised. Data is not encrypted in any way and anyone can manually track all transactions. There is a special site – Bitcoin Block Explorer where users can easily see all the information about the blocks and transactions.

The total amount of money at the entrance of the transaction is always equal to the total amount at the output. The stability of the system is based on the number of users who have an official client running. Until they are the majority, nothing threatens the BTC network.

The smallest amount of BTC is a satoshi, named after Satoshi Nakamoto, BTC's creator. Satoshi is representing 0.00000001 BTC, 100 millionths of a BTC (Mick 2011). If necessary, the protocol and the corresponding software can be changed to work with smaller quantities.

Mining is one of the ways to get electronic coins. At first glance, this is a cost-free method. To start receiving EM with the help of mining, you must be the owner of computer equipment, which has good computing power. It is possible to begin mining only by having established the necessary programme. Its meaning is to solve algorithms that help to find the required number. In the terminology of digital currency, this is called "solve the block." The decision of each block helps to release a certain number of coins.

Mining is the solution to some complex crypto problem, which is solved by the method of a full search. Every year, the algorithm for getting BTCs becomes more complicated to limit the annual emission of cryptocurrency and prevent inflation.

The first set of blockchains created 50 BTCs. In the following, each created block gave 25. A new block of chains is created approximately every 10 minutes. The system was designed so that the maximum number of new BTCs created at the beginning and then reduce their number. It is assumed that the production process will end in 2140 with 21 million. Now, about 15 million BTC have been produced or about 70% of all coins.

The initial value of the virtual currency was about 0.05 $. The maximum cost at the peak was above $1100, but later it dropped to $200. On 2 March 2017, the price of one BTC surpassed the spot price of an ounce of gold for the first time.

It can be concluded that investing in the purchase of BTCs for profit is associated with greater risks of losing money. But there is one assumption they will someday become a scarce commodity because of limited emission. This means that prices will be higher than current ones.

BTCs can also be received or exchanged in the following ways:

• by payment for services and goods;
• by the purchase on the cryptocurrency exchange;
• by exchange BTC between individuals on cryptocurrency exchanges;
• by exchange BTC through WebMoney (WM), Yandex Money, Kiwi, banks, Visa or MasterCard.

One alternative way to get BTC is to buy them on the cryptocurrency Exchange. Such resources help to exchange real money for digital. For example, anybody can easily replenish their account using the e-Payments payment system or bank transfer Digital Securities Exchange or DSX – dsx.uk.

There are two options for storing BTC:

Offline wallet – installed and created on the computer and of course, it's encrypted to avoid hacking. However, there are disadvantages here. If you forget the password for entering the purse or the hard drive will fly on the computer – you will forever lose access to your funds.

Online wallet – all data is stored on the server. If the server is broken, then all the information will be broken. Specificity is similar to the usual KIWI-wallets, WM or Internet banking.

LTC, Litecoin – a successful fork, which is the main backup cryptocurrency. It has a different coin generation algorithm than BTC, which makes it resistant to generation. This makes the currency more popular and evenly distributed among the population.

Litecoin, originally based on the BTC protocol, intended to improve upon its alleged inefficiencies. LTC Litecoin is a successful fork and the main reserve cryptocurrency. It has a good chance to become the currency number one. Litecoin is different from the BTC algorithm for coin generation. This makes it resistant to generation on ASIC, which makes the currency more popular and more evenly distributed among the population. Litecoin is more convenient than BTC for payment transactions because it requires less confirmation from the network (2.5 minutes against 10 minutes in BTC). 31% of all coins were mined by the beginning of 2014. Cryptocurrency with a large market share carries original ideas but do not have universal recognition.

Dogecoin, a clone Litecoin system, is created to reach broader demographics. Dogecoin – actually is one of the five largest cryptocurrencies. Currency is a meme that has appeared exclusively for fun and in the future, the next 2 years can be completely replaced by something more interesting.

ETH is the second most popular cryptocurrency in the world after Bitcoin. ETH runs on a platform of the same name based on blockchain technology. The distributed nature of blockchain technology makes the Ethereum platform secure, and that security enables ETH to accrue value. The Ethereum platform was launched in 2015 by Buterin and Joe Lubin.

Some other samples of cryptocurrency:

- Ripple monetary system – a monetary system based on trust networks (Martin, 2018).
- NXT – conceived as a flexible platform to build applications and financial services around.
- Monero – an open-source cryptocurrency created in April 2014 that focuses on privacy, decentralisation and scalability.

There are many different cryptocurrencies, but this list is constantly increasing. Some currencies appear and disappear, but some work for a long time and are known to us now.

4.3.14 THE ADVANTAGES OF CRYPTOCURRENCY

First, fiat payment-processing companies of today utilise centralised databases to store information related to debit and credit card purchases. However, many large-scale hacks of centralised databases put consumer privacy at great risk.

Blockchain can solve this issue by creating greater data security, making cryptocurrency payments safer for users. If cryptocurrency is to be the future of electronic cash, clearly it must be secure.

1. The most basic thing that can be the pluses is that crypto money is only on the owner computer in an electronic wallet and no one can under any circumstances do anything with them.
2. No control by banks or the state.
3. Open-source cryptocurrency. BTC has the same algorithms that are used in Internet banking. The only difference with Internet banking is the disclosure of information about end users. On the BTC network, all transaction information is shared, but there is no access to the personal information of wallet owners.
4. Cryptocurrency is a P2Pnetwork. There is no main server responsible for all operations in such networks.
5. Unlimited possibilities of transactions – each of the owners of the wallet can pay anyone, anywhere, for anything. Transactions cannot be monitored or prohibited.
6. The commission in this system is lower than in any other. The interest goes to the wallets of miners.

4.3.15 VULNERABILITIES

1. Since cryptocurrency is stored only on a computer, there is a danger of losing all accumulations irretrievably.
2. Significant course volatility and does happen often, leading to net losses.
3. The growth of the BTC exchange rate in some periods has exponential growth and is inflated as a "bubble." Therefore, BTC attracts many speculators who want to make money on the volatility of the exchange rate.
4. Investments in cryptocurrency are associated with great risks and should be considered in the medium and long term.
5. One of the biggest issues that consumers face is that, although online commerce creates possibilities for transactions across borders, there are usually high fees for money conversions.

However, cryptocurrencies can be used globally by online retailers without having to pay fees for sending/receiving funds.

4.3.16 RISKS OF THE CRYPTOCURRENCY MARKET

In the BTC system, it is impossible to appeal and/or cancel transactions, even if it is proved that the owner did not know about them and did not want to conduct them. If the user stole the access password and the BTC s are transferred to another address, the victim will not be able to find out who did this since the recipient's address does not contain identification information (M. Reshevsky, 2011). There is also no mechanism to guarantee a refund if payment is made, but the service or the goods are not received. This is used by scammers. The means of cryptographic protection, which protect cryptocurrency systems, have not yet been tested by time, wide circulation and a hassle-free history. Therefore, safety is not confirmed.

The main BTC exchange, Bitfinex, was hacked and almost 120,000 BTC (about $ 60 million) was stolen in 2016. In 2011, an error was detected in the processing of unconfirmed transactions in the accounting systems of many exchange services, which allowed the crediting of funds without transmission of BTCs (Pagliery 2014). Ignoring this problem led to the bankruptcy of Mt.Gox. Other burglaries of exchange sites and pools of joint extraction were also recorded. At the end of 2013, 96,000 BTCs belonging to users were stolen from the transit accounts of the Sheep Marketplace (Edwards 2013).

In April 2014, Kaspersky Lab reported on the growth of virus attacks aimed at stealing BTCs, including through theft of files with keys. Many countries have not yet decided on their unambiguous attitude to EM. Central banks of most countries are very wary of the development of EM, fearing uncontrolled emissions, the use of electronic payment systems for money laundering and other possible abuses. If we talk about how countries are looking at the cryptocurrency, then we can say that the countries were divided into three camps:

On those who do not approve of the use of the cryptocurrency, as China and Russia did.

Those who created a legal framework that allows the use of the cryptocurrency, along with conventional (the United States, Israel and the UAE).

The use of BTC by criminals has attracted the attention of financial regulators, legislative bodies, law enforcement and the media. The FBI prepared an intelligence assessment, the SEC has issued a pointed warning about investment schemes using virtual currencies and the US Senate held a hearing on virtual currencies in November 2013.

Various potential attacks on the BTC network and its use as a payment system, real or theoretical, have been considered. The BTC protocol includes several features that protect it against some of those attacks, such as unauthorised spending, double spending, forging BTCs and tampering with the blockchain.

Unauthorised spending is mitigated by BTC's implementation of public–private key cryptography. For example, when Alice sends a BTC to Bob, Bob becomes the new owner of the BTC. Eve observing the transaction might want to spend the BTC Bob just received, but she cannot sign the transaction without the knowledge of Bob's private key.

A specific problem that an Internet payment system must solve is double-spending, whereby a user pays the same coin to two or more different recipients. An example of such a problem would be if Eve sent a BTC to Alice and later sent the same BTC to Bob. The BTC network guards against double-spending by recording all BTC transfers in a ledger (the blockchain) that is visible to all users, and ensuring for all transferred BTCs that they haven't been previously spent. Other attacks, such as theft of private keys, require due care by users.

4.3.17 RACE ATTACK

By the rules, the network accepts only one of the transactions. If Alice offers to pay Bob a BTC in exchange for goods and signs a corresponding transaction, it is still possible that she also creates a different transaction at the same time sending the same BTC to Eve. This is called a race attack since there is a race in which the transaction will be accepted first. Bob can reduce the risk of a race attack stipulating that she will not deliver the goods until Alice's payment to Bob appears in the blockchain (Bonadonna 2013).

Another variant race attack (Finney attack) requires the participation of a miner. Instead of sending both payment requests (to pay Bob and Eve with the same coins) to the network, Alice issues only Eve's payment request to the network, while the miner tries to mine a block that includes the payment to Bob instead of Eve. There is a positive probability that the rogue miner will succeed before the network, and the payment to Bob will be rejected. As with the plain race attack, Bob can reduce the risk of a Finney attack by waiting for the payment to be included in the blockchain (Karame, Androulaki, Capkun 2012).

4.3.18 HISTORY MODIFICATION

Ideally, merchants and services that receive payment in BTC should wait for at least one confirmation of that transaction to be distributed over the network, before assuming that the payment was done. The more confirmations, the more difficult it is for an attacker to successfully reverse the transaction in a blockchain. If the attacker is able to gain control of more than 50 per cent of the hashing power then he would be able to prevent new transactions from gaining confirmations, allowing him to halt payments between some or all users. The attacker would also be able to reverse transactions that were completed while they were in control of the network, meaning they could double-spend coins. This case is called a 51% attack. 51% attack refers to an attack on a blockchain if the attacker controls more than half the total network power, in which case it is called a 51% attack (Casey, Vigna 2014).

4.3.19 DEANONYMISATION OF CLIENTS

Deanonymisation is a strategy in data mining in which anonymous data is cross-referenced with other sources of data to re-identify the anonymous data source (Biryukov, Khovratovich, Pustogarov, 2014).

4.3.20 DATA IN THE BLOCKCHAIN

While any digital file can be stored on the blockchain, the larger the size of a transaction, the greater any associated fees become. The growth of BTC in some periods has exponential growth, but in simple language: a «bubble» inflates time, on which you can make good money. Therefore, now BTC attracts many investors and speculators who want to earn money for the volatility of the course in the short term. *The Washington Post* pointed out that the observed cycles of appreciation and depreciation do not correspond to the definition of a speculative bubble (Lee 2013). Therefore, investments in cryptocurrency are associated with greater risks and should be considered in the medium and long term.

Thus, it is possible, to sum up, all the risks of cryptocurrency:

- lack of legal regulation
- priority orientation of legislation to the banking sector in the field of payment systems
- there is a possibility of irrevocable loss of EM in the event of physical destruction of the computer or data carrier on which they were stored
- impossibility to identify the amount and type of money without special electronic devices
- impossibility of direct transfer of a part of the money from one payer to another
- security is not confirmed because the means of cryptographic protection have not passed operational tests
- theft of EM is possible, through innovative methods
- a large number of competing and weakly customer-oriented technologies and the lack of standards
- significant fluctuations in the rate of the cryptocurrency
- cryptocurrency investment is associated with greater risks and should be considered in the medium and long term

It's hard to say which way is true. Free circulation of digital money in the country can easily kill the local currency, but they are also capable of increasing the competitiveness of the country's economy. Thus, they allow making direct investments without the need for their double-conversion into local currency at the entrance and exit. If the banks of developed countries start issuing cheap loans in the cryptocurrency to companies from other countries, it will be both the death of local currency and the development of the local economy.

Cryptocurrency is interesting because it does not belong to a specific person or regulator, and there is no single centre for emissions and supervision. Everything that happens inside the system is the actions of the users themselves and the direct owners of digital money.

Cryptocurrency is an alternative to classical money, with some financial imbalances in the world. American colleges and universities offer their students to attend courses on cryptocurrency, and BTC got into the top technological trends in 2016 and 2017.

4.3.21 Security

While fiat payment processors and businesses often have security flaws that lead to the loss of user funds and other issues, these incidents are not highlighted as much as large-scale cryptocurrency hacks.

As we have seen, even the most secure cryptocurrency wallets can be hacked. With increased security designs in blockchain and education campaigns on how users can keep funds safe, more people will become confident in using crypto for P2P payments.

However, SWIFT does not see blockchain technology as a solution to the problem of delays in international bank payments. According to representatives of the system, blockchain not only violates many regulatory requirements but also unable to ensure the confidentiality of such operations.

4.4 PAYMENT SYSTEMS WORLDWIDE: RISKS, THREATS AND DATA PROTECTION

National systems for interbank operations exist in all major world countries. The United States uses the Fedwire Federal Reserve Banking Network as well as the interbank payment networks CHIPS. The interbank settlements in the EU countries are based on the TARGET system. CHAPS (Clearing Houses Automated Payment System) and BACS (Bankers Automated Clearing Services) are used in the United Kingdom.

4.4.1 Fedwire Is the US Federal Reserve Banking Network

Fedwire (formerly known as the Federal Reserve Wire Network) is a real-time gross settlement funds transfer system owned and operated by the US Federal Reserve System (FRS). This system is used to transfer funds between 6,000 banks, combined in 12 reserve districts with 12 central regional banks.

Central regional banks and some other large banks that are members of the Fedwire have their servers operating online. Smaller banks have Fedwire system terminals. The third group of banks – the so-called "independent" members of the Fedwire system, operate offline and carry out interbank operations on telephone lines connected to them or transmit information directly through another Federal bank (http:/www.fededirectory.frb.org/download.cfm).

Transfers can only be initiated by the sending bank once they receive the proper wiring instructions from the receiving bank. These instructions include the receiving bank's routing number, account number, name and dollar amount being transferred. This information is submitted to the Fed via the Fedwire system. Once the instructions are received and processed, the Fed will debit the funds from the sending bank's reserve account and credit the receiving bank's account. Wire transfers sent via Fedwire are completed on the same day while some are completed instantly (https://www.americanexpress.com/us/foreign-exchange/articles/fedwire-transfers/).

In conjunction with Clearing House Interbank Payments System (CHIPS), operated by The Clearing House Payments Company, a private company, Fedwire is the primary US network for large-value or time-critical domestic and international payments, and it is designed to be highly resilient. CHIPS is subject to heightened regulatory scrutiny by the Federal Reserve Board (http://www.federalreserve.gov/generalinfo/faq/faqbog.htm).

The Fedwire system has grown since its inception, seeing growth in both the number of transfers and total transaction dollar value of about 79% and 207%, respectively, between 1996 and 2016. In 2016, roughly 148.1 million transfers were valued at $766.7 trillion dollars (http://www.federalreserve.gov/generalinfo/faq/faqbog.htm https://www.federalreserve.gov/paymentsystems/fedfunds_ann.htm).

4.4.2 CHIPS (CLEARING HOUSE INTERBANK PAYMENT SYSTEM)

The Clearing House Interbank Payments System (CHIPS) telecommunication system was created in 1970 to replace the paper check settlement system with an electronic settlement system between the New York Bank and foreign customers. All banks are divided into three groups: main banks, settlement banks and banks participants in the CHIPS system. In total, 140 banks are connected to the system, and it works with approximately 10,000 accounts. The CHIPS system works offline. The accumulation and subsequent sending of messages are provided while maintaining data integrity in the central database.

The CHIPS is the primary clearinghouse in the United States for large banking transactions. As of 2015, CHIPS settles over 250,000 trades per day, valued over $1.5 trillion in both domestic and cross-border transactions. CHIPS and the Fedwire funds service used by the Federal Reserve Bank combine to constitute the primary network in the United States for both domestic and foreign large transactions denominated in US dollars. Currently, Fedwire and CHIPS systems serve up to 90% of US interbank domestic payments.

There are two steps to processing funds transfers in CHIPS: clearing and settlement. The clearing is the transfer and confirmation of information between the sending financial institution and receiving financial institution. The settlement is the actual transfer of funds between the payer's financial institution and the payee's financial institution. Settlement discharges the obligation of the payer financial institution to the payee financial institution concerning the payment order. The final settlement is irrevocable and unconditional. That system's rules and applicable law determine the finality of the payment.

The Clearing House Interbank Payments System Fedwire is cheaper than the Fedwire service. But it's not as fast as Fedwire, and the dollar amounts required to use this service are lower. CHIPS is the main clearinghouse for large transactions; the average transaction that uses CHIPS is over $3,000,000.

CHIPS acts on a netting basis. Therefore, payments between parties are netted against each other instead of the full dollar value of both trades being sent. From 9 a.m. to 5 p.m. ET banks send and receive payments. During that time, CHIPS nets and releases payments. From 5 p.m. until 5:15 p.m., the CHIPS system eliminates credit limits, and releases and nets unresolved payments. By 5:15 p.m., CHIPS releases any remaining payments and sends payment orders to banks via Fedwire (https://www.investopedia.com/terms/clearing-house-interbank-payments-system-chips.asp).

4.4.3 BACS

BACS Payment Schemes Limited (BACS) is a telecommunication system that was created in the United Kingdom in 1968. This is the not-for-profit, membership-based industry body and is owned by 16 leading banks and building societies. Later, the system was transformed into the BACSTEL system. The system provides two types of services for subscribers: "scheduled service" (offline messaging) and "on-demand service" for sending short messages via public telecommunication networks.

BACS is responsible for the schemes behind the clearing and settlement of automated payments in the United Kingdom. BACS payment system is of critical importance to the UK financial system.

BACS operates two core schemes namely Direct Debit and Direct Credit. Also, BACS operates a suite of managed services including Cash ISA Transfer Service, Bank Reference Data service and the Current Account Switch Service and Biller Update Service.

BACS Payment Schemes Limited is one of the companies that has been consolidated in 2018 as part of the creation of Pay.UK, along with Faster Payments Scheme Limited and the Cheque & Credit Clearing Company (C&CCC) (https://www.bacs.co.uk/Pages/Home.aspx).

4.4.4 Clearing House Automated Payment System (CHAPS)

The Clearing House Automated Payment System (CHAPS) is a real-time gross settlement payment system used for sterling transactions in the United Kingdom (https://www.bankofengland.co.uk/payment-and-settlement/chaps).

The Bankers Clearing House originally established CHAPS in London in February 1984. With the closure of the Town Clearing, the operating company was renamed CHAPS Clearing Company Limited (informally "CHAPS Co"). Starting 2017, CHAPS is administered by the Bank of England (BoE) and is used by 30 participating financial institutions. Approximately 5,500 additional institutions also engage with the system by way of partnership agreements with the 30 primary members.

Direct participants in CHAPS include the traditional high-street banks, a number of international, and custody banks. Many more financial institutions access the system indirectly and make their payments via direct participants. This is known as an agency or correspondent banking.

CHAPS is one of the largest high-value payment systems in the world, providing efficient, settlement risk-free and irrevocable payments. There are over 30 direct participants and over 5,000 financial institutions that make CHAPS payments through one of the direct participants.

CHAPS allows funds to be transferred almost instantaneously, minimising the risk of loss or theft. Payment obligations between direct participants are settled individually on a gross basis in RTGS on the same day that they are submitted. The speed of CHAPS also substantially eliminates the risk that senders will cancel their transfers before the recipient accepts them. The transfer of funds is irrevocable between the direct participants.

Operating hours: The CHAPS system opens at 6 a.m. each working day. Participants must be open to receive by 8 a.m. and must send by 10 a.m. CHAPS closes at 6 p.m. for bank-to-bank payments. Customer payments must be submitted by 5.40 p.m.

For the most part, CHAPS members are large banks. However, companies may use CHAPs for large or time-sensitive payments to suppliers or tax payments. CHAPS is often used to complete property transactions or for high-value transactions, such as buying a car.

CHAPS transfers are relatively expensive, with banks typically charging as much as £35 for a transfer. For most everyday transactions, CHAPS is unlikely to be economically viable because the associated costs are relatively expensive compared to alternative mechanisms such as wire transfers or electronic funds transfers (EFTs) (https://www.bankofengland.co.uk/payment-and-settlement/chaps).

The benefits of CHAPS payments are:

- Direct access to CHAPS supports the secure and efficient provision of high-value, same-day payments
- There is no minimum or maximum payment limit
- High level of operational resilience based on the Bank's real-time gross settlement infrastructure and the SWIFT messaging network

Settlement risk is eliminated between CHAPS direct participants, at the cost of an increased need for liquidity, making this model best suited to a high-value payment system with the largest potential systemic risk.

4.4.5 INTERNATIONAL PAYMENT SYSTEM TARGET

To meet the needs of monetary policy, the central banks of the European Union created the TARGET payment system. It started conducting operations in January 1999. And since then it has significantly contributed to the implementation of a single monetary policy, the integration of European money markets and the effective implementation of gross settlements within the Eurozone.

TARGET is a trans-European telecommunication automated system for the conduct of international settlements in real time to transportation, security, confidentiality, continuity, timeliness, reliability, the efficiency of payments, automatically convert to euros and transmit any information in EUR to all their customers using various information tools.

The system is designed to work out euro-denominated cross-border payments as if they were internal payments.

The main purpose of the TARGET system is to unite the internal systems of the countries – members of the system unite into an international payment system to transfer large amounts.

The TARGET system consists of the following elements:

- domestic payment systems for the transfer of large amounts in each country-member of this system

- technological connection procedures (Interlinking)
- functions of the European Central Bank

The TARGET payment system processes and carries out international payments in real time in the single Euro currency at low cost, with a high degree of protection and for a short period.

The TARGET system ensures the quick and final payment of all payments if there is enough money. Alternatively, the institutions making the payment are given an overdraft to the system account with the central bank. International payments in the TARGET system, which are processed by national central banks and the ECB, are organised according to the model of "central bank – multilateral correspondent." Payment orders are transmitted using telecommunication lines.

The creation of the European Monetary Union, the TARGET international payment system, and the introduction of the single euro currency opened up opportunities to strengthen Europe in the global economy and at the same time contributed to the strengthening of the European financial system and the global monetary system as a whole.

European banks offer financial institutions a wide range of services in euros and access to all major local and international payment systems in Europe and around the world.

Corporate and private clients have the right, within the framework of the European Monetary Union, to freely choose the euro or any national currency for the denomination of their accounts and payment documents.

In general, the introduction of the euro and the TARGET system encouraged the establishment of common business rules for the implementation of domestic and international settlements in the euro area as well as facilitated the integration of financial market infrastructure.

The functioning of the TARGET system is aimed at achieving three main goals:

- meeting the needs of monetary policy of the European economic community
- increasing the efficiency of intra-European cross-border settlements
- introduction of a reliable and secure mechanism for cross-border settlements

TARGET2 (Trans-European Automated Real-time Gross Settlement Express Transfer System) is the real-time gross settlement (RTGS) system for the Eurozone and is available to non-Eurozone countries. It was developed by and is owned by the Eurosystem. TARGET2 is based on an integrated central technical infrastructure, called the Single Shared Platform (SSP). The SSP is operated by three providing central banks: France (Banque de France), Germany (Deutsche Bundesbank) and Italy (Banca d'Italia). TARGET2 started to replace TARGET in November 2007 (https://www.ecb.europa.eu/pub/pdf/other/ANNEX4TARGET24thprogress.pdf).

TARGET2 is also an interbank RTGS payment system for the clearing of cross-border transfers in the Eurozone. Participants in the system are either direct or indirect. Direct participants hold an RTGS account and have access to real-time information and control tools. They are responsible for all payments sent from or received on their accounts by themselves or any indirect participants operating through them. Indirect participation means that payment orders are always sent to and received from the system via a direct participant, with only the relevant direct participant having a legal relationship with the Eurosystem. Finally, bank branches and subsidiaries can choose to participate in TARGET2 as multi-addressee access or addressable BICs (https://www.ecb.europa.eu/paym/target/target2/html/index.en.html).

4.4.6   THE SWIFT IN THE GLOBAL B2B

International payments involve a complex chain of transactions and payment routes that entail cooperation and coordination between multiple banks and financial institutions. Thus, it is not enough for banks and other financial institutions only to transfer money to each other without having a common protocol and standard by which they can communicate with each other. Society for Worldwide Interbank Financial Telecommunication (SWIFT) was created to provide prompt, reliable, efficient, confidential, and tamper-proof telecommunications services for banks and to work on standardization of forms and methods for the exchange of financial information between countries in the whole world. SWIFT was founded in May 1973 in Brussels as a cooperative society under Belgian law. Its member financial institutions with offices around the world (https://www.swift.com/about-us/discover-swift?AKredir=true) own it.

The SWIFT provides a network that enables financial institutions worldwide to send and receive information about financial transactions in a secure, standardised and reliable environment. SWIFT also sells software and services to financial institutions, much of it for use on the SWIFTNet Network.

The flows of complex chains of international payment transactions are possible by automated payment systems that use the SWIFT standard that enables and ensures that the payments flow smoothly throughout the value chain.

Further, in recent years, the funds from one country to the other are flowing in an almost real-time manner with just minor delays because of the clearinghouses in between. Clearinghouses are financial institutions such as the Central Bank in the EU and the Federal Reserve Bank in the United States, which function as the node for the payments between domestic banks and international banks. There is a common protocol that formed the basis for such communication; this is the SWIFT standard wherein the acronym stands for Society for Worldwide International Funds Transfer wherein this payment standard prescribes the rules and regulations that all participants in the international payment network.

For instance, the sender, the recipient, the intermediary, and the address, and other details are to be captured in a specific format that is standard across banks so that each participant in the payment chain knows exactly what is contained in the payment message.

In the beginning, SWIFT founders designed the network to facilitate communication about Treasury and correspondent transactions only. The robustness of the message format design allowed huge scalability through which SWIFT gradually expanded to provide services to the following institutions (https://www.swift.com/about-us/discover-swift?AKredir=true):

- Banks
- Brokerage Institutes and Trading Houses
- Securities Dealers
- Asset Management Companies
- Clearing Houses
- Depositories
- Exchanges
- Corporate Business Houses
- Treasury Market Participants and Service Providers
- Foreign Exchange and Money Brokers

SWIFT members can be countries and their banking institutions authorised to carry out international banking operations. All members pay a one-time joining fee plus annual support charges, which vary by member classes. SWIFT also charges users for each message based on message type and length. These charges also vary depending upon the bank's usage volume – different charge tiers exist for banks that generate different volumes of messages.

The purpose of the SWIFT identified research, development, implementation, operation, improvement, and development of a system that allows you to transfer data related to international traffic as well as banking information of any kind and content.

Also, SWIFT has additional services. These are backed by the long history of data maintained by SWIFT. These include business intelligence, reference data, and compliance services and offer other income streams for SWIFT.

The main areas of its activity are to provide prompt, reliable, efficient, confidential and protection from unauthorised access telecommunications services for banks and to work on standardisation of forms and methods for the exchange of financial information.

Automation of banking processes at the international level makes it possible to:

- make paperless payment transactions with minimal involvement of people and reduction of operating expenses
- to speed up the exchange of information between state banks through telecommunication lines
- minimise typical types of banking risk (loss of documents, false addressing, falsification of payment documents, etc.)

The majority of international interbank messages use the SWIFT network. Today SWIFT has more than 10,000 live users in 212 countries who exchange on average 4.5 billion messages between them on an annual basis. As of 2015, SWIFT linked more than 11,000 financial institutions in more than 200 countries and territories, which were exchanging an average of over 20 million messages per day (https://www.swift.com/about-us/discover-swift?AKredir=true). SWIFT transports financial messages in a highly secure way but does not hold accounts for its members and does not perform any form of clearing or settlement.

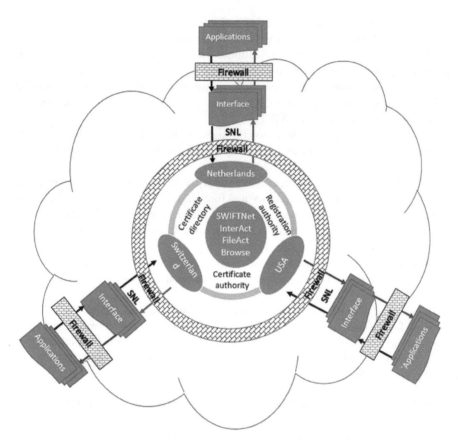

FIGURE 4.19   SWIFT architecture.

Source: Own work based on: Scott S. V., Zachariadis M. 2014.

SWIFT does not facilitate funds transfer. Rather, it sends payment orders, which must be settled by correspondent accounts that the institutions have with each other. Each financial institution, to exchange banking transactions, must have a banking relationship by either being a bank or affiliating itself with one (or more) to enjoy those particular business features (https://www.swift.com/about-us/discover-swift?AKredir=true).

The core of SWIFT system are three OPCs (Operating Centres). One is located in Culpeper, Virginia, USA, the other one in Zoeterwoude, Netherlands, and one in Switzerland. All these centres work with information in real time (Figure 4.19). The Operations centre consists of a message processor of the control processor and a control centre that monitors all system messages. OPC is the core of the network; communication channels between themselves and the corresponding regional processors connect them. These three OPCs or data centres are the core of SWIFT. They are able to handle the traffic of the complete network in case of a failure in one of them. Each of them can monitor the status of the route and regional processors and manage the operation of all network programmes and equipment, connect users and even control the execution of applied tasks (https://www.swift.com/about-us/discover-swift?AKredir=true; Susan V. Scott, Markos Zachariadis 2014).

At the second level are banking institutions with Interface Systems (IS) installed. IS are connected to the network using so-called access points (SAP). Each point can serve several subscribers. The use of leased lines enables message ciphers. SWIFT offers its users a whole range of IS. Also, users can offer their version of IS, but it is necessary to coordinate with SWIFT.

SWIFTNet also provides the following services that fall under the financial marketplace: securities, treasury and derivatives, trade services and payments-and-cash management.

SWIFT connections enable access to a variety of applications, which include real-time instruction matching for treasury and forex transactions, banking market infrastructure for processing payment instructions between banks and securities market infrastructure for processing clearing and settlement instructions for payments, securities, forex and derivatives transactions.

Aimed at services around financial crime compliance, SWIFT offers reporting and utilities like Know Your Customer (KYC), Sanctions and Anti-Money Laundering (AML).

The core of SWIFT business resides in providing a secure, reliable and scalable network for the smooth movement of messages. Through its various messaging hubs, software and network connections, SWIFT offers multiple products and services, which enable its end clients to send and receive transactional messages.

Working in SWIFT gives users the following benefits:

- the system guarantees absolute security of payments with a multi-level combination of physical, technical and organisational methods of protection, complete safety and security of information
- reliability of messaging
- fast message delivery to anywhere in the world in real time
- allows to control and audit all payments and orders passing through the network

*SNL/VPN – SwiftNet Link-VPN connection – the connection between the SwiftNet Link host and VPN box (managed custom-premisses equipment). SwiftNet Link-VPN connection is under the sole responsibility of the user, which must secure and protect it.

- increasing the competitiveness of banks participating in SWIFT
- providing its members with financial protection in case of network outages. SWIFT guarantees the payment of all direct and subsequent costs incurred by the client due to late payment.

4.4.7 Challenges for SWIFT

As technological developments and the needs of banks for more up-to-date services rapidly increased, SWIFT had to keep pace and respond with new products and network upgrades. Consequently, in 1998, not too long after the full deployment of

SWIFT II, the company officially announced their plans for a new TCP/IP network that would offer a series of new IP-based products and services.

The new Secure Internet Protocol Network (SIPN) named SWIFTNet, which was built to replace the old X.25-based network, went live in 2001. The official beginning of the users' migration to the new platform was completed in 2004. The most important development to accompany the new SWIFTNet platform was the addition of enhanced market infrastructure services involving more advanced clearing and settlement instructions as well as links to support STP (straight-through processing) operations. Domestic market infrastructures such as Bundesbank's RTGSPlus system and the BoE's Enquiry Link were the first to fully move to SWIFTNet and use the newly developed messaging services.

Before 2002, SWIFT was an industry cooperative owned by its members and founded to reduce errors and increase efficiency in interbank payments. In 2002, the Member Administered – Closed User Group (MA-CUG), which allowed corporations to access the SWIFT network through member banks, was successfully launched in 2002.

Swift uses a SIPN named SWIFTNet. SWIFTNet platform provides enhanced market infrastructure services involving clearing and settlement instructions as well as links to support STP operations. Nowadays, SWIFTNet is a network of banks and financial institutions. After it became a network phenomenon, SWIFT has outsourced the development of its network. It adopts a multi-vendor model that enables its secure IP network to use the infrastructure of four global network partners who provide a standard offering of managed IP-VPN services. Users that seek to establish a direct connection to SWIFTNet make arrangements with one of its network partners. Connectivity to SWIFTNet demands dedicated interfaces to link to the users' applications, including messaging and communications packages.

These software packages enable users to integrate applications with the services offered and are enhanced with a security layer (a version of PKI). This ensures authenticity, integrity and non-repudiation of emission and reception at the message level. SWIFT offers the requisite standards and rules for compatible interfaces to third-party vendors in order to facilitate the production of competitive products and also provides interface products for the entire range of SWIFTNet services itself. Less costly solutions for indirect connectivity to SWIFTNet are also available.

A crucial step towards leveraging the network and connecting up the content of a transaction with the parties involved was the development of a universal Bank Identifier Code or BIC (Scott, Zachariadis, 2014).

The majority of SWIFT clients have huge transactional volumes for which manual entry of instructions is not practical. The need for automation for SWIFT message creation, processing and transmission is growing. However, this comes at a cost and operational overhead. This creates problems for medium and small banks.

Although SWIFT has been successful in providing software for the same, that too comes at a cost. SWIFT may need to tap into these problem areas for the majority of its client base. Automated solutions within this space may bring in a new stream of income for SWIFT and keep clients engaged in the long run.

All payment instructions and other messages in SWIFT are carried out in a standardised format, and this simplifies the automated processing of documents and avoids errors and disagreements in traditions on paperwork in different countries.

Some measures have been taken to improve the SWIFT system. For example, SWIFT has implemented many generations of security. They implement leading-edge security on a larger scale "ahead of the curve," and other financial services organisations and market infrastructures follow, learning from SWIFT's experience. For example, they were an early adopter of PKI on a large scale and among the fi first to employ Hardware Security Modules (HSM), a special device that is tamper-resistant, rolled out throughout SWIFT's customer sites to digitally sign or encrypt messages.

SWIFT is becoming increasingly popular as security and sustainability issues are now high on the agenda of financial institutions and their regulators. As Mike Fish puts it "where other people try to stay one or two steps ahead, we try to stay two or three steps ahead of the bad guys" (Scott, Zachariadis M. 2014).

The SWIFT system implements some special measures:

- the system checks for permission to use the system terminal
- the system automatically numbers incoming and outgoing messages
- transmission of each message is confirmed individually
- the relationship between the two banks is established by an individual key
- the recipient automatically checks the information
- communication lines between operational centres and regional processors are protected by special crypto devices that ensure message inaccessibility for unauthorised persons.

SWIFT has retained its dominant position in the global processing of transactional messages. It has recently forayed into other areas, such as offering reporting utilities and data for business intelligence, which indicates its willingness to remain innovative. In the short- to mid-term, SWIFT seems poised to continue dominating the market.

4.4.8 Vulnerabilities and Fundamental Principles of the Functioning of Payment Systems

Payment systems are a means of moving funds between banks. They are crucial for the effective functioning of the global financial system. Therefore, one of the necessary conditions for the effective functioning of the global financial system is the stability of international payment systems.

Payment systems may be subject to a variety of risks, such as:

Credit risk – the risk that a member of a payment system fails to meet its financial obligations;

Liquidity – a shortage of funds from a participant in payment systems threatens the fulfilment of its financial obligations within the prescribed period, but in the future, they can be met;

Legal risk – an imperfect and unstable legal base can cause or exacerbate credit risk or liquidity risk;

Operational risk – technical failures and errors may increase credit risk or liquidity risk;

Systemic risk – as a result of the insolvency of one of the participants of payment systems to fulfil their obligations or because of a crisis in the system itself, other participants of the system will not be able to fulfil their obligations. This will lead to the spread of a liquidity crisis and may be a threat to the stability of the financial system as a whole.

In recent years, international standards have been introduced for the creation and operation of payment systems aimed at ensuring economic stability. A major contribution here belongs to the Committee on Payment and Settlement Systems (CPSS) of the central banks of the countries of Group 10, whose working group in May 1998 defined the fundamental principles of the functioning of payment systems.

The main points of the report can be summarised as follows:

A necessary condition for the safe interaction of participants in payment systems is the existence of a reasonable legal framework in all relevant jurisdictions.

The rules and procedures of payment systems should be transparent so that its participants can better understand the causes and consequences of each of the financial risks, which, in turn, should ensure their prevention.

To manage credit and liquidity risks and their limitations, payment systems must clearly define the necessary rules and procedures regarding the respective responsibilities of the system operator and participants of payment systems. Such rules and procedures provide for the responsibility for managing risks and their limitations and must ensure that all participants have both incentives and opportunities to manage and limit each of the risks they generate. There are analytical and operational risk management techniques. Analytical include current monitoring and analysis of credit risk and liquidity risk caused by participants in payment systems. The operational risk management techniques include the establishment by participants of payment systems of overdraft limits or the introduction of front coverage or collateral, as well as management of transaction queues and the like.

Payment systems must ensure final settlement on the day of value, best of all, during the day. Over the period between the acceptance of the payment system and the final settlement, participants may experience credit or liquidity risks. This principle encourages the acceleration of settlement on a specific value date and does not prevent the system from accepting it in advance.

Payment systems of multilateral netting should ensure timely completion of daily settlements in the event of insolvency of the participant with the largest obligations. In this case, the threat of a lack of liquidity for other participants in payment systems is intensifying. Therefore, one of the standards implies the ability of the PS to withstand the insolvency of the participant with the highest net receivables position.

In most cases, mutual transfer of assets fulfils participants' obligations. The most common and dangerous type of these assets is the balance on the account of the central bank. If the settlement assets are claims against other credit institutions that may cause credit risks, the PS is exposed to a crisis of confidence, which in turn generates a systemic risk. Accounts in the central bank are in this respect the safest settlement assets precisely because of the absence of credit risk.

PS should guarantee a high level of security and operational reliability and have mechanisms for quick analysis of unusual situations for the timely completion of daily payment processing. To do this, it must meet recognised safety standards, adequate cost of operations, maintain a high level of operational stability, which is achieved not only by high-class technical equipment and software but also by qualified staff.

PS should provide a user-friendly and cost-effective way to make payments. The liquidity of the system is the most important condition for its continuous operation. Recipients prefer daily calculations, wanting to get funds that can be used immediately. However, senders seek to avoid costs associated with an increase in liquidity required at the beginning of a business day. If the system has an inadequate mechanism for servicing intraday liquidity, it is at risk of a slow turnover or a stop when each participant expects the other to pay first. To be effective, participants must be encouraged to pay immediately. Technological and functional procedures that provide payment services must meet all types of services required by users, taking into account the level of economic development of the relevant market.

PS should provide objective and transparent membership criteria, which contributes to an efficient and cheap payment service. The procedure for withdrawing a participant from the system at his request or the decision of the system operator should be clearly defined.

Since the PS can potentially influence the financial and economic development of a country, it must have effective, accountable and transparent governance, regardless of whether it is done by the central bank or the private sector.

International payment flows go smoothly as long as all participants in the value chain do their part in addition to adhering to the SWIFT protocol. Further, the global payment value chain is efficient mainly because globalisation has led to the liberalisation of the banking rules and regulations that have enabled banks anywhere to deal with other banks everywhere and anytime and every time.

Finally, the next time you send or receive an international payment, just think about what it takes to enable your payment and imagine bits and bytes of data and information stream across the world so that your payment is processed smoothly and successfully.

4.4.9 PAYMENT SYSTEMS AND PAYMENT-PROCESSING SERVICES

Modern business has changed the traditional forms of payment and moved to the Internet. This led to the development of a variety of electronic payment systems. The payments flow across the world and banks underpin global commerce and trade. Online shopping on international portals or receiving payments from abroad, global supply chains of corporations with international suppliers and customers, all these transactions would be dealing with a complex network of institutions and banks that route the payments from one end of the supply chain or the value chain to the other.

Besides, nations trade with each other because central banks transact with each other, as well as banks in different countries, deal with each other, then they are all participating in the international payment system that is the bedrock of global payment flows.

So, who and what are the constituents and components of the international payment system?

To start with, banks and financial institutions form the first level of international payment wherein they hold accounts of other global banks who in turn hold accounts of the former. This enables the banks to send and receive payments from each other as they can simply debit their accounts and credit the other bank's account with them and this, in turn, leads to payments flowing to the recipient bank that debit the sending bank and credit their account.

Thus, the international payment system is a system of settlements between financial institutions, business organisations and Internet users in the process of buying and selling goods and services via the Internet.

The functions of electronic payment systems are the following:

• Opening and maintaining virtual customer accounts
• Providing customers with the opportunity to replenish their virtual accounts in various ways (by bank transfer, depositing cash, postal transfer, activation of cards issued by the payment system, etc.)
• Conducting transactions between customer accounts, storing transaction data
• Securing accounts (preventing unauthorised access) and protecting customer information
• Consulting customer support
• Uninterrupted functioning of the programmes of the complex of the payment system

B2B EC payment system facilitates the acceptance of electronic payment for online transactions. B2B payment systems have become increasingly popular due to the widespread use of Internet-based shopping and banking. The main advantage of payment systems and services on the Internet is the ability to work online 24 hours and 7 days a week (Table 4.5).

All of them have applications for mobile versions. However, not everyone issues plastic cards and not everyone allows withdrawing cash through an ATM.

Some companies enable financial transactions to take place over the Internet, such as PayPal. Many of the intermediaries permit consumers to establish an account quickly and to transfer funds into their online accounts from a traditional bank account (typically via ACH transactions), and vice versa, after verification of the consumer's identity and authority to access such bank accounts. Also, the larger intermediaries further allow transactions to and from credit card accounts, although such credit card transactions are usually assessed a fee (either to the recipient or the sender) to recoup the transaction fees charged to the intermediary.

The speed and simplicity with which cyber – intermediary accounts can be established and used have contributed to their widespread use, although the risk of abuse,

TABLE 4.5
Payment Systems and Payment-Processing Services

Payment/Merchant Systems and Services	Online	POS	Mobile	Withdraw Fee
Centralised systems of fiat currency based on networks				
PayPal	+	+	+	2.5%
Alipay	+	+	+	0.55%
Google Pay	+	+	+	1.5% or $. 31
Apple Pay	+	+	+	1.5%
based on plastic cards				
Payoneer	+	+	+	2%
Skrill	+	-	+	2.5%
Systems of digital currency centralised				
EasyPay	+	+	+	1% and >
WebMoney	+	-	+	0,8% and >
QIWI	+	+	+	From 1% to 3%
decentralised				
Bitcoin, BTC and its forks Litecoin, LTC Ripple Monetary System Peercoin, PPC etc.	+	+	+	Depends On Service Provider

Source: Own work.

theft and other problems with disgruntled users frequently accusing the intermediaries themselves of wrongful behaviour is associated with them.

PayPal is an electronic payment system founded in December 1998. It is used as an alternative payment system for small businesses and online trading. PayPal acts as an intermediary between the seller and the buyer, ensuring the highest reliability of payment-by-payment cards VISA, MasterCard, American Express and other payment systems. PayPal has done a better job of fighting abuse than did e-gold, now they are fighting the same Internet fraud as e-gold (PayPal https://www.paypal.com/us/).

The system is very common in most countries of the world. An average of 18,000 new users is connected to the system every day. More than 230,000,000 people in 203 countries use PayPal to pay for purchases and to transfer money to any recipient who has an e-mail address.

PayPal has some variants of programmes to work with clients in different countries. The choice of the programme depends on the conditions of national legislation and the loyalty of the national regulator. For example, a one-way programme for making payments only works in some post-Soviet countries.

The PayPal Zero programme assumes the possibility of crediting, entering and withdrawing funds in currency, but the user can't keep a balance on the PayPal account. The funds must be automatically credited to the card tied to the account.

The SRW (Send-Recieve-Withdrawal) programme, besides the above, allows keeping a balance in your PayPal account in the currency and transferring it to the card when the user deems it necessary. All calculations are carried out only at a cross border and only in currency. The next programme Local Currency provides for all of the above as well as enables payments not only in the global but also in local currency.

PayPal helps ensure the confidentiality of information when making transactions on the Internet. The PayPal security service guarantees the control of bank accounts, the authorisation of the user's card and the user's IP addresses. The system considers fraud in terms of risk management. PayPal developed a monitoring system to combat fraud, used by artificial intelligence to detect potentially fraudulent transactions. Transaction security and fraud protection system are also guaranteed by an additional security key implemented by two-factor protection – the password and six-digit code are automatically generated or sent to the client's mobile phone.

The PayPal system does not require entering information about the customer's credit card when making each purchase. Information about the financial capabilities of the client is never provided to third parties. The customer's credit card number and bank account number will be invisible to the merchants. Besides, anti-fraud specialists ensure the protection of client data against possible attacks by intruders in advance.

Customers can make payments through the Internet directly from a bank after the bank account is combined with his PayPal account. Adding a bank account is part of the verification that confirms the ownership of the bank account after having completed the necessary steps in PayPal.

Alipay is a mobile app that allows consumers with bank accounts, cards, gift cards, etc. to pay for their purchases worldwide. The buyer needs an Alipay online account. Sellers in most countries can open an account with Alipay for their online stores, and they can add Alipay support in their shop's retail POS. Alipay supports TR in 14 major foreign currencies (https://global.alipay.com/index.htm).

The fee is set to modest 0.1% for withdrawals of over RMB 20,000, and merchant are charged 0.55% transaction fee.

Google Pay (Google Wallet) (https://pay.google.com/about/#friends) upgraded into Android Pay Google-Checkout was upgraded into Google-Wallet, then Google-Wallet was upgraded into Android Pay. Android Pay (or Google Wallet) is used by Google-based services, products and supported in retail shopping centres, markets and POS. Google Wallet allows users to send money from Wallet to other users, relatives, etc. via their Android or iOS-based phone, it also allows receiving money. Buyers for purchasing use android Pay (G Pay), which are available mostly on Google Android OS-based phone. Google does not charges (https://support.google.com/pay/merchants/answer/6288977?hl=en) sellers (or takes away) fee from payment that buyer pays. Google Wallet fund may be added into Wallet from another Wallet account or received from another Android Pay user, and, the fee for receiving fund is $0 (zero) (https://support.google.com/pay/answer/7643913?hl=en&visit_id=637108133140111929-3809918766&rd=2). Google Wallet and Android Pay mobile apps both forcefully require access to GPS geolocation. Google Wallet can read contacts list, modify systems settings, etc. Such an app needs to ask the user, before each access, and single contact needs to be copied out of the user's contacts list and pasted manually into GW when needed. If the seller or merchant's PT/POS supports NFC, then it will also accept Google Pay-based payments. If NFC support is not present in PT/POS then Google Pay will not work.

Apple Pay: it is used, e.g. in iTunes stores or Apple Store, Apple-based services, products, and it is also supported by many retail shopping centres, markets and POS. Apple initially charged around 0.15%–0.30% fee from each payment paid by the buyer (using their Credit/Debit cards), and the rest ended up going into the seller's hand. This was changed in September 2015, Apple now charges around 15% + $0.15 from each payment, before giving the rest of the amount to the seller. Also, banks take-away around a 2% fee from Apple's portion for each (Apple Pay) transaction. If the seller or merchant's PT/POS supports NFC, then it will also accept Apple Pay-based payment. If NFC support is not present in PT/POS, then Apple Pay will not work (https://www.apple.com/apple-pay/).

Skrill is the next popular Internet payment system. It is an open and transparent payment system, with a high degree of reliability and customer protection. This service was founded in 2001 in the United Kingdom and was named Moneybookers. In 2010, the service acquired a new name Skrill Limited. This system is regulated by the financial supervisory authority FCA and has permission to issue EM (Skrill https://www.skrill.com/).

This system is popular all over the world and covers more than 30 million users from more than 200 countries. The annual turnover of the company is more than 10 billion US dollars.

Skrill allows opening an electronic purse, which is available in 40 currencies. Skrill purse can use for purchases and payment of various services: freelance, casino, forex, bookmakers. Also, customers can pay for purchases in online stores, make money transfers and withdraw funds from a bank card. The client can be funding his electronic purse through the Neteller payment system, VISA, MasterCard, Maestro or Swift bank transfer from his bank account. He can withdraw and cash out the funds to a linked bank card, to the bank account or own a Skrill card. In addition, clients can get Skrill Prepaid Mastercard. But Skrill's offering of and support to the Skrill Prepaid Program is limited to residents of the European Economic Area.

Skrill paid close attention to customers' personal information to prevent fraudulent and illegal actions on the part of customers and companies as well as according to the requirements of financial supervision authorities. To open an account, the user must be 18 years old or more. There are also restrictions for residents of some countries. The user is assigned a personal identification number (ID) after registration.

Much attention is paid to the safety of users and their settlements. The company fully compensates for all losses for the user in case of illegal access to the wallet by third parties. Customers can claim payments from the insurance fund in the event of bankruptcy of the company. The payment system can close the account if there is a suspicion of fraudulent activity and can block the account if exchange operations to other EM, e.g. QIWI, WebMoney, Yandex Money, BTC and others, are carried out.

As Skrill Limited is regulated by the financial supervisory authority FCA, so its privacy policy includes:

- Financial supervision
- Open information about users
- A transparent system of calculations

- High reliability for customers and payments from the insurance fund
- Blocking the account for withdrawal and exchange in exchangers for other electronic payment systems, such as WebMoney, QIWI, Yandex Money
- Closing of the account in case of suspicion of fraud

For transactions involving currency conversion Skrill adds a fee of up to 4.49% to the wholesale exchange rates (Skrill https://www.finder.com/skrill). Skrill automatically deducts these fees from the amount your friend or family member receives on their end. You will also pay to withdraw money from your account.

- 1.9% transaction fee
- up to 4.49% currency conversion fee
- up to 7.5% withdrawal fee (varies by payment method)

For example, if you are transferring $1,000 from your Skrill account to a friend in the United Kingdom, Skrill will deduct a transaction fee of 1.9% ($19), along with a 3.99% ($39.90) currency conversion fee. Your friend will receive $941.10.

There are also fees for loading funds to your Skrill account. The price depends on the method you use:

- Bank transfer: Free
- ACH: 6%
- Credit card: 2.9%
- Paysafecard: 7.5%

If you use your credit card for gambling purposes your issuer may charge a 'cash advance' fee.

Payoneer. The other payment system that provides EC payment services, online money transfers is Payoneer. This system provides financial services for businesses in the whole of the world. Payoneer is a registered Member of the Service Provider (MSP) of MasterCard Incorporated and is a MasterCard Member Service Provider around the world. Moreover, the system issues debit cards (https://inc42.com/buzz/payoneer-india/; www.ecommercetimes.com. Retrieved 2019-02-01).

Payoneer connects entrepreneurs and professionals in 200 countries (https://www.cnbc.com/2017/05/16/payoneer-2017-disruptor-50.html) promoting and guaranteeing unimpeded of their international money transfers and online payments. The company allows millions of entrepreneurs and professionals to enter new markets (https://www.skrill.com/).

Payoneer users have the opportunity to receive funds to their account at a local bank or e-wallet as well as through a prepaid MasterCard debit card that can be used at ATMs or the point of sale. The platform has more than 150 currencies and offers services with a low currency conversion fee ((https://www.cnbc.com/2017/05/16/payoneer-2017-disruptor-50.html www.ecommercetimes.com. Retrieved 2019-02-01.). MasterCard and Bank of America provide user security in the Payoneer payment system.

The most core obligation at Payoneer is to protect customers' funds and prevent money laundering. Payoneer guarantees that all payee disbursements are made through a fully compliant, secure and tightly audited payments platform that is recognised and valued by financial regulators all around the world.

Payoneer operates under a robust, risk-based compliance programme that addresses the regulatory requirements of each country that is involved in the cross-border payment. The system follows anti-money laundering policies and procedures based on fundamentals from regulations.

Payoneer provides comprehensive risk management and deploys multiple layers of risk technology, both in-house and third party. The system uses various procedures to protect customers' business and Payoneer against different fraud scenarios such as registration fraud, account takeover and other activities (https://www.cnbc.com/2017/05/16/payoneer-2017-disruptor-50.html). However, nobody can guarantee users from cards to be hacked and stolen funds.

WebMoney Transfer is one of the most widely known centralised digital currency payment systems. It is a universal, global, non-banking information system for the transfer of property rights based on EM. Its history began in 1998.

The WM system has a universal flexible structure that allows users to perform secure calculations in real time. WM users can pay for goods in e-shops that support the WM payment form, pay off with other system participants, transfer WM to bank accounts and create your stores (using Shop Creator) that will function in this system.

According to the internal statistics of WM, the number of transactions in the system amounted to more than 160 million and the volume – more than 17 billion dollars by 2014 (https://www.webmoney.ru/rus/information/statistic/index.shtm). The number of registrations in the WM system exceeded the mark of 31 million accounts in December 2015 (http://passport.wmtransfer.com/asp/WMCertify.asp).

WM system allows:

- pay for goods and services on the network
- discuss terms of trade operations with partners with the help of voice service, videoconference, protected WM-mail
- receive and issue loans in WM title signs
- create your digital checks for payment of goods and services in online stores
- exchange electronic currencies at a favourable exchange rate
- distribute software products and e-books in a copy-protected format
- make calculations by e-mail, use a mobile phone as a purse

WM uses also EM nominated in US dollars, euros, and Russian and Belarusian rubles with guaranteed non-resident institutions.

Emission of certain type title signs is carried out by the Guarantor organisation that holds and manages the issue of securities and establishes the exchange equivalent.

WebMoney Transfer charges a fee of 0.8% of the payment amount for every transaction, but not less than 0.01 WM (https://www.webmoney.ru/rus/information/statistic/index.shtm).

WM Transfer does not charge a fee for transactions between purses of the same type and belonging to the same WMID.

WM charges the fee of 0.8% of the payment amount for every transaction, but not less than 0.01 WM. Owners of D purses are charged the fee of 0.1% of the amount of each credit they provide in the course of credit transactions, but not less than 0.01 WMZ. (https://wiki.wmtransfer.com/projects/webmoney/wiki/WebMoney_Transfer_fee)):

> The company WM Transfer Ltd is the owner, administrator and developer of the WM system. It is providing its organisational and technological integrity. The company Computing Forces are handled by the development of software and technical support for the system operation.

The WebMoney Transfer system allows for instant secure transactions. Identification system acting in the system allows uniquely identifying and recording all the operations performed. Customers can conduct secure correspondence with other participants, discuss details of transactions and comment on the conduct of transactions using the built-in confidential message service.

Security of the WM transaction is provided at the system level. The funds are always on the sender's WM purse or in the WM purse of the recipient when the transaction is made and do not require a credit card or bank account. Transactions cannot be cancelled.

The list of security settings for accounts in the WM System includes the following authentication methods:

- Login and password
- Files with secret keys
- Personal digital certificates
- SMS verification code
- E-NUM, an internal service for generating a one-time password

A purse can be funded in the System:

- by bank transfer
- by transfer with online bank
- through the exchange WM Transfer
- by postal order
- through the INDX exchange
- exchange of system title-boards for EM of payment systems GoldMoney, Standard Reserve
- payment by Western Unión System
- purchase and activation of WM-cards

Withdrawal money from the system can be done in one of the following ways:

- by bank wire transfer
- by transfer using IMTB Online Bank
- through the exchange office
- by postal order

- through the stock exchange
- payment by Western Unión system
- exchange of system title signs for EM of payment systems GoldMoney, Standard Reserve
- by a credit card (to a card account)

WM supports online settings in several types of purses that store information about the property rights of the respective types using e-money, the so-called WM headers that are stored by the respective owners of electronic "wallets" (WebMoney www. wmtransfer.com):

WMR – RUR Bearer's bank cheque in Russian rubles, R-Purse

WME – EUR Electronic money in Euros – E-Purse

WMZ – USD Goods certificate, in US dollars, Z-Purse

WMU – UAH (Bank account claims in Ukrainian hryvnia), U-Purse

WMY – UZS (Uzbekistani som) Y-Purse

WMB – Electronic Belarusian rubles B-Purse

WMS – Kyrgyzstani som S-Purse

WMG – Warehouse receipt for stock gold in a certified storage area, G-Purse

WMV – Prepaid transfer in Vietnamese đồng, V-Check

WMK – a receipt for the right to receive EKZT from the guarantor for a certain amount, K-Purse

WMX – retains ownership of the publication of records in the global public database of bitcoin.org X-Purse.

Transfer of funds is possible only for the same type of purses, and the exchange of different title signs is made at special exchange offices.

WM is considered the most democratic system because it does not impose any special requirements for the user. Therefore, we can say that it is fully consistent with the declared title "global system."

WM has a built-in ability lending. There are two special types of purses for lending operations: WMC to indicate the amount of the loan issued and WMD to indicate the amount of the loan received.

At the same time, the system has many drawbacks. All payments between system participants are made only between the same electronic "purses." The system does not check users' registration information and it may even be fictitious.

Bitcoin Payment System: These payment-processing services are used by BTC supporting trading services or by some retail shopping centres+markets and POS and by many online (centralised+decentralised) shopping centres/markets/ stores. The BTC transaction fee "Cost very little." To transfer BTC virtual currency from one BTC wallet to another, and to include the transfer in BTC blockchain (decentralised distributed database) and to receive verification (or proof or confirmations) on that transfer very quickly (within 15 minutes or 1:30 hour), then there is a variable higher fee rate which is charged by BTC miners. But currently, the minimum fee for miners is close to or around ฿0.00001 BTC per KB (kilobytes) of data/info for a confirmed BTC transfer. A typical BTC transaction may contain around 0.5 KB (or 512 bytes) of data. Some BTC mining service providers also support free or low-cost BTC transfer (usually for a transaction that has less than 1 KB data), though verification might be slightly delayed (BitPay https://bitpay. com/pricing/) (https://en.bitcoin.it/wiki/Free_transaction_relay_policy; https:// en.bitcoin.it/wiki/Software#Shopping_Cart_Integration_in_eCommerce-Systems). Sellers who cannot run their own BTC mining hardware, to include a transaction into the blockchain, or sellers who cannot integrate plugin, for receiving BTC-transaction verification, for a sale/purchase, then such sellers have to use third-party services from other BTC exchange or other BTC merchant service processor, and their processing fees are much higher. A seller should not ship out or deliver products or services, before receiving a sufficient number of confirmations (>3) on a BTC/XBT payment.

Thus, payment systems on the Internet are subject to both financial and non-financial risks. These risks concern both users of payment systems and operators of the system. Analysis of the risks of payment systems is also advisable to proceed based on the classification of risks in their areas of origin, the mechanisms of calculation, their distribution over time. This makes it possible to assess the degree of each type of financial risk and to choose the methods of managing them.

In developing and implementing risk management measures in payment systems, it is desirable to be guided by some general principles:

- mandatory identification of system users
- transparency of mutual settlements
- control access to the system
- risk must be managed with minimal costs
- it is necessary to be flexible in determining ways to achieve the goal
- stimulating the most economical solutions to risk management
- publication of errors in the payment system, fraud, as well as centralised analysis of the parameters and causes of errors
- periodic verification of measures to counter fraud with the introduction of the necessary changes in the payment process

The types of payment systems risks, their degree, and management measures should also be considered taking into account the issues: who manages the system and who is the guarantor (central bank or private organisation); how payments are made – on a gross or net basis if it provides a daily loan.

This approach to the classification of payment system risks, in our opinion, is optimal, since it allows us to focus on the key differences in the types of risks inherent in these systems, and, accordingly, the mechanisms of risk management.

The process of risk management is important. It involves identification of exposure to risk, risk assessment, choice of risk management methods and their application, the ultimate goal of which is to achieve the optimum profit-risk ratio for the user.

4.4.10 DATA PROTECTION IN E-COMMERCE

Huge volume transactions are happening in EC every day. Many of these require suppliers to have access to customer data. Therefore, one of the main problems of EC is data preservation and protection. Internet platforms store very much information that is collected directly from customers and retailers. Customers' data is stored on centralised servers and is vulnerable to hackers. Hackers usually target administrators, users and employees of online stores using a variety of malicious methods. As result, the industry faces 32.4% of all successful threats each year.

Therefore, many users have a good reason to be concerned about the transfer of their personal data. In addition, very often the confidential data is used illegally for advertising purposes or even transferred to third parties.

With the consumer at the centre of growing international EC, it is highly recommended that businesses stay up on data protection issues. Trust is essential for business successful expansion. Failure to keep an online retail business safe on EC platforms can affect sales and damage a store's reputation. Once it becomes known that an e-shop cannot be relied on to keep user data secure, no one wants to buy here again. All of this emphasises that built-in data protection and customer privacy help build trust and business.

The term "data protection" originally came from Europe and originated in connection with privacy protection legislation. The European Union in 2018 passed an important law called the General Data Protection Regulation. The law affects how retailers are allowed to process customer information as well as the rights of customers to access their data and know how it is used. EC stores will need to rethink their approach to storing customer data.

In this part, we have tried to list down the common threats EC faces and how to be safe from them https://www.ionos.com/digitalguide/websites/digital-law/data-protection-in-e-commerce/ https://www.scalefast.com/blog/customer-data-and-privacy https://www.getastra.com/blog/knowledge-base/ecommerce-security-threats/ https://www.cloudways.com/blog/ecommerce-security-tips/ https://www.javatpoint. com/security-threat-to-e-commerce

https://www.kratikal.com/blog/top-5-cyber-threats-to-e-commerce-security/ https://phoenixnap.com/blog/ecommerce-security-threats:

1. Financial Frauds
   a. Credit/Debit Card Fraud
   b. Transaction Fraud
2. Phishing
3. Spamming
4. DOS and Distributed Denial of Service (DDoS) Attacks
5. Malware
6. Exploitation of Known Vulnerabilities
   a. SQL Injection
   b. Cross-site Scripting (XSS)
7. Bots

8. Brute Force Attacks
9. Man in The Middle
10. e-Skimming

1. **Financial Fraud**

There are two main forms of financial fraud in EC. The first is credit cards stolen and unauthorised payments. The second is transactions on insecure systems that are aborted or redirected.

a. **Credit/Debit Card Fraud**

This happens when a cybercriminal uses stolen credit cards to buy goods from an online store. Typically, in such cases, shipping and billing addresses are different. It is possible to detect and restrict such activity in the store by installing AVS – Address Verification System.

Another form of credit card fraud is when a fraudster steals your personal information and identity to obtain a credit card.

One of the major threats associated with a debit/credit card is ATM. They can steal card details from the ATM. Some of the important methods that criminals use to obtain information about our card are:

Skimming

This is the process of connecting a data reader to an ATM card reader. When a customer inserts their card into an ATM card reader, the information is copied from the magnetic stripe to the device. Thus, criminals will find out the card number, name, CVV number, card expiration date and other details.

Vishing/phishing

Phishing is an activity in which a fraudster obtains a user's confidential information, password, usernames and credit card information, often maliciously.

Wishing is an action in which a fraudster received confidential information about a user by sending an SMS to his mobile. It seems to the user that these SMS and calls are coming from a reliable source, but in reality, they are fake. The main purpose of vishing and phishing is to obtain a customer's PIN, account information and passwords.

b. **Transaction Fraud**

Every second online the shoppers make financial transactions, and bank support do these more convenient and secure. However, this does not protect against fraud because of users' carelessness. They from time to time forget to check their bank records and give cybercriminals opportunities to make unauthorised payments.

Bad gamblers commit unauthorised transactions, which leads to large losses for the business. Some hackers are also involved in refund frauds when they submit fake refund requests.

Online shoppers are realising the importance of website security tokens like the HTTPS protocol. However, such indicators can often be faked. This type of spoofing can make it difficult to determine if a website is providing a secure service. Consumers should be informed and vigilant on the Internet. EC organisations must take additional security measures. The following solutions are very effective in protecting the EC domain from threats:

1) Online shops need to secure the payment gateway. Online store owners should avoid storing customer credit card information in their database. Instead, they can allow trusted and reliable third-party resources to process payment transactions outside the website. For example, PayPal and Stripe. This provides the best security for the personal and financial data of customers. It is also important to ensure that the payment gateway provider takes security very seriously and ensures connected to it to prioritise security.

2) Any EC business looking to secure transactions and build a good reputation must take steps to ensure security. The PCI Security Standards Council has issued a strict set of best practices to keep EC websites secure and improve the safety of online payments. It specifies what type of web hosting to use, determines the required security level while payment processing and so on.

2. **Phishing**

Phishing is the reception of fake e-mails from banks or payment systems, addressed to a company or a customer. This is a widely used trick and form of deception used by hackers. This requires the execution and inadvertent provision of login information or personally identifiable information.

Phishing is difficult to prevent because this is a broad category and does not require the use of force. Moreover, some security breaches do not occur on the site's side but on the client's side. They can use weak passwords or pass confidential information to phishing sites and fall into the hands of hackers.

The solution to phishing protection is user education. Users need to be aware of data security's importance. Therefore, it is imperative to provide best-in-class security training to employees so they can take action against the ever-evolving cyberattacks.

For retailers, the best way to counter phishing is to educate their customers about the risks of unsafe security practices. Customers need to know how to identify e-mails, and what they might be asked for in an e-mail, and what they might never be asked about. This needs to encourage customers to ask for confirmation if they receive questionable e-mails. Also needs to require the client to create strong passwords and tell them about how phishing works.

3. **Spam**

Some scammers may send infected links via e-mail or social media inboxes. They can also leave these links in their comments or blog posts and contact forms. They want to access databases through request forms. Once users click on these links, they will direct them to the spam sites, where the user can become a victim. These links can also affect site speed.

The anti-spam solution is to train employees and download spam filtering tools and antivirus software and update them regularly, and use Google reCAPTCHA. The reCAPTCHA is a free service from Google that helps protect websites from spam and abuse.

4. **DOS and DDoS Attacks**

Many EC websites have incurred losses to disruptions in their website and overall sales because of DDoS attacks. Here is how it works: the servers are receiving a stream of requests from many untracked IP addresses, resulting in a crash. This organised attack overwhelms the store's hosting and prevents the site from loading for most visitors. This is mainly done to prevent the site from focusing on important visits.

Sometimes, the end goal can damage the store's reputation. Most often, a DDoS attack is accompanied by a blackmail requirement to pay a certain amount to the attack will be disabled.

DOS and DDoS attacks can be resisted by backing up databases and sites using security plugins.

The website owner should always make regular data backups. This is very important to do so that the business can quickly recover from an attack. The backup and restore plugin will help with this. Security plugins are especially important for maintaining WordPress sites, ensuring secure plugin installation and securing the site's front end. They protect sites from DDoS attacks, malware and hacking by informing users of threat detection in real time.

Content Delivery Networks (CDNs) are another hosting option for an EC website. They improve processes by storing content on servers located across the country in data centres known as points of presence. These data centres have their security, which means they add another layer of security.

5. **Malicious Software**

Hackers can develop malicious software and install it on a victim's IT system without their permission. These programmes can easily delete any sensitive data that may be present on infected systems and can infect the victim's website. Various types of malwares want to infiltrate the backend to steal sensitive site data and customer information. These include spyware, viruses, Trojans, ransomware, malicious adware, XSS, SQL injections aimed at credit card information and personal information. Malicious JavaScript coding is the most common. WordPress sites using WooCommerce and Shopify are regularly targeted by malware injections via widgets and plugin updates. The solution is to use professional antivirus software, switch to HTTPS, secure servers and admin panels, and use SSL certificates when using multi-layered security.

To avoid any malicious attack on the site, it is necessary to keep an eye on any suspicious activity. The solution to this problem can be professional antivirus software, SSL certificates, secure servers and admin panels and multi-layered protection.

Anti-Malware is a program that detects, removes and prevents infection of computer and IT systems with infectious software (malware). Since malware is a general term for all kinds of infections, including worms, viruses, trojans, etc., an effective anti-malware tool will help.

On the other hand, Antivirus is a program designed to protect against viruses. Although many antivirus programs have been designed to prevent infection by other malware. Protecting your PC and other additional systems with antivirus helps keep these infections in check.

To protect the admin panel and the server, users should always use and often change complex passwords. It is also good to restrict user access and define user roles. Each user should only have access to his roles in the admin panel. In addition, it should be configured so that the panel sends notifications whenever a foreign IP address tries to access it.

Make sure they follow the best practices for securing servers.

6. **Exploitation of Known Vulnerabilities**
   Often an online store is vulnerable to SQL injection and XSS. Let's take a quick look at these vulnerabilities:
   a. SQL injection
      This is a malicious technique when a hacker attacks the request forms to access the victim's database. They destroy the victim's database with an infectious code, collect data and then erase the trail.

   b. **Cross-site Scripting (XSS)**
      Attackers can place a malicious piece of JavaScript in an online store to target visitors and customers on the Internet. Such a code can access customer cookies and perform calculations.

      Every EC company must adhere to certain security standards. Therefore, it is important to regularly check the health and safety of EC websites so that hackers do not try to do any real damage to the website. Regular Vulnerability Assessment and Penetration Testing (VAPT) can reduce the risk of cyberthreats by detecting and patching exploitable vulnerabilities.

7. **Bots**
   Bots can be both good and bad. The good ones crawl the web and determine the site's search engine rankings. Bad Bots can crawl websites for inventory and pricing information and change prices on the site, freeze popular items in shopping carts and thereby reduce site sales and total revenues. Some cyber-criminals develop special bots that can scan the victim's website to obtain information about the available products and prices. The victim's competitors can hire such hackers. They can use the data to lower prices on their websites.

   To protect against Bad Bots, a company should protect open APIs and mobile apps, and regularly check traffic sources for spikes, and then block those hosting providers and proxy services.

8. **Brute Force and Password Cracking**
   Brute force attacks target the admin panel of an online store and crack the password. These rogue programmes connect to the site and try thousands of combinations to get the victim's password. Always use strong, complex passwords that are difficult to guess. Also, always change your passwords frequently.

Active Defence

An online store can be attacked at any time, regardless of its underlying security level. Therefore, inbound traffic must be monitored and analysed. When visit requests are considered fraudulent, they must be completely blocked. This protection prevents a DDoS attack from slowing down site crawling or significantly impacting site performance.

Strong passwords and multi-factor authentication are equally important. It should be required that more complex passwords and multi-factor authentication be used internally for administrator access. This setting requires the logged-in user to associate their access password with another form of authentication, such as the authentication code sent in a text message. It is also needed to creating regular backups of the site: this way, if someone gains unauthorised access and makes drastic changes, the site can quickly be returned to previous backups.

9. The Man in the Middle

A hacker can eavesdrop on the communication between the online store and the user. If a user is connected to a vulnerable Wi-Fi or network, such attackers can take advantage of this.

EC sites must be SSL certified as this is the Google standard. It is a free and fairly straightforward way to add more layers of encryption and security to on-site transactions.

The Secure Sockets Layer certificate is an essential cybersecurity measure that protects website data from any type of cyberattack. An SSL certificate places a padlock and HTTPS on a web address, creating an encrypted link to prevent attackers from intercepting information or communication.

The web host should have a firewall for the servers, but it is also good to have one specifically for the site and computer. Many security plugins have built-in firewalls.

10. Electronic Skimming

Electronic skimming is the infection of checkout pages with malicious software. The aim is to steal customers' personal and payment information.

It is very important to update software regularly. The software works just as well as the latest version, so if it's not updated on the recommendation of the vendor, your EC site and your business are at risk. Schedule upgrades and update all programmes, software and plugins regularly.

Brand Monitoring

It is important to keep an eye on malicious activity against a website or application to avoid cyberattacks. Implementing a dedicated strict brand monitoring tool will help track all online fraudulent activities on behalf of the brand. It will also help protect your website and application from phishing and copyright infringement.

The top EC security threats we have looked at are potentially devastating not only to retailers but also to customers. For this reason, it is necessary to act appropriately and develop strategies to address them.

Summary

Operating conditions of orgaisations are determined by the globalisation processes, the rapidly changing and turbulent environment and the growing competitive pressure. An organisation's ability to maintain its position is often determined by its ability to take new opportunities brought by the development of informatics technologies and information techniques. The significance of this dimension of the development of contemporary organisations is manifested, in particular, in the aspect of the evolutionary transformation of industrial economy towards the so-called knowledge-based economy (e-business, virtual enterprise, networking enterprise). The achievement of an organisation's operating objectives and winning competitive advantage depends largely on its ability to adapt its organisational solutions, methods of operating, employee skills and tools, mainly ICT tools, to the challenges set by the modern environment of the information stage of the civilisational development. In other words, new opportunities brought by the development of information technologies and techniques give competing organisations chances for success and increasingly often become the basis for success. In turn, the development of informatics technique, telecommunications and the so-called multimedia cause tremendous changes to the environment which become the reason for the increasing importance of ICT in organisations. The evolution of the role of resources in economy shows changes leading towards a relative decrease in the importance of matter and energy in the post-industrial era and an increase in the importance of information and knowledge as key factors. The modern-day reality is dominated by information. Information and knowledge derived from it, as well as the ability to use it, are becoming a strategic resource in the context of an organisation's competitiveness and ability to create innovation. Information and knowledge are today the foundation of economy, culture and politics. Information technology is entering every sphere of life, while the civilisational change is measured by the fact that "the human mind is becoming a direct production force, not just a decision-making element in the production process". One can observe the emergence of a society which is referred to as information society[1], where information technologies determine the conditions of work, life and development. These technologies encompass "information and telecommunication techniques" which include the following:

- informatics and telecommunications equipment,
- telecommunications infrastructure,
- software,
- informatics systems and structures,
- methods of information processing.

The concept of information and communication technologies encompasses a family of technologies for processing, gathering and transmitting information

DOI: 10.1201/9781003271345-5

electronically. The term informatics technologies is narrower as it concerns technologies related to computers and software, but not to communication or network technologies. The technological development makes both these concepts increasingly more coherent. At the same time, they are the driving force behind the civilisational, social and economic development. Information and telecommunication techniques are under constant and dynamic development. This entails creation of new organisations and new unique workplaces, as well as a greater role of information technologies in management. Information technology (IT) is a key factor that determines an organisation's success, giving it the ability to improve effectiveness and efficiency. The digital environment plays a particularly important role in Europe, as investments in ICT account for half of the growth in organisations' productivity. The rapidly changing environment entails departure from and modification of traditional business models. The advent of the Internet era implies emergence of Internet and virtual organisations. According to current observations, transition to an electronic platform leads to at least partial levelling of chances for start-up organisations, allowing them to compete for customers with much larger and well-established rivals. The matter of availability of tools of the information era is connected with the issue of informatics infrastructure which – due to significant costs of implementation – should be subject of investments at local, regional and national levels.

Utilisation of digital capabilities requires a change in the way an organisation's functioning is defined. Deployment of ICT implies transformation of the entire process – from product design up to customer service. Digitalisation offers an advantage of flexibility, reduced production costs and better workplace organisation.

The use of Internet to run economic activity is becoming increasingly popular. E-business can complement a traditional organisation or be a venture launched online from the very start. The following models of e-business should be listed:

- transferred models – where the Internet is used for facilitating business processes and improving access to markets and customers (e.g. on-line stores),
- innovative models – where the Internet determines the existence of the business (e.g. Internet search engines),
- new forms of cooperation, competition and specialisation.

Cloud computing is another example of using modern informatics technologies and the main trend in the development of informatics innovations. All services based on virtual servers provide for decreasing the costs of investments in hardware IT solutions. Cloud-based services allow businesses, especially small ones, to use the latest technological solutions without the needs to invest large sums in purchases of software and infrastructure. This solution contributes to reducing general operating costs (expenditures on hardware and software and payroll costs) and enhancing flexibility, and thus represents an optimal support for their development. At present, effective market operations require own website as an important marketing tool. Websites are increasingly often used for presenting price lists, product or service catalogues as well as publishing information on job vacancies (with the option to upload job applications).

Electronic trade (e-commerce) is another important flexibility-building technique for contemporary enterprises which operate in the rapidly changing and turbulent environment. Social media represent a modern technique for marketing communication and cooperation between organisations, customers and business partners. Electronic mail and social media portals more and more often limit or even eliminate previously used telephone contacts. In particular, because of their increased popularity, social media portals are used by organisations to promote their products, offering such advantages as creating groups of loyal customers and effective acquisition of new ones. Furthermore, by communication in social media, organisations encourage sharing ideas which they can later use when creating and developing products and services. The literature describes this model of acquiring resources based on online provision of products and services as crowdsourcing. It is a relatively new communication idea which offers the possibility to use knowledge held by large groups of people, integrating them with a given organisation or person in order to conduct productive activities. Social media are increasingly often used in the process of workforce recruitment.

At present, new ICT technologies are considered to be among the most effective management and innovation tools, and a major economic growth factor. In this context, the processes aimed at intensifying the use of digital technologies imply the perspective of organisations' development in terms of process optimisation, sales market expansion, creation and development of innovative products and more effective use of the human capital. Particular advantages in the process of market competition and development are offered to small organisations which are just starting their activities. The possibility of versatile use of information from various sources were previously reserved mainly for large organisations which could spend large sums on launching data gathering and processing systems (infrastructure, qualified personnel). The development of information technologies has radically changed this state of affairs. Thanks to the widespread use of the Internet as a business tool, a large portion of useful information, which was previously hard to get or simply unavailable, has now become available. This requires efforts to be made to support the processes of digitalisation, particularly in small organisations.

Some revolutionary changes are taking place in the area of culture as a method of communication. Their deepest foundation lies in the transition from analogue encryption to digital encryption of at least one element of the communication path, as it is a condition for deploying the latest telecommunication technologies (however, people tend to omit the fact that digital encryption is excellently suitable for manipulation, thus creating previously unknown social and cultural opportunities and threats). Communication lies at the basis of human interactions. Without it, there would be no human being or society. On the other hand, transport of tangible media of culture is becoming obsolete and replaced by transport of thoughts. In front of our eyes, cultures are merging with the media culture. Telecommunications ever more strongly determines the shape of civilizational and cultural processes. It redefines such idea as civilisation and culture. One can therefore venture to say that the Internet is becoming a new platform for intercultural communication.

Since the 1980s, the global economy has been referred to as "globalisation". This is closely related to the development of information societies, while determining the global phenomena and processes by the degree of development of these societies. A great majority of specialists in the field believe that the progress in the economic globalisation is synchronised with the development of information societies. Contemporary information societies are subject to the effects of globalisation. It should also be noted that the degree of development of information societies affects and determines the pace and nature of global processes.

The result was the following: Information technology for the financial market have been reviewed and systematized. There were systematized E-commerce tools, international payment systems and modern money systems. The risks of modern financial market instruments were also considered and the security rules for using banking services, e-commerce and payment systems were proposed.

Significant amounts of information and the inability to quickly process and control it in manual mode created the need for special software. Thus, a new information technology market for managing financial flows and electronic commerce emerged. The rapid development of the financial management technologies has created modern business proposals such as digital and virtual currencies, crowd-funding, peer-to-peer lending, mobile banking, online investment and new payment systems.

New information technologies allow firms to increase competitiveness using financial products and services, thus increasing their value. IT users receive significant savings and choice of investment options.

At the same time, new IT creates a challenge for regulators, who should monitor how this or that technology affects the financial sector. An example is the cryptocurrency market that created chaos until the middle of 2018 and led to significant losses for participants in the currency exchange market.

E-commerce systems on the Internet are subject to both financial and non-financial risks. These risks concern both users of payment systems and operators of the system. Analysis of the risks of payment systems is also advisable to proceed based on the classification of risks in their areas of origin, the mechanisms of calculation, their distribution over time. This makes it possible to assess the degree of each type of financial risk and to choose the methods of managing them.

Further, the global payment value chain is efficient mainly because globalization has led to liberalization of the banking rules and regulations that have enabled banks anywhere to deal with other banks everywhere and anytime and every time.

So, the sent or received international payment is processed smoothly and successfully because of bits and bytes of data and information streaming across the world and is under control banks' security systems.

NOTE

1 A society is becoming more information-based when it reaches the level of development and the scale of complexity of its social and economic processes which require application of new techniques for gathering, processing, transmitting and using large quantities of information generated by these processes. Information as well as the resulting knowledge and technologies become the primary production factor.

References

Aasheim C.H.L., Lixin L.I., Williams S. 2019. Knowledge and skill requirements for entry-level information technology workers: A comparison of industry and academia. *Journal of Information Systems Education*, 20.3, p. 10.

Adamczewski P. et al. 2017. Środowisko SMAC jako determinanta zarządzania 3.0. *Przedsiębiorczość i Zarządzanie*, 18.10.1, pp. 11–22.

Agarwal M. 30 Jun 2016. *New York Based Payments Platform Payoneer Re-Enters Indian Market*. Inc42. https://inc42.com/buzz/payoneer-india/

Alipay, *China's leading third-party online payment solution*. https://global.alipay.com/index.htm

Al-Laham, M., Al-Tarawneh, H. and Abdallat, N. 2009. *Development of Electronic Money and Its Impact on the Central Bank Role and Monetary Policy*. http://iisit.org/Vol6/IISITv6p339-349Al-Laham589.pdf

Allweyer T. 2020. *IT-Management: Grundlagen und Perspektiven für den erfolgreichen Einsatz von IT im Unternehmen*. BoD–Books on Demand.

Alpar P. et al. 2019. Bedeutung von Informationssystemen und grundlegende Begriffe. [In:] *Anwendungsorientierte Wirtschaftsinformatik*. Wiesbaden, Springer Vieweg, pp. 3–23.

Amazon Local Register. (n.d.). https://local.amazon.com/merchants/products/localregister

Anderl R. 2018. Informationstechnologie. [In:] *Dubbel*. Berlin, Heidelberg, Springer Vieweg, pp. 1997–2011.

Andrzejewski K. 2019. Security information management systems. Management sciences. *Nauki o Zarządzaniu*, 24.4, pp. 1–9.

Apple Pay. (n.d.). https://www.apple.com/apple-pay/

Apple Watch works with Apple Pay to replace your credit cards. (n.d.). https://www.theverge.com/2014/9/9/6127587/apple-watch-works-with-apple-pay-to-replace-your-credit-cards

Arana-Solares I.A. et al. 2019. Contextual factors intervening in the manufacturing strategy and technology management-performance relationship. *International Journal of Production Economics* 207, pp. 81–95.

Audit Report. Treasury.gov. 10 November 2015. https://www.treasury.gov/about/organizational-structure/ig/Audit%20Reports%20and%20Testimonies/OIG-16-006.pdf

Babik W. 2017. Organizacja i recepcja informacji w środowisku cyfrowym w świetle ekologii informacji. *Bibliotheca Nostra*, 2.48.

Bacs. (n.d.). https://www.bacs.co.uk/Pages/Home.aspx

Baun C.H. 2019. Grundlagen der Informationstechnik. [In:] *Computer Networks/Computernetze*. Wiesbaden, Springer Vieweg, pp. 3–13.

Behringer S. 2017. Unternehmen in der Krise. [In:] *Unternehmenssanierung*. Wiesbaden, Springer Gabler, pp. 1–35.

Benker T., Jürck C. 2016. Das betriebliche Informationssystem. [In:] *Geschäftsprozessorientierte Systementwicklung*. Wiesbaden, Springer Vieweg, pp. 25–32.

Berdowska A., Mikuláš P. 2020. *Technologie cyfrowe wspomagające komunikację organizacji*. Uniwersytet Ekonomiczny w Katowicach, Prace Naukowe, pp. 126–147.

Bergemann D., Morris S. 2019. Information Design: A Unified Perspective. *Journal of Economic Literature*. 57 (1), pp. 44–95.

Biehl B. 2020. Bereiche der Kreativwirtschaft. [In:] *Management in der Kreativwirtschaft*. Wiesbaden, Springer Gabler, pp. 3–23.

Biryukov A., Khovratovich D., Pustogarov I. 2014. *Deanonymisation of clients in Bitcoin P2P network*. *ACM Conference on Computer and Communications Security* http://orbilu.uni.lu/handle/10993/18679, (12.11.2017).

Bitpay. (n.d.). https://bitpay.com/pricing/

Blickle G. 2019. Anforderungsanalyse. [In:] *Arbeits-und Organisationspsychologie*. Berlin, Heidelberg, Springer, pp. 235–249.

Bombała B. 2017. Zagadnienie wiedzy i organizacyjnej kreatywności-ujęcie fenomenologiczne *Education of Economists & Managers*, 44, pp. 2.

Bonadonna E. 2013. *Bitcoin and the Double-spending Problem*. Cornell University. http://blogs.cornell.edu/info4220/2013/03/29/bitcoin-and-the-double-spending-problem/, (12.11.2017).

Brătianu C. 2017. Foreword: The knowledge economy: The present future. [In:] *Management Dynamics in the Knowledge Economy*, 5.4, pp. 477–479.

Brenner W., Broy M., Leimeister J.M. 2017. Auf dem Weg zu einer Informatik neuer Prägung in Wissenschaft, *Studium und Wirtschaft*. Informatik-Spektrum, 40.6, pp. 602–606.

Brzeziński S., Bubel D. 2016. Asymilacja standardów funkcjonowania organizacji inteligentnych w procesach zarządzania na przykładzie niemieckich przedsiębiorstw. *Studia i Prace Kolegium Zarządzania i Finansów, Szkoła Główna Handlowa*, 148, pp. 85–97.

Buchholz U., Knorre S. 2019. Risikomanagement. [In:] *Interne Kommunikation und Unternehmensführung*. Wiesbaden, Springer Gabler, 2019. pp. 177–198.

Bühler P., Schlaich P., Sinner D. 2019. Datenschutz–Datensicherheit. [In:] *Datenmanagement*. Heidelberg, Berlin, Springer Vieweg, pp. 80–97.

Cahill J.M. et al. 2019. *Server farm management*. U.S. Patent Application No 16/238, p. 30.

Calvo-Amodio J., Rousseau D. 2019. David. The human activity system: Emergence from purpose, boundaries, relationships, and context. *Procedia Computer Science*, 153, pp. 91–99.

Capurro R. 2017. Ethik der Informationsgesellschaft. [In:] *Homo Digitalis*. Wiesbaden, Springer VS, pp. 127–148.

Casas J.A., Ortega-Ruiz R., Monks C.P. 2020. Cyberbullying: A changing phenomenon. [In:] *Online Peer Engagement in Adolescence*. Routledge, pp. 71–84.

Casey M.J., Vigna P. 2014. Short-Term Fixes To Avert 51% Attack. Money Beat. *Wall Street Journal*. https://blogs.wsj.com/moneybeat/2014/06/16/bitbeat-a-51-attack-what-is-it-and-could-it-happen/ (12.11.2017).

Chan L. et al. 2019. Survey of AI in cybersecurity for information technology management. [In:] *Technology & Engineering Management Conference (Temscon)*, IEEE, pp. 1–8.

Chandrashekhar A.M., Muktha G., Anjana D. 2016. Cyberstalking and Cyberbullying: Effects and prevention measures. *Imperial Journal of Interdisciplinary Research*, 2.3, pp. 95–102.

Chang F.-M. 2020. Optimization analysis of management operation for a server farm. *Quality Technology & Quantitative Management*, 17.3, pp. 307–318.

Chaps https://www.bankofengland.co.uk/payment-and-settlement/chaps

Chaum D. 1982. *Blind signatures for untraceable payments*. Santa Barbara, CA, Department of Computer Science, University of California.

Chaux E. et al. 2016. Effects of the cyberbullying prevention program media heroes (Medienhelden) on traditional bullying. [In:] *Aggressive Behavior*, 42.2, pp. 157–165.

Clearing House Interbank Payments System (CHIPS) https://www.investopedia.com/terms/clearing-house-interbank-payments-system-chips.asp

Çoklar A.N., Yaman N.D., Yurdakul I.K. 2017. Information literacy and digital nativity as determinants of online information search strategies. [In:] *Computers in Human Behavior*, 70, pp. 1–9.

Dallinger U. 2017. *Kommunikation*, Verstehen, Verständigung. Hermeneutische Wissenssoziologie. Standpunkte zur Theorie der Interpretation, p. 237.

Data protection in e-commerce. (n.d.). https://www.ionos.com/digitalguide/websites/digital-law/data-protection-in-e-commerce/

Davletkireeva L.Z., Novikova T.B., Prasolova E.A. 2019. Development of Basic Model of IT Enterprise Architecture: Audit of Problems and Methods of Their Solution. [In:] *International Multi-Conference on Industrial Engineering and Modern Technologies (FarEastCon)*, IEEE, pp. 1–5.

Davydov V. Rudetskaya M. 2015. *A. V. Electronic commerce: Textbook. allowance / Khabarovsk: Pacific Publishing House.* State University, p. 149.

De Haes S.et al. 2020. COBIT as a Framework for Enterprise Governance of IT. [In:] *Enterprise Governance of Information Technology.* Cham, Springer, pp. 125–162.

Detrixhe J. 2020. *Central banks are contemplating a world without cash* https://www.g4scashreport.com/

Digital Currencies. 2015. https://www.bis.org/cpmi/publ/d137.pdf

Directive 2009/110/EC of the European Parliament and of the Council of 16 September 2009 on the taking up, pursuit and prudential supervision of the business of electronic money institutions amending Directives 2005/60/EC and 2006/48/EC and repealing Directive 2000/46/EC, Official Journal L 267, 10/10/2009 P. 0007 - 0017. https://eur-lex.europa.eu/legal-content/en/ALL/?uri=CELEX:32009L0110

Donlea T. 2015. *Risk Management Solutions for E-commerce,* http://losspreventionmedia.com/insider/data-protection/risk-management-solutions-for-E-commerce/ (12.11.2017).

Easytrip, O2 launch mobile toll payments service in the Republic of Ireland. (n.d.).

Ecommerce Introductory Guide to International eCommerce, Part 1: Customer Data and Privacy. (n.d.). https://www.scalefast.com/blog/customer-data-and-privacy

Ecommerce Security and Protection Plan for Your Online Store. 2020. Saud Razzak https://www.cloudways.com/blog/ecommerce-security-tips/

E-commerce Security Threats That Are Getting Stronger By The Day! Jinson Varghese. (n.d.). https://www.getastra.com/blog/knowledge-base/ecommerce-security-threats/

Edwards J. 2013. *A Thief Is Attempting To Hide $100 Million In Stolen Bitcoins — And You Can Watch It Live Right Now. Business Insider.* http://www.businessinsider.com/a-thief-is-attempting-to-hide-100-million-in-stolen-bitcoins-and-you-can-watch-it-live-right-now-2013-12, (12.11.2017).

Eickhoff T. et al. 2019. Intelligentes Informationsmanagement für verfügbarkeitsorientierte Geschäftsmodelle. [In:] *Entwicklung datenbasierter Produkt-Service Systeme.* Berlin, Heidelberg, Springer Vieweg, pp. 45–108.

El Emary I.M.M., Brzozowska A., Bubel D. 2020. *Management of organizational culture as a stabilizer of changes: Organizational culture management dilemmas.* CRC Press.

Electronic Fund Transfer Act (Regulation E). Federal Deposit Insurance Corporation. https://www.fdic.gov/news/news/financial/2009/fil09066.pdf

Electronic Money. (n.d.). https://www.investopedia.com/terms/e/electronic-money.asp

Elm W.A. 2018. *Das Management – Informationssystem als Mittel der Unternehmensführung.* Walter de Gruyter GmbH & Co KG.

Erner M., Hammer S. 2019. Strategisches Management 4.0. [In:] *Management 4.0–Unternehmensführung im digitalen Zeitalter.* Berlin, Heidelberg, Springer Gabler, pp. 123–170.

Federal Reserve. January 16, 2009. *Board of Governors FAQ.* Federal Reserve. http://www.federalreserve.gov/generalinfo/faq/faqbog.htm

Fedwire Funds Service-Annual. (n.d.). *Federal reserve.gov. Board of Governors of the Federal Reserve System.* https://www.federalreserve.gov/paymentsystems/fedfunds_ann.htm

Fedwire Participant Directory. (n.d.). http://www.fededirectory.frb.org/download.cfm

Ferstl O.K., Sinz E.J. 2019. *Software-Konzepte der Wirtschaftsinformatik.* Walter de Gruyter GmbH & Co KG.

Fox C. 2018. Understanding the New ISO and COSO Updates. *Risk Management,* 65.6, pp. 4–7.

Free transaction relay policy – Bitcoin Wiki. (n.d.). https://en.bitcoin.it/wiki/Free_transaction_relay_policy[1]

Friedl G., Pedell B. 2020. Burkhard. Integriertes Controlling mit SAP-Software. [In:] *Controlling mit SAP®.* Wiesbaden, Springer Vieweg, pp. 189–217.

Friedrichsen M., Wersig W. 2020. Digitale Kompetenz–Handlungsoptionen und Perspektiven. [In:] *Digitale Kompetenz.* Wiesbaden, Springer Gabler, pp. 289–304.

From your wallet to Google Wallet: your digital payment options, The Conversation, 26-05-2013 http://theconversation.com/from-your-wallet-to-google-wallet-your-digital-payment-options-14540

Furmanek W. 2002. Kluczowe umiejętności technologii informacyjnych (eksplikacja pojęć). [In:] *Dydaktyka informatyki*, p. 250.

Gadatsch A. 2020. Modellierung und Analyse von Prozessen. [In:] *Grundkurs Geschäftsprozess-Management*. Wiesbaden, Springer Vieweg, pp. 87–151.

Gadatsch A., Mangiapane M. 2017a. Sicherheitsanforderungen herausarbeiten. [In:] *IT-Sicherheit*. Wiesbaden, Springer Vieweg, 2017. pp. 23–32.

Gadatsch A., Mangiapane M. 2017b. Vier Dimensionen der IT-Sicherheit. [In:] *IT-Sicherheit*. Wiesbaden, Springer Vieweg, pp. 17–22.

Gansmeier D., Forsthofer R. 2019. Studie zur Rezeption des Modells der "Lernenden Organisation"nach Senge bei Mitarbeitern und Führungskräften in einem Unternehmen des öffentlichen Dienstes. [In:] *Nachhaltigkeit im interdisziplinären Kontext*. Wiesbaden, Springer, pp. 51–68.

Gasparski W. 2019. Działania przedsiębiorcze a prakseologia i etyka. *Prakseologia*, 161, pp. 5–28.

Gibbons R., Prusak L. 2020. Knowledge, stories, and culture in organizations. [In:] *AEA Papers and Proceedings*, pp. 187–192.

Gleißner W. 2017. Grundlagen des Risikomanagements: mit fundierten Informationen zu besseren Entscheidungen. *Vahlen*.

Glenc P. 2020. Automatyzacja analizy cyfrowej komunikacji organizacji. *Prace Naukowe, Uniwersytet Ekonomiczny w Katowicach*, pp. 108–125.

Glinkowska B. 2012. *Wybrane aspekty zarządzania wiedzą w małych i średnich przedsiębiorstwach*. Zeszyty Naukowe Uniwersytetu Szczecińskiego. *Finanse, Rynki Finansowe, Ubezpieczenia*, 56, pp. 339–350.

Google Pay. (n.d.). https://pay.google.com/about/#friends

Gräfrath B., Huber R., Uhlemann B. 2020. *Einheit. Interdisziplinarität. Komplementarität: Orientierungsprobleme der Wissenschaft heute*. Walter de Gruyter GmbH & Co KG.

Gruyter D. 2019. *Integrierte Datenverarbeitungssysteme für die Unternehmensführung*. Walter de Gruyter GmbH & Co KG, 2019.

Gryncewicz W. 2007. Podejście infologiczne w doskonaleniu jakości informacji. Prace Naukowe Akademii Ekonomicznej we Wrocławiu. Informatyka Ekonomiczna, 11.1156, *Informatyka ekonomiczna: wybrane zagadnienia*, pp. 158–168.

Gunia G. 2019. Zintegrowane systemy informatyczne przedsiębiorstw w kontekście Przemysłu 4.0. *Zarządzanie Przedsiębiorstwem*, 22.2.

Hahn D. 2020. Risikomanagement. [In:] *Risiko-Management in Kommunen*. Wiesbaden, Springer Gabler, pp. 13–46.

Hanschke I. 2019. *Informationssicherheit und Datenschutz systematisch und nachhaltig gestalten: Eine kompakte Einführung in die Praxis*. Springer-Verlag.

Hanschke I., Schwarz C. 2019. Informationssicherheit – lean & agil. *Wirtschaftsinformatik & Management*, 11.4, pp. 216–223.

Hernes M. et al. 2019. Reprezentacja wiedzy kolektywnej organizacji w systemach informatycznych zarządzania. *Przedsiębiorczość i Zarządzanie*, 20.4.1, pp. 77–87.

Hoffmann M.J. 2019. *Betriebliche Informationswirtschaft und Datenverarbeitungsorganisation: Analyse und Konzeption von Organisationssystemen*. Walter de Gruyter GmbH & Co KG. http://www.dab-europe.com

Huber E., Hellwig O., Quirchmayr G. 2016. Wissensaustausch und Vertrauen unter Computer Emergency Response Teams – eine europäische Herausforderung. *Datenschutz und Datensicherheit - DuD*, 40.3, pp. 162–166.

Hügelmeyer P., Glöggler A. 2020. Integre Gestaltung von Veränderungsprozessen. [In:] *Integrität in der Führung*. Berlin, Heidelberg, Springer Gabler, pp. 171–194.

Huszlak W., Skrzypek A. 2019. Dojrzałość i doskonalenie organizacji. *Bezpieczeństwo. Teoria i Praktyka*, 37.4, pp. 209–215.

Hyodo N. et al. 2020. Resilient Virtual Network Function Placement Model Based on Recovery Time Objectives. *21st International Conference on High Performance Switching and Routing (HPSR)*. IEEE, pp. 1–7.

Impact of technology on the financial sector. (n.d.). https://www.kemplittle.com/news/impact-of-technology-on-the-financial-sector/

Irawan S. et al. 2019. Hybrid Soft System Methodology (SSM) and Becerra Approach for Modeling Knowledge Management System. *Journal of Physics: Conference Series. IOP Publishing*, p. 012055.

Jabłońska M. 2019. Personalizacja internetu: zagrożenie czy naturalny proces rozwoju sieci? *Com. press*, 2 (1).

Jacob M. 2019. Digitalisierung und Nachhaltigkeit in Unternehmen. [In:] *Digitalisierung & Nachhaltigkeit*. Wiesbaden, Springer Vieweg.

Jaffe J.M., Tippins S., Wesley D. 2000. Risk Management for the Internet, E-commerce Series, San Diego, Volume 26, No. 2. https://www.soa.org/Library/Proceedings/Record-Of-The-Society-Of-Actuaries/2000-09/2000/January/rsa00v26n278pd.aspx, (12.11.2017).

Jecker C., Huck-Sandhu S. 2020. Von der Information zur Orientierung. Zur (neuen) Rolle der internen Kommunikation in Selbstorganisationen. [In:] *Der Mensch in der Selbstorganisation*. Wiesbaden, Springer Gabler, pp. 351–371.

Kalisz D., Szyran-Resiak A. 2019. Organizacja wirtualna w erze społeczeństwa informacyjnego. *Zeszyty Naukowe PWSZ w Płocku, Nauki Ekonomiczne*.

Karame G.O., Androulaki E., Capkun S. 2012. *Two Bitcoins at the Price of One? Double-Spending Attacks on Fast Payments in Bitcoin*. International Association for Cryptologic Research. http://eprint.iacr.org/2012/248.pdf (12.11.2017).

Kärtner J. 2019. Zur Theorie und Typologie der Erfolgsmedien: On the Theory and Typology of Success Media. *Zeitschrift für Soziologie*, 48.2, pp. 116–135.

Kautt Y. 2019. Zum Begriff der visuellen Kommunikation. [In:] *Soziologie Visueller Kommunikation*. Wiesbaden, Springer VS, pp. 31–42.

Kels P. 2019. Zur Digitalisierung und Algorithmisierung von Arbeit im Kontext wissensbasierter Organisationen. *Digitalisierung der Wissensarbeit: Interdisziplinäre Analysen und Fallstudien*, p. 34.

Kęsy M. 2019. Jakość kształcenia w ujęciu standardów cywilizacyjnych społeczeństwa informacyjnego. *Dydaktyka informatyki*, 14, pp. 120–134.

Kilian K.J. et al. 2018. Epistemiczne układy odniesienia– nowe spojrzenie na racjonalność naukową. [In:] *ΣΟΦΙΑ. Pismo Filozofów Krajów Słowiańskich*, 18, pp. 37–58.

Kizza J.M. 2017. Computer crime investigations and ethics. [In:] *Ethical and social issues in the information age*. Cham, Springer, pp. 339–353.

Klinger J. et al. 2020. Informationsmanagement. [In:] *Management im Gesundheitswesen*. Wiesbaden, Springer Gabler, pp. 185–199.

Klinkel S., Rahn J., Bernhard R. 2017. Schlüsselkompetenzen für die Entwicklung digitalvernetzter Lösungen. *Prozesse, Technologie, Anwendungen, Systeme und Management*, pp. 267–280.

Kofler T. 2018. Digitalisierungsaspekte. [In:] *Das digitale Unternehmen*. Berlin, Heidelberg, Springer Vieweg, pp. 73–99.

Kollmann T. 2019. Die Grundlagen des E-Procurement. [In:] *E-Business*. Wiesbaden, Springer Gabler, pp. 139–258.

Korombel A., Nowicka-Skowron M. 2017. Innowacje i działalność innowacyjna polskich przedsiębiorstw w świetle krajowych i zagranicznych badań. *Zeszyty Naukowe Wyższej Szkoły Humanitas. Zarządzanie*, 4, pp. 9–19.

Kral G. 2004. Psychologie und Internet – einige persönliche Betrachtungen. [In:] *Die Praxis der Psychologie*. Vienna, Springer, pp. 273–280.

Krebs J. 2019. *Uninformative Information: Informationsübertragung als irreführende Leitmetapher der Informationsgesellschaft.* Transcript Verlag.

Kubiak T. 2017. Media społecznościowe jako źródło informacji rynkowej. *Marketing Instytucji Naukowych i Badawczych*, 2/24, pp. 1–58.

Kühn A., Kühn F.H. 2017. Schlüsselkompetenz Kommunikation: Pulsschlag der Veränderung. [In:] *Veränderungsintelligenz*. Wiesbaden, Springer Gabler, pp. 481–540.

Kura K. et al. 2019. Optimal control for disease vector management in SIT models: an integro-difference equation approach. *Journal of Mathematical Biology*, 78.6, pp. 1821–1839.

Kuzmenko E. 2019. Industrial enterprise risk management [In:] *Проблемы научной мысли*, 8.1, pp. 50–55.

Lambert S.L. et al. 2017. Assembly FG: An educational case on MRP II integrated within ERP. *Accounting Perspectives*, 16.1, pp. 43–62.

Lambertz M. 2018. *Die intelligente Organisation: das Playbook für organisatorische Komplexität.* BusinessVillage.

Langefors B. 1980. Infological models and information user views. *Information Systems*, 5.1, pp. 17–32.

Lee T. 2013. When will the people who called Bitcoin a bubble admit they were wrong. *The Washington Post*. https://www.washingtonpost.com/news/the-switch/wp/2013/11/05/when-will-the-people-who-called-bitcoin-a-bubble-admit-they-were-wrong/?utm_term=.38d8b80e06c0 (12.11.2017).

Lenhard T.H. 2020. *Datensicherheit: technische und organisatorische schutzmanahmen gegen datenverlust und: computerkriminalitätincludes digital download.* Morgan Kaufmann, 2020.

Lenk K. 2017. Wissensmanagement als Brücke zwischen Informationstechnik und Verwaltungsrealität. [In:] *Verwaltung, Informationstechnik & Management.* Nomos Verlagsgesellschaft mbH & Co. KG, pp. 87–100.

Liu A. 2014. Beyond Bitcoin: A Guide to the Most Promising Cryptocurrencies. *Vice Motherboard*. Archived from the original on 24 December 2013. Retrieved 7 January 2014. https://web.archive.org/web/20131224084601/http:/motherboard.vice.com/blog/beyond-bitcoin-a-guide-to-the-most-promising-cryptocurrencies

Lombardi O., Holik F., Vanni L. 2016. What is Shannon information? *Synthese*, 193.7, pp. 1983–2012.

Lovick S. 2020. *What Is The Sharing Economy?* https://www.businessbecause.com/news/insights/6736/what-is-the-sharing-economy

Lutz T. 2019. *Das computerorientierte Informationssystem (CIS): eine methodische Einführung.* Walter de Gruyter GmbH & Co KG.

Lyre H. 2017. Der Begriff der Information: Was er leistet und was er nicht leistet. [In:] *Berechenbarkeit der Welt?* Wiesbaden, Springer VS, pp. 477–493.

Macdonald, S., Jarvis, L., Lavis, S.M. 2019. Cyberterrorism today? Findings from a follow-on survey of researchers. *Studies in Conflict & Terrorism*, 1–26.

Maciąg R. 2008. Nowe techniki informacyjne jako modelowanie rzeczywistości: podstawowe pytania badawcze. [In:] Wilk E., Kolasińska-Pasterczyk I., *Nowa audiowizualność: nowy paradygmat kultury?* Kraków, Wydawnictwo Uniwersytetu Jagiellońskiego pp. 271–286.

Madauss B.J. 2017. Risikomanagement im Projekt. [In:] *Projektmanagement.* Berlin, Heidelberg, Springer Vieweg, pp. 663–690.

Mammes I. et al. 2019. Technology, Information Technology and Natural Science as Basics for Innovation. [In:] *Zur Bedeutung der Technischen Bildung in Fächerverbünden.* Wiesbaden, Springer Spektrum, pp. 93–109.

Mangat M. 2020. *Top eCommerce Security Threats with Solutions for 2020* https://phoenixnap.com/blog/ecommerce-security-threats

Martin A. 6 June 2018. *Ripple and Swift slug it out over cross-border payments. Financial Times.* https://www.ft.com/content/631af8cc-47cc-11e8-8c77-ff51caedcde6

Martínková I. 2017. *Body Ecology: Avoiding body–mind dualism. Loisir et Société/Society and Leisure*, 40.1: pp.101–112.

Marz O. et al. 2019. Informationstechnologie im Kontext der Wirtschaft. [In:] *IT-Investitionen verstehen und bewerten*. Berlin, Heidelberg, Springer Gabler, pp. 7–17.

Matysek M. et al. 2019. Holistyczne ujęcie zarządzania ryzykiem bezpieczeństwa informacji w organizacjach sektora publicznego. *Zarządzanie Publiczne*, 3 (47), pp. 175–189.

Meggle G. 2019. Theorien der Kommunikation Eine Einführung. [In:] *Kommunikationstheoretische Schriften*. Mentis Verlag, pp. 29–35.

Melnyk L. G., Brukhanova M.V. 2010. *Social and economic problems of the information society*. Sumy, University Book.

MetaStock (n.d.). https://www.metastock.com/

Meter D.J., Bauman S. 2018. Moral disengagement about cyberbullying and parental monitoring: Effects on traditional bullying and victimization via cyberbullying involvement. *The Journal of Early Adolescence*, 38.3: pp. 303–326.

Meyer S. 2020. *Evolving Ecommerce: 14 Trends Driving Online Retail In 2020. Bigcommerce*. https://www.bigcommerce.com/blog/ecommerce-trends/#14-ecommerce-trends-leading-the-way, (12.11.2017).

Mick J. 2011. *Cracking the Bitcoin: Digging Into a $131M USD Virtual Currency. Daily Tech*. http://www.dailytech.com/Cracking+the+Bitcoin+Digging+Into+a+131M+USD+Virtual+Currency/article21878.htm, (12.11.2017).

Mihelj S., Leguina A., Downey J. 2019. Culture is digital: Cultural participation, diversity and the digital divide. *New Media & Society*, 21.7, pp. 1465–1485.

Mobipay – Fujitsu Spain. (n.d.). https://www.fujitsu.com/es/about/resources/case-studies/mobipay_en.html

Möller C.H. 2019. WSIS: Der Weltgipfel zur Informationsgesellschaft. [In:] *Kommunikationsfreiheit im Internet*. Wiesbaden, Springer VS, pp. 155–193.

Müller K.W. 2017. Internetsucht – das lange missverstandene Phänomen. [In:] *Internetsucht*. Wiesbaden, Springer Spektrum, pp. 9–15.

Neuhaus M. 2019. Perspektiven des organisatorischen Wandels und des Veränderungsmanagements. [In:] *Wandel in Managementberatungen*. Wiesbaden, Springer Gabler, pp. 73–126.

Nogalski B., Niewiadomski P. 2019. Samoocena dojrzałości w strategicznym zarządzaniu zasobami ludzkimi-spojrzenie przez pryzmat modelu ciągłego doskonalenia. *Studia i Prace Kolegium Zarządzania i Finansów*, 175: pp. 15176–15176.

Nonaka I., Nishihara A.H. 2018. Introduction to the concepts and frameworks of knowledge-creating theory. [In:] *Knowledge creation in community development*. Cham, Palgrave Macmillan, pp. 1–15.

Nonaka I., Nishihara A.H., Kawada H. 2018. Knowledge-based management theory. [In:] *Knowledge creation in public administrations*. Cham, Palgrave Macmillan, pp. 1–21.

North K., Brandner A., Steininger T. 2016. Die Wissenstreppe: Information–Wissen–Kompetenz. [In:] *Wissensmanagement für Qualitätsmanager*. Wiesbaden, Springer Gabler, pp. 5–8.

O2– O2 money – The O2 Wallet service closed on 31 March 2014. https://www.o2.co.uk/money

Ogonowski P. 2019. *Mobile Commerce: How to Get 3X More Revenue From M-Commerce*. https://www.growcode.com/blog/mobile-commerce/

Ogonowski P., 2020. *The Top 40 Ecommerce Trends for 2020*. https://www.growcode.com/blog/ecommerce-trends/

Osterhage W. 2018. Telematik. [In:] *Sicherheitskonzepte in der mobilen Kommunikation*. Berlin, Heidelberg, Springer Vieweg, pp. 139–151.

Pagliery J. 2014. *Bitcoin: And the Future of Money*. https://www.amazon.com/Bitcoin-Future-Money-Jose-Pagliery-ebook/dp/B00ME3PW36

Pallavi Dutta Top 5 Cyber Threats to E-commerce Security. (n.d.). https://www.kratikal.com/ blog/top-5-cyber-threats-to-e-commerce-security/

Panasiewicz L. 2004. Kontrowersje w sprawie zarządzania wiedzą. *Ekonomika i organizacja przedsiębiorstwa*, 7, pp. 42–49.

Panasiewicz L. 2019. Rozwój zdolności dynamicznych z perspektywy zarządzania wiedzą. *Marketing i Rynek*, 12, pp. 12–17.

Passport-Verification Service. WebMoney. (n.d.). http://passport.wmtransfer.com/asp/ WMCertify.asp

Payoneer. 16 May 2017. *Payments without borders*. Englewood Cliffs, New Jersey, CNBC. https://www.cnbc.com/2017/05/16/payoneer-2017-disruptor-50.html

Payoneer. 2019. Taking Prepaid Debit Cards to the Next Level. www.ecommercetimes.com. Retrieved 2019-02-01.

PayPal. (n.d.). https://www.paypal.com/us/

PDSnet. (n.d.). https://www.pdsnet.co.za/

Persson P. 2018. Attention manipulation and information overload. *Behavioural Public Policy*, 2.1, pp. 78–106.

Podolski P. et al. 2019. Manipulacja informacją na rynkach finansowych: przyczynek do analizy na przykładzie rynku kapitałowego w Polsce. *Ekonomia Międzynarodowa*, 26, pp. 112–133.

Poljak R., Poščić P., Jakšić D. 2017. Comparative analysis of the selected relational database management systems. *40th International Convention on Information and Communication Technology, Electronics and Microelectronics (MIPRO)*. IEEE, pp. 1496–1500.

Pospiech M. 2019. *Marco. Aufgabengerechte Informationsbereitstellung in Zeiten von Big Data: Konsequenzen für ein Informationsmanagement*. Springer-Verlag.

Quartz/oz.com/Data: Central banks G4S World Cash Report. (n.d.). https://www. g4scashreport.com/https://qz.com/1810727/central-banks-are-researching-digital-currencies-to-replace-cash/

Reinhold T. 2016. Zur Verantwortung der Informatik in einer technologisierten Gesellschaft. Sicherheit und Frieden (S+ F), *Security and Peace*, 2016, 253–256.

Reshevsky M. 2011. Gold rush XXI century // *ComputerBild: magazine*. – 2011. – August 15 (No. 17). C. 64–69.

Role of Information Technology (IT) in the Banking Sector. (n.d.). https://www.mbaknol.com/ business-finance/role-of-information-technology-it-in-the-banking-sector/

Romanowska M. 2016. Determinanty innowacyjności polskich przedsiębiorstw. *Przegląd Organizacji*, 2.913, pp. 29–35.

Romeike E., Hager P. 2020. Risiko – Management in der Informations- und Kommunikationstechnologie (IuK). [In:] *Erfolgsfaktor Risiko-Management 4.0*. Wiesbaden, Springer Gabler, 2020. pp. 479–520.

Rot A. et al. 2011. Kwantyfikatywne i kwalifikatywne metody analizy ryzyka na potrzeby bezpieczeństwa systemów informatycznych w organizacji. *Informatyka Ekonomiczna*, 20, pp. 189–203.

Rozkrut A. et al. 2018. Kompetencje cyfrowe społeczeństwa informacyjnego. *Studia i Prace WNEiZ US*, 54/3, pp. 347–360.

Sala J., Tańska H. 2019. Kreowanie i przygotowywanie systemów informatycznych w przedsiębiorstwach MMSP jako główne czynniki rozwoju polskiego społeczeństwa informacyjnego. [In:] *Nierówności społeczne a wzrost gospodarczy*, 58, pp. 198–208

Saltis S. 2020a. The *Future of eCommerce: eCommerce Trends To Watch For In 2020 Core dna*. https://www.coredna.com/blogs/ecommerce-trends#3, (15.12.2020).

Saltis S. 2020b. *D2C Benefits: Here's Why Manufacturers Are Going D2C Core dna*. https:// www.coredna.com/blogs/direct-to-consumer-benefits (15.12.2020)

Saraswat A. 2015. *Risk Management in E-commerce*, https://www.linkedin.com/pulse/ risk-management-E-commerce-alok-saraswat

Schlagwein D., Schoder D. Spindeldreher K. 2019. Consolidated, systemic conceptualization, and definition of the "sharing economy". *Journal of the Association for Information Science and Technology*. doi: 10.1002/asi.24300.

Scott S.V., Zachariadis M. 2014. *The Society for Worldwide Interbank Financial Telecommunication (SWIFT) Cooperative governance for network innovation, standards, and community*. London and New York, Routledge, p. 192.

See how long it takes to send or receive money – Google Wallet Help. (n.d.). https://support.google.com/pay/answer/7643913?hl=en&visit_id=637108133140111929-3809918766&rd=2

Sharing Economy. (n.d.). https://www.investopedia.com/terms/s/sharing-economy.asp#:~:text= The%20sharing%20economy%20is%20an,%2Dbased%20on%2Dline%20platform

Sienkiewicz P. 2019. Wartość informacji w systemach zarządzania organizacją. *Automatyka, Akademia Górniczo-Hutnicza im. Stanisława Staszica w Krakowie*, 13, pp. 593–599.

Silitschanu P. *B2B Payments Learning: What are Fedwire Transfers?* americanexpress.com. American Express Company. https://www.americanexpress.com/us/foreign-exchange/articles/fedwire-transfers/

Skowron-Grabowska B., Szczepanik T., Besta P. 2019. Knowledge Management in Intelligent Organizations. *System Safety: Human-Technical Facility-Environment*, 1.1, pp. 1012–1019.

Skrill. (n.d.-a). https://www.finder.com/skrill

Skrill. (n.d.-b). https://www.skrill.com/

Society for Worldwide Interbank Financial Telecommunication. (n.d.). https://www.swift.com/about-us/discover-swift?AKredir=true

Software – Bitcoin Wiki. (n.d.). https://en.bitcoin.it/wiki/Software#Shopping_Cart_Integration_in_eCommerce-Systems

Song M. et al. 2019. Effects of aggressive traits on cyberbullying: Mediated moderation or moderated mediation? *Computers in Human Behavior*, 97, pp. 167–178.

Starcevic V., Aboujaoude E. 2017. Internet addiction: Reappraisal of an increasingly inadequate concept. *CNS Spectrums*, 22.1, pp. 7–13.

Statista 2019. https://www.statista.com/

Stefanowicz B. 2017. Informacja, wiedza, mądrość – podejście infologiczne. *Współczesne Problemy Zarządzania*, 1.2017, pp. 11–22.

Steinhardt I., Schneijderberg C.H. 2019. Legitimität von Daten und Wissen der Qualitätssicherung bzw. des Qualitätsmanagements. [In:] *Qualitätssicherung und Qualitätsmanagement an Hochschulen*. Rainer Hampp Verlag, pp. 183–204.

Stroińska E., Trippner-Hrabi J. 2017. *Wykorzystanie systemów informatycznych w zarządzaniu wiedzą – dobre praktyki*. Studia i Prace WNEiZ US, 47, pp. 261–270.

Suchanek A. 2020. Unternehmensverantwortung: Primum non nocere. [In:] *Entgrenzte Verantwortung*. Berlin, Heidelberg, Springer, pp. 109–123.

Sytnyk N.V. 2008. *Banking information systems: Textbook. manual*. Kyiv: KNEU. p. 384.

Taguchi Y., Yoshinaga T. 2018. System Resource Management to Control the Risk of Data-Loss in a Cloud-Based Disaster Recovery. [In:] *42nd Annual Computer Software and Applications Conference (COMPSAC)*, IEEE, pp. 210–215.

Target. (n.d.). https://www.ecb.europa.eu/pub/pdf/other/ANNEX4TARGET24thprogress.pdf

Ten eCommerce Trends 2020. https://10ecommercetrends.com/

The differences between cryptocurrencies, virtual, and digital currencies. (n.d.). https://thenextweb.com/hardfork/2019/02/19/the-differences-between-cryptocurrencies-virtual-and-digital-currencies/

The Top Ecommerce Trends You Need to Know About for 2020. https://www.sellbrite.com/blog/ecommerce-trends-2020/

Thielscher C.H. 2020. Wirtschaft, Gerechtigkeit und Ethik. [In:] *Wirtschaftswissenschaften verstehen*. Springer Gabler, Wiesbaden, pp. 15–49.

This Day in Tech: Google Wallet launches. (n.d.). https://www.cnet.com/news/this-day-in-tech-google-wallet-launches/

Threat to E-Commerce. (n.d.). https://www.javatpoint.com/security-threat-to-e-commerce

Tiemeyer E. (ed.) 2020. *Handbuch IT-Management: Konzepte, Methoden, Lösungen und Arbeitshilfen für die Praxis.* Carl Hanser Verlag GmbH Co KG.

Transaction fees – Play Console Help. (n.d.). https://support.google.com/googleplay/android-developer/answer/112622?hl=en2

Turban E., King D., McKay J., Marshall P., Lee J., Vielhand, D. 2008. *Electronic Commerce 2008: A Managerial Perspective.* London, Pearson Education Ltd. p. 550.

Turriago-Hoyos A., Thoene U., Arjoon S. 2016. *Knowledge workers and virtues in Peter Drucker's management theory. SAGE Open,* 6.1, 2158244016639631.

Ullah F., Sepasgozar S. M. 2019. A study of information technology adoption for real-estate management: A system dynamic model. *Innovative Production And Construction: Transforming Construction Through Emerging Technologies,* pp. 469–484.

Urbanowska-Sojkin E. 2017. System informacyjny w wyborach strategicznych przedsiębiorstw. *Ekonomika i Organizacja Przedsiębiorstwa,* 12, pp. 240–256.

Urbanowska-Sojkin E., Weinert A. 2019. Wykorzystanie systemów IT w informacyjnym wspomaganiu wyborów strategicznych w przedsiębiorstwach działających w różnych sektorach. *Przegląd Organizacji,* 4, pp. 58–67.

Urbanowska-Sojkin E. et al. 2014. Zarządzanie ryzykiem wobec wyzwań z otoczenia. *Prace Naukowe Uniwersytetu Ekonomicznego we Wrocławiu* 366, pp. 560–571.

Vanderschuren L. et al. 2017. Punishment models of addictive behavior. *Current Opinion in Behavioral Sciences,* 13, pp.77–84.

Vartanova E., Gladkova A. 2019. *New forms of the digital divide. Digital media inequalities: Policies against divides, distrust and discrimination,* pp. 193–213.

Venmo pricing. (n.d.). https://venmo.com/about/fees/

Virtual currency. (n.d.). https://www.investopedia.com/terms/v/virtual-currency.asp

Virtual currency schemes – a further analysis. ecb.europa.eu. February 2015. https://www.ecb.europa.eu/pub/pdf/other/virtualcurrencyschemesen.pdf

Virtual Currency Schemes (PDF). ecb.europa.eu. October 2012. https://www.ecb.europa.eu/pub/pdf/other/virtualcurrencyschemes201210en.pdf

Webmoney. (n.d.). https://www.webmoney.ru/rus/information/statistic/index.shtm

WebMoney_Transfer_fee. (n.d.). https://wiki.wmtransfer.com/projects/webmoney/wiki/WebMoney_Transfer_fee

Weinstein A. 2018. *Superior Customer Value: Finding and Keeping Customers in the Now Economy.* Routledge.

What is TARGET2?. (n.d.). https://www.ecb.europa.eu/paym/target/target2/html/index.en.html

Wiegerling K. 2016. Umfassende IT-Systeme. [In:] *Handbuch Medien-und Informationsethik.* Stuttgart, JB Metzler, pp. 217–226.

Wölfling K., Müller K.W., Dreier M. 2020. Computerspiel-und Internetsucht. [In:] *Verhaltenstherapiemanual: Kinder und Jugendliche.* Berlin, Heidelberg, Springer, pp. 317–320.

Wölfling K. et al. 2017. Internetsucht und internetbezogene Störungen. *Psychotherapeut,* 62.5: pp. 422–430.

Zakrzewski L., Kamińska B. 2010. Business Intelligence a zarządzanie wiedzą. [In:] *Przedsiębiorczość i zarządzanie,* XII. 1, pp. 11–37.

Zumkeller D. 2002. *Telekommunikation. Telematik und Verkehr im Jahre 2020 – Ein Zukunftsbild unserer Mobilität.* Universität Kaiserslautern, Fachgebiet Verkehrswesen, pp. 00–4.

Index

Note: Pages in *italics* refer to figures and **bold** refer to tables.

A

Anthropoinfosphere, 107
API-driven E-commerce, 133
Artificial Intelligent (AI), 132
Augmented reality, 130, 132, 136

B

Bitcoin Payment System, 200
Blockchain technology, 127, 132–133, 137–138, 175, 180

C

Centralized electronic money systems, 171
COBIT methodology, 77, *80*
Cognitive chain, 19
Communications techniques, 4
Computer technique, 11, **15**, 17, 50
Computer-aided management systems, 31
Cryptocurrency, 123, 127, 138, 144, 162, 170–180, 212
Cryptocurrency market, 123, 127, 144, 177, 212
Cryptocurrency Wallet, 170, 171, 180

D

Data processing, 4, 10–14, 16, 17, 36, 41, 46, 48–50, 52–55, *58*, 59, 66, 67, 72, 84, 168
Data protection in e-commerce (Credit/Debit card fraud, Skimming, Phishing Vishing/Phishing, SPAM, DOS and DDoS Attacks, Malware, Man in The Middle, Brute force attacks, SQL Injection Electronic Skimming), 202–207
Database, 4, 23, 25, 35, 37, 39, 41, 43–47, 49, 51–61, 63–65, 67, 85, 87, 88, 124, 133, 138, 155, 157, 161, 171, 173, 176, 181, 200, 204–206, 220
Decentralised electronic money systems, 170, 171
Digital currency, 150, 170–174, 194, 198
Digital money, 170–172, 179
Digital money system, 170–171
Digital signatures, 151, 172
DIKW hierarchy, 18
Direct-to-Consumer (D2C), 126–127, 130, 136, 220

E

E-commerce business models, 123
E-commerce payment systems, 153
Electronic auctions, 139
Electronic commerce (E-commerce), 123, 212, 215, 222
Electronic exchange, 142
Electronic Funds Transfer (EFT), 165, 183
Electronic Money (E-money), 151–154, 158, 161, 170–171, 200, 213, 215
Electronic trading systems, 139
E-shop (Internet-shops, online store), 128, 140, 198, 202

F

Financial frauds, 202
Financial management technologies, 123, 212
Foreign exchange markets, 144

G

Global information network, 5
Global market, 5, 12, 64, 67, 124, 145

H

Hard knowledge, 30–32
Hard methods, 14–**15**
Headless E-commerce (Headless EC), 132–134, 137
Hidden knowledge, 30

I

Infological approach, 20–21, 25
Informatics, 1, 3–7, 9–17, 19, 21, 23, 25, 27, 29, 31, 33, 41–48, 50–52, 54–55, 59–60, 63–71, 73–77, 79, 81–87, 89, 91–94, 96–99, 104–105, 107–109, *111*, 113, 115–117, 119, 121, 209–210
Informatics security, 76
Informatics system, 10, 12–17, 21, 76–77, 79, 81–87, 89, 91–99, *101*, 103, 105, 107, 109, *111*, 113, 115, 117, 119, 121, 209

Informatics technology, 1, 3–5, 7, 9, 11, 13, **15**,
    17, 19, 21, 23, 25, 27, 29, 31, 33, 47,
    65, 68, 84
Informatics tools, 4, 48, 105
Information, 1–33, 35–73, 75–81, 83–91, 93–95,
    97–103, 105, 107–125, 127–130,
    133–137, 139–140, 143–144, 151–152,
    154–155, 159, 162–163, 165, 167–170,
    173, 175–177, 180–181, 183–188, 190,
    192–193, 195, 198, 200, 202–207,
    209–222
Information processing, 3–4, 9–11, 54–55, 63, 72,
    76, 83–84, 209
Information Security Management System
    (ISMS), 75–76, 83
Information security policy, 75–76, 83
Information Services, 75–76, 83
Information system, 10–18, 20, 25–26, 32, 35,
    40–44, 46, 48, 50, 52, 54–55, 57–59,
    62, 68, 72, 76–77, 79–80, 83–85,
    88–89, 91, 143, 198, 213, 218, 221
Information technique, 10–11, 13–18, 26, 30, 33,
    48–50, 52–57, 69, 209
Information technology, 1–6, 8–9, 41, 44, 55, 79,
    123, 143–144, 165, 209–210, 212–215,
    218, 220, 222
Internet applications, 124
Internet banking, 150
Internet banking risks, 167
Internet banking vulnerabilities, 167
Internet clearing systems, 151
Internet exchange, 139, 142
Internet payment methods, 151
IT risk management, 89–92, 95, 97–99

L

Langefors infological theory, 20

M

Machine Learning, 132, 134
Mail advertising, **141**
Management, 2, 4–6, 8, 10–20, 22–24, 26, *28*,
    30–33, 36–38, 40–44, 46–50, 52,
    54–60, 62–*70*, 72, 74–92, 94–108, 110,
    112, 114, 116, 118,120, 122–124, 126,
    128, 130, 132–134, 136, 138, 140,
    143–144, 146, 148, 150
Management informatics system, 43, 60, 63, 69
Management information system, 12, 43, 50, 59
Management methods, 5, 13, 50, 63, 93, 201
Management process, 17, 37, 41, 63, *80*, 89, 91,
    95, 97, 100–*101*, 105, 122, 168
Management systems, 10, 31, 41, 43, 46, 48, 59,
    75–76, 213, 220
Mechanical Trading System (MTS), 144

Mobile banking, 123, 150, 165, 112
Mobile Payments, 131–133
Mobile Shopping, 66, 132

O

Online Auction, 139
Online payment systems, 150
Organisation, 2–6, 8–18, 20–22, 24–30, 32–33,
    35–84, 86, 88–94, 96–108, 110, 112,
    114, 116, 118, 120, 122, 124–128, 130,
    132–134, 136, 138–140, 142, 144, 146,
    148, 150, 152, 154, 156, 158, 160, 162,
    164, 168, 170, 172, 174, 176, 178, 180,
    182, 184, 186, 188, 190, 192–194, 196,
    198–202, 204, 206, 209–211, 214,
    216–218

P

Payment systems, 123, 126, 137, 150, 153–154,
    160, 163, 167–168, 177, 179–180,
    182–185, 190–194, 197–201, 204,
    212
Peer-to-Peer (P2P) economy, 123
Praxeological rules, 1
Principle of intersubjective verifiability of
    statements, 1
Process of learning, 30
Progressive web apps (PWA), 131, 133

R

Risk management, 76, 81, 89, *90*–92, 94–95,
    97–107, 122, 167–168, 191, 195, 198,
    201, 215, 217–218, 220
Risk management methods, 92, 201
Risk management standards, 104
Risks of payment systems, 167, 201, 212
Risks of the cryptocurrency market, 177

S

Safety rules, 153
Sharing economy, 138, 218, 221
SMAC systems, 65–67
Smart organisation, 63–65, 67
State-of-the-art information technologies, 5
SWIFT, 154, 180, 183, 185, 190, 192, 196, 218,
    221

T

Technology, 1–9, 11–13, **15**, 17, 19, 21, 23,
    25, 27, 39, 31, 33, 41–42, 44, 47,
    55–56, *58*–59, 61–62, 65–66, 68, 74,
    79–*80*, 84, 98, 100–*101*, 106, 120,

123, 128, 132–138, 143–145, 151,
160, 164–166, 168, 171, 175, 180,
198, 209–210, 212–215, 217–218,
220–222
Technology skills, 1–2, 8–9, 123
Telecommunication Services, 124
Teleinformatics, 4–5, 63–65
Teleinformatics technologies, 63
Telematics, 4–5
The cryptocurrency market, 123, 127, 144, 177, 212

The elasticity of demand, 125
Theory of codes and teletransmission, 25
Types of knowledge, 30

V

Virtual Currencies, 170–174, 177, 212
Virtual money system, 170
Virtual reality, 60, 132, 135
Voice Commerce, 132, 134

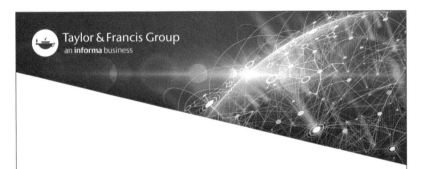